W9-BAX-463

WITHDRAWN

HOW *to* USE

re® 6

SAMS

201 West 10
Indianapolis

Douglas Dixon

JA   '02

ll Color

How to Use Adobe® Premiere® 6

International Standard Book Number: 0-672-32166-1

Library of Congress Catalog Card Number: 2001091651

Printed in the United States of America

First Printing: July 2001

04   03   02   01   4   3   2

Trademarks

All terms mentioned in this book that are known to be trademarks or service marks have been appropriately capitalized. Sams Publishing cannot attest to the accuracy of this information. Use of a term in this book should not be regarded as affecting the validity of any trademark or service mark.

Warning and Disclaimer

Every effort has been made to make this book as complete and as accurate as possible, but no warranty or fitness is implied. The information provided is on an "as is" basis. The author and the publisher shall have neither liability nor responsibility to any person or entity with respect to any loss or damages arising from the information contained in this book or from the use of the files available on the Web site.

Acquisitions Editors
Jennifer Kost-Barker
Betsy Brown

Development Editor
Jonathan Steever

Managing Editor
Charlotte Clapp

Project Editor
Elizabeth Finney

Copy Editor
Mary Ellen Stephenson

Indexers
Kelly Castell
Sheila Schroeder

Proofreader
Anthony Reitz

Technical Editor
Alan Hamill

Team Coordinator
Amy Patton

Interior Designer
Gary Adair

Cover Designers
Aren Howell
Nathan Clement

Page Layout
Stacey DeRome
Mark Walchle

Contents at a Glance

Contents

About the Author

Douglas Dixon is a technologist and author who has worked in the "Video Valley" of Princeton, New Jersey, for more than 20 years, at the bleeding edge where advanced consumer video applications meet personal computers.

As a technology leader at Sarnoff Corp., and previously as a software product manager at Intel, Doug has extensive experience developing multimedia and Web technology into consumer products.

As a technology writer, Doug is a contributing editor for *Camcorder and Computer Video* and *Digital Photographer* magazines. His writing has covered video editing and streaming media technology and tools, DV and DVD, desktop and handhelds, as well as consumer and professional products. While he writes about new and cutting-edge technology, Doug's focus is on making technology understandable and useful for real people. For more on these topics, see his Manifest Technology Web site at **www.manifest-tech.com**.

Doug has published technical articles related to his projects in publications ranging from ACM and IEEE journals to *Computer Graphics World*. He also is active in professional activities and has spoken at local, regional, and national meetings, from user groups to Comdex and the ACM SIGGRAPH Conference.

Dedication

To my mother and father, who helped start me on the journey, and to my family, Connie, Karin, and Brian, who make the trip so special.

Acknowledgments

Not surprisingly, I would like to thank the team at Adobe who brought us version 6 of Premiere. It has been a real pleasure working with such a clean application, especially because it makes it so fun and easy to mess around with video on DV, and so painless to help out friends with quick productions. Thanks also to the team at Sams Publishing, who brought together this book and were great to work with, especially Jennifer Kost-Barker, who got this puppy rolling; Betsy Brown, who kept it on track; Jon Steever, who made sure it all fit together; Mary Ellen Stephenson, who kept the words straight; and Elizabeth Finney, who pushed it to the end. And thanks to Neil Salkind and Studio B for their support and perseverance in developing this opportunity.

After all, this is a very exciting time to be in the technology business, especially as digital video becomes accessible and affordable on consumer PCs. I would like to thank Bob Wolenik, Tony Gomez, and Mark Shapiro for the opportunity to cover these developments for Miller Magazines, and Rich Rein and Barbara Fox for the great learning experience of writing for the *U.S. 1* newspaper in Princeton. And thanks to Andy van Dam and my compatriots back at the Computer Science program at Brown University for making writing a natural part of technology education.

Tell Us What You Think!

As the reader of this book, *you* are our most important critic and commentator. We value your opinion and want to know what we're doing right, what we could do better, what areas you'd like to see us publish in, and any other words of wisdom you're willing to pass our way.

I welcome your comments. You can e-mail or write me directly to let me know what you did or didn't like about this book—as well as what we can do to make our books stronger.

Please note that I cannot help you with technical problems related to the topic of this book, and that due to the high volume of mail I receive, I might not be able to reply to every message.

When you write, please be sure to include this book's title and author as well as your name and phone or fax number. I will carefully review your comments and share them with the author and editors who worked on the book.

Email: **graphics@samspublishing.com**

Mail: Mark Taber
          Associate Publisher
          Sams Publishing
          201 West 103rd Street
          Indianapolis, IN 46290 USA

The Complete Visual Reference

Each chapter of this book is made up of a series of short, instructional tasks, designed to help you understand all the information that you need to get the most out of your computer hardware and software.

Click: Click the left mouse button once.

Double-click: Click the left mouse button twice in rapid succession.

Right-click: Click the right mouse button once.

Drag: Click and hold the left mouse button, position the mouse pointer, and release.

Pointer Arrow: Highlights an item on the screen you need to point to or focus on in the step or task.

Selection: Highlights the area onscreen discussed in the step or task.

Type: Click once where indicated and begin typing to enter your text or data.

Drag and Drop: Point to the starting place or object. Hold down the mouse button (right or left per instructions), move the mouse to the new location, and then release the button.

Drag

Drop

Each task includes a series of easy-to-understand steps designed to guide you through the procedure.

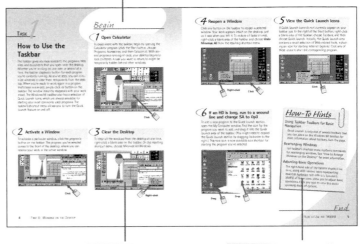

Each step is fully illustrated to show you how it looks onscreen.

Extra hints that tell you how to accomplish a goal are provided in most tasks.

 Key icons: Clearly indicate which key combinations to use.

Menus and items you click are shown in **bold**. Words in *italic* are defined in more detail in the glossary. Information you type is in a `special font`.

If you see this symbol, it means the task you're in continues on the next page.

Continues

Introduction

Welcome to Adobe Premiere 6! Premiere has a long history as the leading cross-platform video editing application for Windows and Macintosh. And, although Premiere has always had power and professional features aplenty, now it is even easier to use for creating quick and fun digital video productions.

My goal with this book is to help you get started with using Premiere, and become familiar with the range of its capabilities. With this book, you can use Premiere to quickly and easily create your own video productions with professional touches. The book takes you through all of the major features of Premiere, basic and advanced, which can enable you to

- Capture high-quality video from your DV camcorder.
- Organize your audio and video clips and edit them into a complete production.
- Enhance your work with transitions and effects, titles and animations.
- Save and share your productions as digital video files.
- Output streaming media formats to share on the Web.

Each topic is illustrated with step-by-step screen shots, annotated to illustrate the operation being demonstrated. Premiere is a cross-platform application, so the examples in this book apply equally well to Premiere's Macintosh version (even though most of the screenshots are taken from the Windows version). When there are differences between the two versions, particularly with keyboard and mouse shortcuts, the text describes operations for both systems.

Who Should Use This Book?

If you are just starting out with digital video on the desktop, then this book can get you started quickly with Premiere 6, capturing video, performing simple edits, and exporting your productions for the desktop or Web. Premiere provides convenient tools like the Storyboard and Title windows to help get you going, and then provides lots more room for growth as you start taking advantage of its more sophisticated features.

Plus, Premiere makes it very convenient to use its advanced features—for example, by using floating palettes to list transitions and effects and group them in categories, and by providing preview capabilities in the Title and Effects dialogs. And Premiere's extensive undo capability and History palette makes it easy to learn and experiment with the different options.

If you are stepping up from an entry-level video editing application, this book will show you how Premiere 6 frees you from the limitations of more basic tools. For example, now you can have more than one or two video and audio tracks, choose from a much wider range of transitions and effects, customize the screen layout for your working style, and generally have much more control over editing your production.

Finally, if you are upgrading from version 5, this book demonstrates the significant improvements offered in Premiere 6, especially with built-in support for capture from DV camcorders, output to all the major Web formats, a collection of After Effects plug-ins, and a dedicated Audio Mixer. This version of Premiere also offers an enhanced interface, with more convenient access to controls through command buttons and extensive keyboard shortcuts.

Book Organization

This book is organized into 16 parts, or chapters, each focusing on a major feature in Premiere. Each part contains approximately five to nine tasks, which take you step by step through performing a particular operation in Premiere. Each task presents the operation in a series of steps, each illustrated with a Premiere screen shot annotated to highlight the action being performed. In this way, you can easily see and understand how to use the Premiere controls to perform the task.

Parts 1 to 4 get you started quickly with using Premiere by taking you through the process of importing, organizing, and editing material into a simple production. They also introduce the Premiere user interface components and conventions (projects, bins, clips, the Storyboard, the Timeline, and so on). The illustrations for these parts all use the sample media clips provided with Premiere, so that you can follow along exactly with the steps in the book.

After you become familiar with the basics of using Premiere, Parts 5 through 7 show how to save and share your productions by exporting video and audio to different desktop and Web formats. They also explain how to capture your own material to edit, especially digital video from a DV camcorder, and also output the final production back to DV.

In the second half of the book, Parts 9 through 16 then introduce more sophisticated techniques for trimming and editing your audio and video clips. These parts also demonstrate additional features in Premiere for enhancing your productions, from titles and overlays, to audio and video effects, to motion animations.

By covering each of the major features in Premiere, this book also shows you the wealth of additional capabilities and options you can use to create more sophisticated and professional results. You can get started quickly, and then still have plenty of room to grow in the future.

Learn More About Using Premiere

To learn more about using Premiere, check the Adobe support Web site for technical tips and tutorials. Also check the Adobe site periodically for new upgrade releases and support for problems or bugs:

Adobe Premiere—Product Information and Tutorials

   www.adobe.com/products/premiere

Adobe Support—Technical Guides and Tutorials

   www.adobe.com/support

Adobe Support—Downloads

   www.adobe.com/support/downloads

Adobe Support—Searchable Knowledgebase

   www.adobe.com/support/database.html

For more information on desktop video topics, including video editing tools, file and compression formats, DV, and streaming media, also visit my Manifest Technology Web site:

   www.manifest-tech.com

Task

PART 1

Getting Started with Adobe Premiere

*W*elcome to Adobe Premiere! The best way to learn a new program is to dive right in and get started, but Premiere can be intimidating at first look. It is such a powerful and complex video editing tool, with so much flexibility and so many options.

But the good news is that Premiere really is easy to use for basic editing operations. This chapter will get you started by taking a tour of the steps involved in using Premiere: setting up your *workspace*, importing audio and video *clips* into a Project window, organizing the clips into *bins*, assembling them into a *project* in the Timeline window, and *previewing* the resulting *program* in the Monitor window.

Along the way, I will introduce the Premiere user interface and organizational elements, including menus, windows, buttons, and other controls. Premiere provides lots of options for how you work, so go ahead and experiment, and even customize the work area the way that you prefer.

To make sure that you can follow what is happening in the book, these first few parts use only the sample video clip files that are included with Premiere and installed with it on your hard disk. If you have not done so already, go ahead—install Premiere (using the instructions that came with your software), and let's get started. ●

A Quick Tour of Premiere

Adobe Premiere is a powerful video editing tool, but with that power comes lots of options and controls, and different kinds of windows filling the screen. In this task, you will take a quick tour of how to use Premiere, to get a sense of the basic windows and controls and how to work through a video production.

Begin

1 Select the Initial Workspace

The first time you start Premiere, it displays the **Initial Workspace** dialog. Just click **Select A/B Editing** to configure your default *Workspace* layout of windows and tools for using Premiere. (*A/B Editing* simply means editing your clips in pairs—A and B—possibly with a transition from one to the next.) If you have already run Premiere, then skip to the next step.

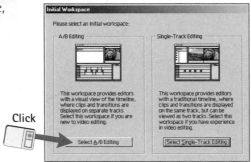

Click

2 Select the Project Settings

After you have selected your initial workspace, Premiere displays the **Load Project Settings** dialog. Here, you specify your Project settings to match the type of material that you will be working with. For the moment, select a basic file format: **Multimedia QuickTime** (for Macintosh users) or **Multimedia Video for Windows** (for Windows users). Then click the **OK** button to set up your *Project*.

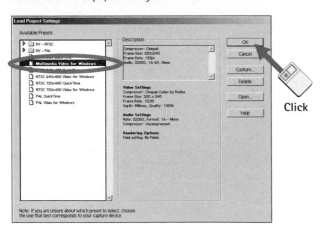

Click

3 Select the A/B Editing Workspace

Premiere opens a new empty project with the default workspace window layout. After you have worked in Premiere for a while and have moved around the different windows, the screen layout can become cluttered and disorganized. To restore the workspace layout to the default arrangement, pull down the **Window** menu and choose **Workspace, A/B Editing**.

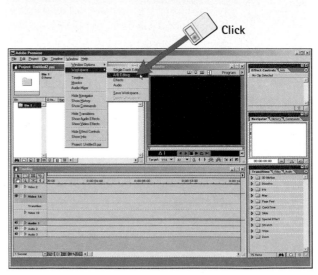

Click

4 Import a Clip

The **Project** window at the top left of the Premiere work area contains a collection of *bins* (folders of clips) to be used in the project. Sample clips are installed with Premiere in the **Sample Folder** on your hard disk. To import a clip file into the bin area, pull down the **File** menu and choose **Import, File**. In the **Import** dialog, navigate to the **Sample Folder**, typically installed under `C:\Program Files\Adobe\Premiere 6.0\` `Sample Folder` (Windows) or `Macintosh HD:` `Applications: Adobe Premiere 6.0:` `Sample Folder:` (Macintosh). Then click to select the file `Cyclers.avi` (Windows) or `Cyclers.mov` (Macintosh) and click **Open**.

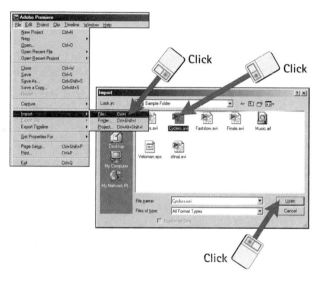

Click

Click

Click

5 Add to the Timeline

The **Timeline** window along the bottom right of the Premiere work area is where you assemble your production by organizing and editing your clips, and add transitions, effects, and titles. To add the **Cyclers** clip to the Timeline, drag it from the bin area in the **Project** window to the **Video 1A** track in the Timeline.

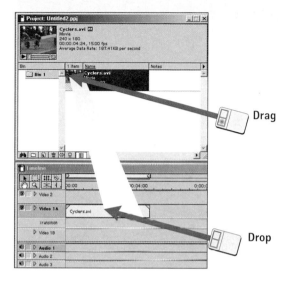

Drag

Drop

6 Play in the Monitor Window

The **Monitor** window to the right of the **Project** window is where you can preview the *program* that you are editing on the Timeline. Click the VCR playback controls along the bottom of the window to play through the Timeline.

Click

How-To Hints

Floating Palette Windows

The three smaller windows down the right side of the Premiere window are tool *palettes*. Although the **Project**, **Timeline**, and **Monitor** windows are contained in the main Premiere window, the palette windows actually float above the Premiere window. This makes them easy to position off to the side of the screen for convenient access when you need them, but can also be disconcerting when you move the Premiere window and the palettes stay floating in their original positions.

End

How to Manage Projects

Premiere organizes your editing activities into *Projects*, which include the collection of material that you are using, the edits that you have performed on them, and even the layout of windows in the work area. You can save an editing project in process and then reload it later to continue working.

Begin

1 Play the Thumbnail

The **Project** window is where you load, organize, and access the clips that you are going to use in your project. The clips are organized into bins or folders, from which you can access and drag them to be edited. For a quick preview of the contents of a clip, simply click the **Cyclers** clip to select it (from Task 1), and a thumbnail viewer appears in the top-left corner of the **Project** window. Click the **Play** button to preview the clip in the thumbnail window.

Click

2 Save Your Project

To save your project, pull down the **File** menu and choose **Save**. Premiere will display the **Save File** dialog. Navigate to the **Sample Folder**, type **Sample Project** as the name for the project file, and click **Save**. Premiere creates project files in Windows with the extension **.PPJ**.

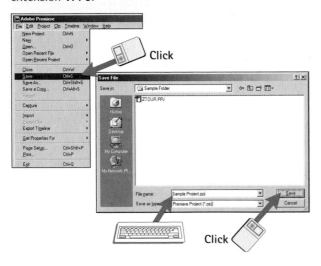

Click

Click

3 Start a New Project

To start a new project, pull down the **File** menu and choose **New Project**. If you have not saved your current project, Premiere will display a dialog asking whether you want to do so now. Premiere then displays the **Load Project Settings** dialog. Select **Multimedia QuickTime** (for Macintosh users) or **Multimedia Video for Windows** (for Windows users). Then click **OK**.

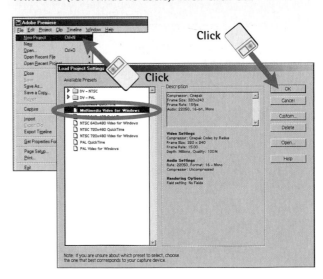

Click

Click

4 Open an Existing Project

To open a project that you saved previously, pull down the **File** menu and choose **Open Recent Project**, and then the **Sample Project** name that you saved previously (or pull down the **File** menu and choose **Open**).

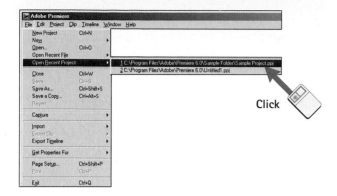

Click

5 Save Your Workspace

To save your own custom workspace layouts, pull down the **Window** menu and choose **Workspace**, **Save Workspace**. Premiere then will display the **Save Workspace** dialog. Type a name for your workspace and press **Save**.

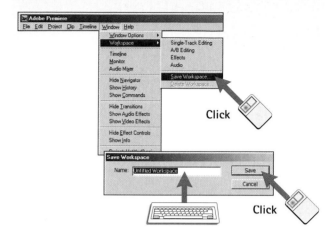

Click

Click

6 Resuming an Existing Project

The next time that you start up Premiere, it will display the **Load Project Settings** dialog again. If you want to resume working on an existing project, click **Open** and then use the **Open** dialog to navigate to your saved project file (**.PPJ** under Windows). Premiere then reopens your project back to the bin contents and window layout that were last saved.

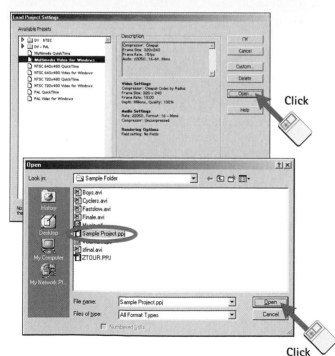

Click

Click

How-To Hints

Save Your Projects

It's a good idea to periodically save your work as you are editing with Premiere. The Premiere project file is not very large because it contains only references to the media that you are editing, and not actual video files. Go ahead and experiment with Premiere—just save your Project first.

Auto Save

You can also have Premiere automatically save your Project at specified intervals. You can save to the same file, or even better, save a series of files to archive each state of your project over a period of time. To set the Auto Save options, pull down the **Edit** menu and select **Preferences, Auto Save and Undo**. See Part 2, "Importing and Organizing Clips," for more on **Undo**.

End

How to Organize Clips in Project Bins

Use the Project window in Premiere to organize your collection of clips for editing, and to see information about your clips. You can import both individual clip files and entire bins of clips, and organize them into one or more bins.

Begin

1 Import a Folder of Clips

To import an entire folder of clip files into the Project, pull down the **File** menu and choose **Import, Folder**. In the **Browse for Folder** dialog that appears, navigate to the **Sample Folder**, click the folder name to select it, and then click **OK**.

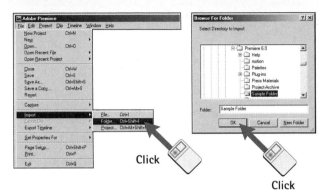

Click

Click

2 Organize Your Bins

When you import clips, they are added to the contents of the current bin. You can organize your bins separately, or by nesting them hierarchically inside one another. Drag the **Sample Folder** bin from inside the **Bin 1** bin to the bottom of the *bin view* in the left panel of the **Project** window.

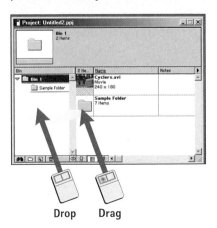

Drop   Drag

3 Display the List View

The **Project** window provides several different views of the clips in each bin. Use the three buttons below the clip panel to switch between **Icon**, **Thumbnail**, and **List** views. Click the rightmost **List View** button to see a list of the clips in the **Sample Folder** bin.

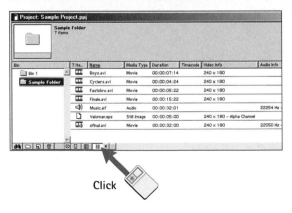

Click

4 Create a New Bin

Premiere displays the list of clips with information about their format. Click the **New Bin** folder button under the left bin pane to create a new bin folder. Premiere then displays the **Create Bin** dialog. Enter **Bin 2** as the name, and click **OK**. You can also rename bins by clicking their name and typing new text.

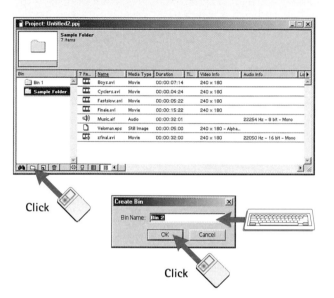

Click

Click

Click

5 Delete a Bin

Premiere adds the new bin to the Project window. To delete the new bin, select it, and then click the **Delete** button below the bin pane, or press the **Delete** key. Deleting a clip, or an entire bin full of clips, does not delete the actual clip files from your disk; it just deletes the references to them from your project.

Click

6 Save Your Project

Before going on, this is a good time to save your project again. Pull down the **File** menu and choose **Save**. The current project bins and settings will be saved so that you can continue working with them later.

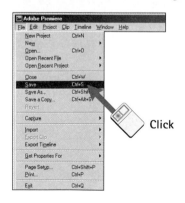

Click

How-To Hints

Window Menus

Premiere provides several different ways to access the available menu options for each window. Click the triangular window **Menu** button near the upper-right corner of each window or palette to access the common commands and display options for that window.

Pop-Up Context Menus

For quick access to the most useful menu options available for a specific window, or to an object within a window, right-click (Windows) or Control-click (Macintosh) on the window or object to display a pop-up *context menu*.

End

How to Play Clips in a Clip Window

Now that you have organized the clips for your project into bins, you can view individual clips and prepare them for inclusion in the Timeline. Clips are displayed in individual Clip windows with controls for playback and editing.

Begin

1 Open a Clip Window

To view a clip, double-click the **zfinal** clip in the **Sample Folder** bin, or select it, pull down the **Clip** menu, and choose **Open Clip**. You can open multiple clip windows, and switch between them by clicking them or by selecting them from the **Window** menu.

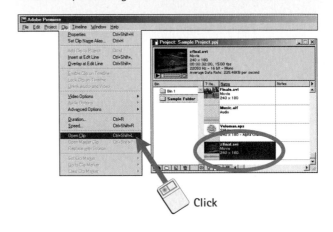

Click

2 Play the Clip

Premiere opens the clip in a separate **Clip** window, with the name of the clip in the title bar. To play through the clip, use the playback control buttons at the bottom of the **Clip** window. Click the triangular **Play** button to start playback, and the square **Stop** button to stop playing. Click the **Loop** button to loop repeatedly through the clip. Click the **Frame Back** and **Frame Forward** buttons to step backward and forward through the clip, respectively. Click and hold a **Frame** button to scan through the clip, or press **Shift** as you click to jump five frames at a time.

3 View the Timecode

The Clip window displays the total **Clip Duration** (in seconds and frames) to the left of the play controls. The **Current Clip Location** *timecode* appears to the right. This shows your current location in the clip, corresponding to the **Set Location** triangular *shuttle slider*.

4 Jog and Shuttle in the Clip

To jump to a general area of the clip, click the corresponding point along the shuttle slider area under the video. To *shuttle* rapidly through the clip, click and drag the **Set Location** blue triangular shuttle slider to the left (backward in clip) or right (forward). To *jog* though the individual clip frames, click and drag the cursor right or left in the **Frame Jog** striped jog tread area.

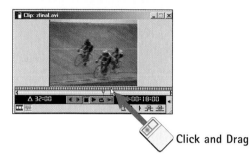

Click and Drag

5 Adjust the Volume

To quickly adjust audio volume during playback of the clip, click the **Set Volume** button on the bottom right of the window. Clicking the button cycles through medium and high volume and mute.

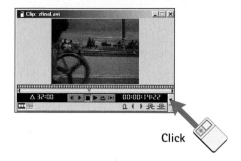

Click

6 View Audio Controls and Images

Besides video files, the **Sample Folder** bin contains two other types of files: Audio and Still Image. Double-click the **Music.aiff** clip to open a **Clip** window that displays the audio file with the audio waveform and playback controls. Double-click **Veloman.eps** to open a second **Clip** window that displays the still image file.

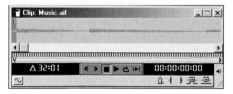

How-To Hints

Using Keyboard Shortcuts

Premiere provides lots of keyboard shortcuts to simplify playing back clips. Just press the **Spacebar** to start and stop playback. Use the **Left** and **Right** cursor control keys to step through frames, and the **Up** and **Down** cursor keys to jump to the beginning and end of the clip.

Entering a Timecode

To move to a specific timecode, click the **Current Clip Location** display, type in a new time, and press **Enter** (Windows) or **Return** (Macintosh). You can also enter the time on the numeric keypad as consecutive digits without colons.

End

5

How to Add Clips to the Timeline

After you have organized your clips in bins in the Project window, you can begin arranging the clips into a sequence in the Timeline window. You can then enhance your presentation by adding other components such as transitions, effects, titles, overlays, and background audio.

Begin

1 Add a Video Track

To start building your production, first, open the project you saved in Task 3. Open the **Sample Folder** bin and then click the icon for the **Boys** video file and drag it to the **Video 1A** row in the **Timeline** window.

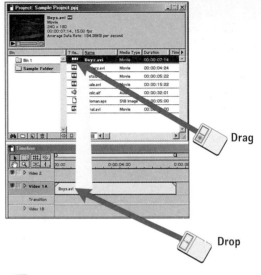

Drag

Drop

2 Add a Second Video Track

To add a second video clip to be played in sequence after the first clip, click the **Cyclers** video file, drag it to the **Video 1A** row in the **Timeline** window, and place it immediately after the **Boys** clip.

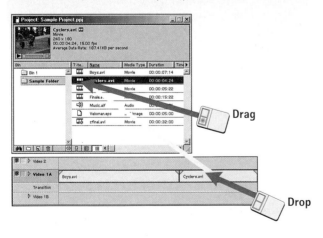

Drag

Drop

3 Add an Audio Track

To add an audio music track to play with these silent video clips, click the **Music** audio file and drag it to the start of the **Audio 1** track.

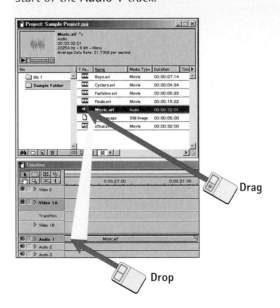

Drag

Drop

4 Scroll the Timeline

The video files have disappeared! The music file is much longer than the video clips, so the **Timeline** window scrolled to the end of the full production. Use the scrollbar at the bottom of the window to scroll back to the beginning of the production.

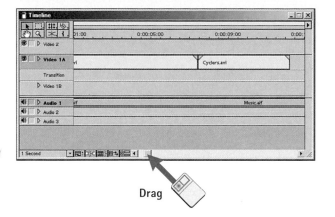

Drag

5 Zoom the Timeline

To change the Timeline display so that the entire production fits in the window, use the **Zoom** menu at the bottom left of the window to zoom the Timeline display out to **2 Seconds**.

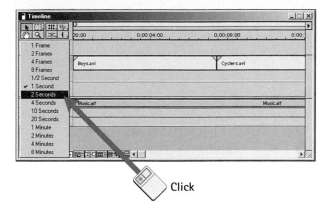

Click

6 View the Full Timeline

Now the entire contents of the Timeline are visible in the window.

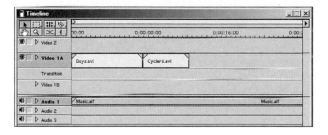

How-To Hints

Quick Scrolling

To quickly zoom the Timeline display in and out, use the **Hand Tool** button (hand icon) in the tool area at the top left of the **Timeline** window. To select the hand tool, click it, or press the **H** key. Click and drag the hand cursor to scroll the Timeline.

Quick Zooming

To quickly zoom the Timeline display in and out, use the **Zoom Tool** button (magnifying glass icon) in the tool area at the top left of the **Timeline** window. To select the zoom tool, click it, or press the **Z** key. The cursor changes to a magnifying glass with a plus sign ("+"), and you can then click to zoom in on the Timeline. To zoom out and see more of the program, hold down the **Alt** (Windows) or **Option** (Macintosh) key to change the cursor to a minus sign ("-"), and then click to zoom out.

End

How to Preview a Program on the Timeline

After you have started editing your production, or *program*, on the Timeline, you can also play it in its current form in the Program Monitor window at the top right of the Premiere work area. The Monitor window and the Timeline are synchronized, so that they move together as you play or shuttle in either area.

Begin

1 Playing the Program

The **Monitor** window has much the same play controls and time displays as the **Clip** window (from Task 4). To play the current program on the Timeline, use the **play control** buttons at the bottom of the **Monitor** window.

2 Using the Edit Line

As the program plays in the **Monitor** window, the corresponding position is displayed in the Timeline by the vertical *edit line*. The *time ruler* along the top of the **Timeline** window displays the current time of the edit line. Moving the edit line in the Timeline changes the corresponding frame displayed in the **Monitor** window.

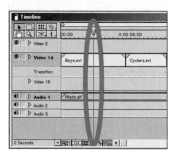

3 Dragging the Edit Line

To move the edit line, first position the cursor in the time ruler; the cursor changes to a triangle. Click anywhere in the time ruler to jump the edit line to that position, or click and drag the triangle to the left or right to shuttle through the program. By dragging the triangle off either side of the window, you can shuttle to the beginning or end of the program.

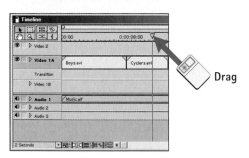

Drag

4 Using the Navigator Palette

Premiere provides another method for displaying and moving around in the Timeline layout. The **Navigator** palette on the right of the work area offers a graphical view of the entire Timeline. The **Current View** box (in green) shows the area currently visible in the **Timeline** window, and the **Edit Line** (in red) shows the current position of the edit line. If the **Navigator** palette is not currently visible, click the **Navigator** tab in the **Palette** window, or pull down the **Window** menu and choose **Show Navigator**.

5 Scrolling in the Navigator Palette

You can use the **Navigator** palette not only to view the Timeline, but also to move the **Timeline** and **Monitor** window displays. Click and drag on the **Current View** box (in green), using the hand cursor to scroll the Timeline window to the corresponding area of the project. Or hold down **Shift** to click and drag the **Edit Line** (in red), using the triangle cursor to move the edit line through the project.

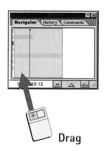

Drag

6 Zooming in the Navigator Palette

You can also zoom the Timeline display from the **Navigator** palette. Click the **Zoom Out** and **Zoom In** buttons (small and large mountain icons) at the bottom of the palette to zoom the Timeline. You can also click and slide the zoom slider between the buttons to adjust the zoom level.

Click

How-To Hints

Current Timecode

To keep track of where you are in the program, Premiere displays the corresponding timecode in both the **Program Location** of the Monitor window and the **Timecode** area at the bottom left of the Navigator palette. You can also jump directly to a timecode by typing in either of these fields.

Current Zoom Level

To keep track of your zoom level as you zoom in and out in the **Timeline** window, watch the **Zoom** menu at the bottom left of the **Timeline** window. Premiere displays the zoom level, with the Timeline displaying a period ranging from 1 Frame to 8 Minutes of the clip.

End

Task

PART 2

Importing and Organizing Clips

As we saw in the quick tour of Premiere in Part 1, "Getting Started with Adobe Premiere," Premiere organizes your editing activity into a Project. This includes the media clips you are working with (organized in bins in the Project window), the edits that you have performed on them (sequenced on the Timeline window), and even your current arrangement of windows in the Premiere work area (saved as a Workspace).

The first step in working with a Project is to import and organize your source media clips, including video, audio, and images. To assist in the editing process, it is useful to build a library of your clips, organized in whatever way is helpful for you—perhaps by topic, or theme, or date. The Premiere Project window provides powerful organization capabilities, including multiple ways of viewing clips and clip information and the ability to import and collect clips into bins as a hierarchy of nested folders. As you organize your clips, you can also add your own text notes and labels, and then use Premiere's search tools to find clips matching the specific characteristics.

The tasks in this part step you through using the Project window to import, organize, view, and search clips. They also demonstrate the wide variety of the user interface options provided by Premiere, including program, window, and pop-up menus; command buttons; and text input.

The final task also introduces the Premiere Undo capability and History palette so that you can feel free to experiment with the different features as you work on a Project, try different operations, and then easily back them out and start over. ●

How to Use the Project Window

In the Project window, you can import, organize, and view the clip files that you plan to edit together into your production. After you assemble the clips, you can then trim, edit, and view them in the Clip, Timeline, and Monitor windows.

Begin

1 Open a Project

To open the Project you saved in Part 1, pull down the **File** menu, choose **Open Recent Project**, and then open the **Sample Project** name that you saved (or choose Open from the **File** menu).

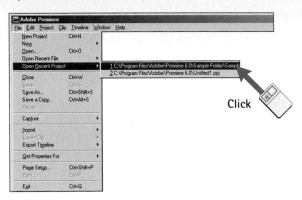

2 Select a Bin

The bin area on the left side of the **Project** window displays a hierarchical view of the bin folders that you have imported and added to your Project. Click the **Sample Folder** bin to select it.

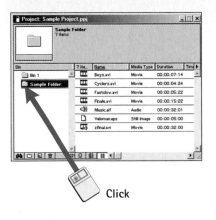

3 Select a Clip

The **Clip** area on the right side of the **Project** window displays the media clip files contained in the currently selected bin. Premiere provides several different options for customizing your view of the clips. Click on the **Cyclers** movie file to select it.

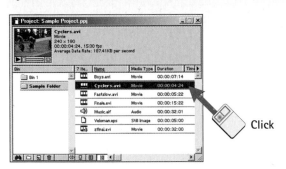

4 Preview the Clip

The preview area at the top of the **Project** window displays information about the current clips, and provides a thumbnail viewer for playing through the clip. Click on the triangular **Play** button to play through the clip.

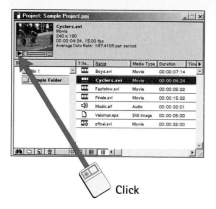

Click

5 Pull Down a Window Menu

Premiere provides several different ways to access the available menu options for each window and pane within a window. Click the triangular window **Menu** button near the upper-right corner of the **Project** window to access common commands and options.

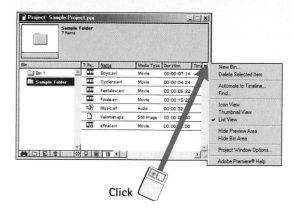

Click

6 Pop Up a Context Menu

Premiere also provides pop-up context menus for quick access to the most useful menu options available for a specific area within a window. Right-click (Windows) or Control+click (Macintosh) on the preview and bin areas to see the available options. Some of the common commands are also available as buttons at the bottom of the bin and clip areas.

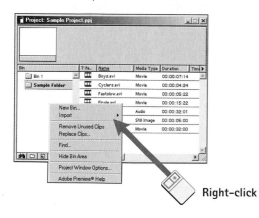

Right-click

How-To Hints

Resizing and Hiding Panes

You can resize the bin and clip areas by clicking and dragging the **Resize Bin Area** button (two arrow icons) at the bottom of the **Project** Window. You can also use the window or context menus to **Hide** or **Show** the preview or bin areas.

Poster Frames

By default, Premiere uses the first frame of a clip for the thumbnail icon. You can choose a different poster frame to visualize the clip, especially if the clip begins with a fade up from black. In the Preview thumbnail, click the **Set Poster Frame** button to the right of the slider, or select it from the pop-up context menu.

End

How to View Clip Information

As you assemble your clips in the **Project** window, Premiere provides several options for displaying information about the clips. These include summary information in the clip lists, detailed clip Property information, and even a Data Rate graph to show how the frames in the clip are compressed.

Begin

1 Preview a Clip

To see basic information about a clip in the **Project** window, view the clip in List view, or click on the clip so it is displayed in the preview area, with the thumbnail viewer and clip information.

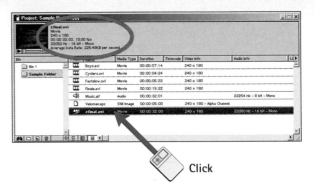

Click

2 Display the Info Palette

Premiere also displays summary information about the currently selected object in the *Info palette* along the right side of the work area. If the palette is hidden, click on the **Info** tab in the **Palette** window, or pull down the **Window** menu and choose **Show Info**. The **Info** palette is especially useful for viewing information about clips in the Timeline.

Click

3 Display Clip Properties

To see more detailed information about a clip, select it in the clip or preview area, and then pull down the **Clip** menu and chose **Properties**, or choose **Properties** from the pop-up context menu.

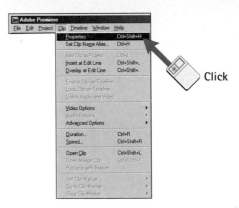

Click

4 View the Properties Window

The clip **Properties** window displays details on the clip file on disk, and the audio and video tracks in the file. To display a graph of the clip data rate, click the **Data Rate** button at the bottom left of the **Properties** window.

Click

5 View the Data Rate Graph

The **Data Rate** graph shows the data rate of each frame in the file (as individual bars), and the average data rate (as the white line). You can see at a glance whether the clip can be played successfully at a specific target data rate.

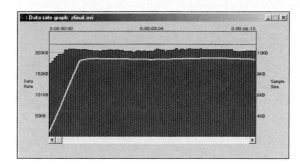

6 Display File Properties

To find out information about a file even before you open it, pull down the **File** menu and choose **Get Properties For, File**. Premiere then opens the **Properties** dialog for that file.

Click

How-To Hints

The Data Rate Graph

The Data Rate graph can be very useful in understanding how well your clips will play on different computer systems, and over the Internet, at different data rates. The graph lets you study in detail how well each individual frame of the clip was compressed. For files compressed with independent keyframes, and difference frames between the keyframes, the keyframe sizes are in red, and the difference frame sizes are in blue.

End

How to Import Clips

Premiere offers several options for importing clips into your Project, either individually or in groups. After you organize your clips into bins in the Project window, you can then save the bins to use with other Projects.

1 Import a Clip

To import an individual clip file into your Project, first select **Bin 1** as the destination bin, and then pull down the **File** menu and choose **Import**, **File** (or choose it from the pop-up context menu). In the dialog, go to the **Sample Folder** (from Task 1), and then click to select the **Fastslow** file and click **Open**.

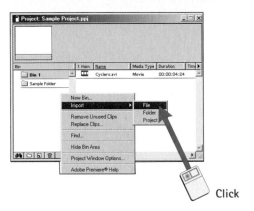

Click

2 Import a Folder

To import an entire folder of clip files into your Project, first select **Bin 1** as the destination bin, then pull down the **File** menu and choose **Import**, **Folder** (or choose it from the pop-up context menu). In the **Browse for Folder** dialog, navigate to the **Sample Folder**, click on the folder name to select it, and then click **OK**.

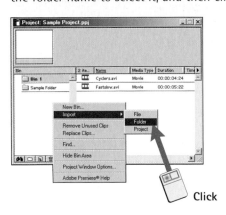

Click

3 Explore Nested Bins

Click on the triangular icon to the left of the **Bin 1** icon to show the bins nested within it. Notice that you now have two copies of the **Sample Folder** in your Project, which can be useful when organizing clips across multiple bins.

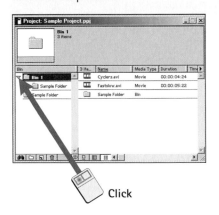

Click

4 Export the Bin

Once you go through the effort of organizing a group of clips into a bin, you can also save the bin for use in other Projects. Click on the bin folder icon to select **Bin 1** and then pull down the **Project** menu and choose **Export Bin from Project** (or use the pop-up context menu).

Click

5 Save the Bin File

In the **Save File** dialog, navigate to the folder where you want to save the bin, enter **Sample Bin** as the name, and click **Save**. Premiere creates bin files in Windows with the extension **.PLB**.

Click

6 Import the Bin File

To use the saved bin file in a Project, pull down the **File** menu and choose **Open**. In the **Open** dialog, set the file type to **Premiere Bin (*.plb)**, select the **Sample Bin** saved bin file, and click **Open**. Premiere opens the bin in a separate **External Bin** window. You can then copy individual clips or even the entire bin into your Project.

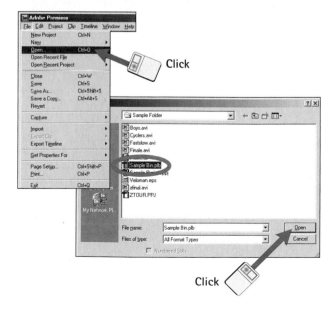

Click

How-To Hints

Bin Windows

You can also open multiple Bin windows for the bins in your Project, which can be helpful when you are organizing clips across multiple folders. To open a bin in a separate window, click on the bin to select it and choose **Open Bin in New Window** from the pop-up context menu. The Bin windows provide an alternate view of the bins in the Project, so changes in one view are reflected in the other.

End

TASK 4

How to Organize Bins

You can use the Project window in Premiere to organize and group your clips into bins. Bins act like file folders, and can be moved, copied, renamed, and otherwise rearranged to help you organize your clips.

Begin

1 Create a New Bin

To add a new bin folder to a Project, click the **New Bin** button (folder icon) under the bin area (or use the **Project** window menu or pop-up context menu). In the **Create Bin** dialog, type the name **Bin 2** for the new bin, and click **OK**.

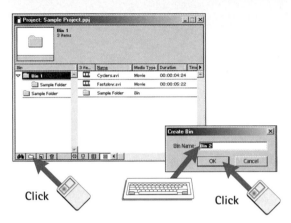

Click

Click

2 Rename a Bin

To rename a bin folder, click the **Sample Folder** name nested under **Bin 1** in the bin area, and enter a new name as **Sample 2** by editing the name field in place. You can also click on the folder icon in the bin or clip areas and select **Rename Bin** from the window or pop-up context menu to display the **Bin Alias** dialog.

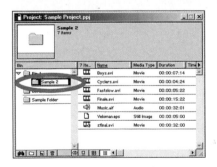

3 Select Clips

To select an individual clip, click the clip icon or thumbnail in the clip list. To select multiple clips in the **Sample 2** bin, click the **Cyclers** clip name and drag the cursor down and over to select and highlight a group of three clips.

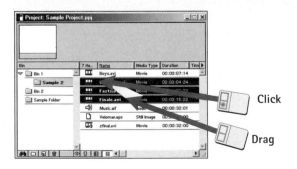

Click

Drag

4 Move the Clips

Once you have selected an individual clip or group of clips, you can move the selected item between bins. Click and drag with the hand cursor from the icon area to the left of the names to the **Bin 2** folder.

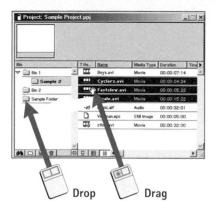

Drop   Drag

5 Move a Bin

Similarly, you can move entire bins, along with their contents to nest them hierarchically. To move the **Sample 2** bin, click on the folder icon for the bin, either in the left bin area or in the right clip area, and drag and drop it onto the **Bin 2** folder.

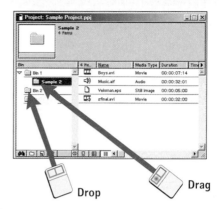

Drop   Drag

6 Delete a Bin

To clean up your Project, delete the new bins. Click on the **Bin 2** folder to select it, and then click on the **Delete** button (trash can icon) below the bin pane (or press the **Delete** key). You can also select **Clear** from the pop-up context menu. Deleting a clip, or even an entire bin full of clips, does not delete the actual clip files from your disk; it just deletes the references to them from your Project.

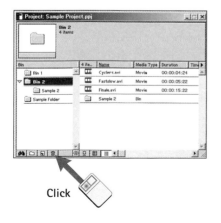

Click

How-To Hints

Cleaning Up

An easier way to clean up your Project after you have been experimenting is to simply close the Project and throw away any changes, and reopen it to the last saved version. Or simply pull down the **File** menu and select **Revert**. When the warning dialog asks if you want to discard your changes to this Project, click **Yes**.

Cut, Copy, and Paste

Another way to move and copy both clips and bins is through the clipboard **Cut**, **Copy**, and **Paste** commands. You can select these from the **Edit** or pop-up context menus, or use the normal Windows or Macintosh keyboard shortcuts.

End

How to View Clips

As you organize your clips in bins, Premiere provides three different ways to view the contents of the bins, and additional options to customize the views. Select the different views in the Project window menu or click on the view buttons below the clip area.

Begin

1 Select the Icon View

To view and organize your clips as icons, select the **Sample Folder**, and then click the **Icon View** button. You can drag the icons around to organize them, or select **Clean Up View** from the Project window or pop-up context menu to move them back into a grid layout. You can also select specific clips using the common methods, including making multiple selections with Control+Click (Windows) and Shift+Click (Macintosh).

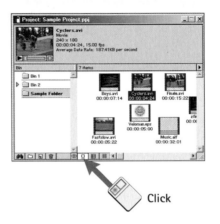

Click

2 Select Icon Options

To customize the Icon view, select **Project Window Options** from the **Project** window menu or pop-up context menu. From the **Size** list, choose the size to display each icon, and select **Snap to Grid** to force the icons to line up in a grid layout. Deselect **Draw Icons** to not display a thumbnail of each clip, which can make the Project window display faster.

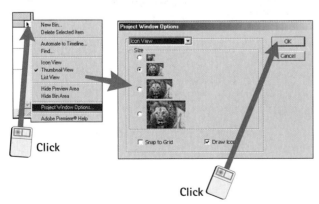

Click

Click

3 Select the Thumbnail View

To view your clips as thumbnails in a list with additional information, click the **Thumbnail View** button. You can then sort the list according to the entries in each column by clicking on the column headings.

Click

4 Select Thumbnail Options

To customize the thumbnail view, select **Project Window Options** from the **Project** window or pop-up context menu. From the **Icons** list, choose the size to display each icon, and deselect **Draw Icons** to not display a thumbnail of each clip. In the **Fields** area, change the names of the fields used to enter descriptive information about each clip.

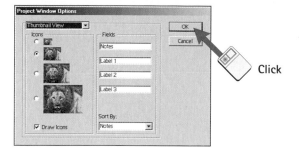

Click

5 Select the List View

To view your clips in a terse list with descriptive information about each clip, click the **List View** button. Click on the column headings to sort the list.

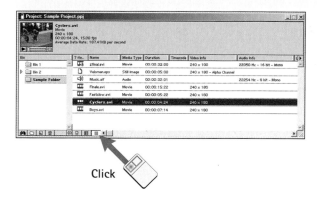

Click

6 Select List Options

To customize the List view, select **Project Window Options** from the **Project** window or pop-up context menu. From the **Fields** list, select the information about each clip that will be displayed in the List view.

How-To Hints

Using Clip Views

In the List view, you can review all the information about your clips, including attributes such as media type and duration, as well as additional user information in the Notes and Label fields. The Thumbnail view shows a thumbnail of each clip along with some basic information; you can add your own information here. Use the Icon view to organize and reorder your clips before moving them to the Timeline.

End

How to Label and Search

The more you organize your clips with bins, the more useful they become for later work as you save and share them with other Projects. You can also add your own annotations by entering text notes and labels for the clips. Then sort your clips using the annotation text or search the clip information and annotations with the **Find** command.

Begin

1 Display the Thumbnail View

To enter notes and labels about your clips, first click on the **Thumbnail View** button to display the clips.

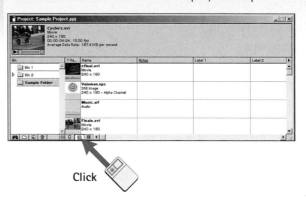

Click

2 Enter Clip Notes

Click in the **Notes** field for the clip and type the text of your notes or comments about the clips.

3 Enter Clip Labels

Premiere also provides three other **Label** fields in which you can enter additional information to help identify and organize your clips. To enter a label, click in the **Label 1** field and type **My Label** as the text of the label.

4 Rename Notes and Label Fields

You can also change the name of the Notes and Label fields. When using the Thumbnail or List views, select **Project Window Options** from the **Project** window pop-up context menu and type new names into the **Fields** area.

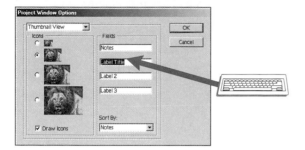

5 Search for Clips

Additional information entered in the Notes and Label fields can help you search for specific clips within a Project. Click on the window you want to search, pull down the **Edit** menu, and choose **Find** (or use the **Project** window menu or pop-up context menu) to display the **Find** dialog. You can also click on the **Find** button (binoculars icon).

Click

6 Select Find Options

In the **Find** dialog, click the left drop-down **Find** menu to select the field to search. Click the middle drop-down menu to search for matches to the specified text, or to search for fields that do not match the text. Then enter the text to search for in the right field. In the **And** line, you can specify a second text search field. Then click **Find** to begin the search, or **Find Again** when continuing a search for the next matching item.

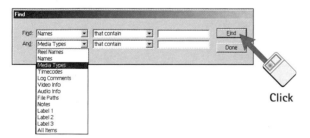

Click

How-To Hints

Notes and Labels

The predefined Notes and Labels fields can actually be used in any way that is helpful. Enter long notes into any of the fields to annotate the clip for later use. Enter a series of keywords to help search for specific clips, or just enter one word to sort the clips in the list displays. In this way, you can organize and annotate collections of clips into bins that can be reused in many different Projects.

End

How to Undo and Change History

Now that you have become experienced with using Premiere to import and organize clips into bins, and seen how easy it is to add, move, copy, and delete clips and even entire bins, it is time to also learn how to recover from mistakes. Premiere offers a variety of ways to undo and roll back a series of actions, which also makes it easy to experiment with changes.

Begin

1 Undo

To undo your last action, pull down the **Edit** menu and click on **Undo**. The name of the action also appears in the menu, such as Text Editing. Premiere remembers up to your last 99 actions across all open windows, so you can sequentially undo them step by step.

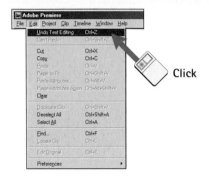
Click

2 Display the History Palette

Even better, Premiere displays the list of your recent actions in the *History palette* along the right side of the work area. If the palette is hidden, click on the **History** tab in the **Palette** window, or pull down the **Window** menu and choose **Show History**.

Click

3 Go Back In History

The **History** palette displays each action that has been performed on the Project, with the most recent at the bottom. To jump back to a previous state, click the name of the tool or command used in that state. All of the more recent states below it in the list are then dimmed.

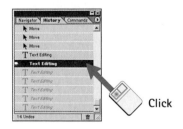
Click

 4 Change History

After you step back to a previous state, you can still move to a different state, whether older (above) or newer (below, and dimmed). You can also choose to start working again at that previous state, in which case the dimmed history list is discarded, and a new list starts.

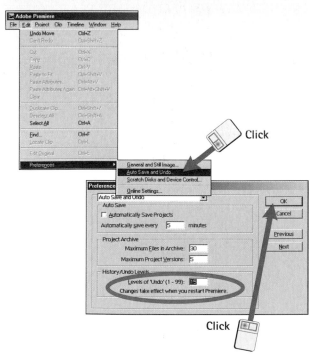

5 Delete History

You can also step back in the **History** palette to a previous state, and delete the states that followed it. Click on the most recent state that you want to preserve, and then open the **Palette** window menu and choose **Delete**, or press the **Delete** button (trashcan icon) at the bottom-right corner.

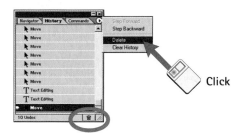

Click

6 Set Undo Properties

To review your Undo and **History** palette setting options, pull down the **Edit** menu and select **Preferences, AutoSave and Undo**. You can set the number of Undo levels (and the number of levels saved in the history palette) from 1 to 99.

Click

Click

Task

Assembling Clips Using the Storyboard and Timeline

*A*fter you have imported your media clips into your Project, and organized them into bins, it is time to begin assembling your production on the Timeline. The easiest way to lay out your clips on the Timeline is to make a rough cut, in which you first arrange the clips roughly in order, and then fine-tune your production by positioning and trimming them more precisely.

You can get started quickly with Premiere by just clicking and dragging clips into position on the Timeline. You can also use the new Storyboard window to arrange the clips into sequence before moving them into the Timeline. Premiere also provides a new Automate to Timeline command to automatically lay out a group of clips on the Timeline, and even overlap them with a default transition.

In this part, you'll insert clips into the Timeline individually and in groups, move and delete them, and automate the layout with the Storyboard. This is all you will need to make your first video productions. See Parts 9, 10, and 11 for more on trimming clips and advanced editing techniques. ●

How to Add Clips in the Timeline

The most direct way to add and organize individual clips in the Timeline is just to click and drag them. You can drag clips from a bin in the Project window, from a Clip window, and within the Timeline window.

Begin

1 Open the Sample Project

To start working with a clean slate, pull down the **File** menu and choose **Open Recent Project**, and then choose the **Sample Project** file. Or, if the Project is already open, pull down the **File** menu and choose **Revert**.

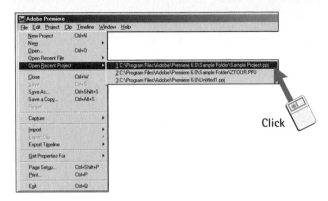

Click

2 Drag from the Project

Select the **Sample Folder** bin in the **Project** window, and then click and drag the **Cyclers** clip to the **Video 1A** track in the **Timeline**.

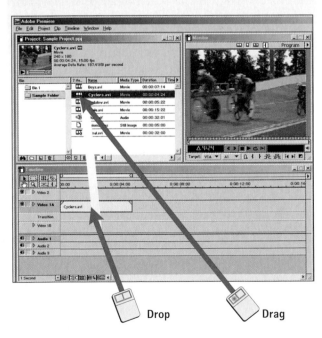

Drop   Drag

3 Drag from a Clip Window

You can also drag to the **Timeline** from a **Clip** window. Double-click to open the **Fastslow** clip in a **Clip** window, and then drag from the video area to drop the clip after **Cyclers** in the **Video 1A** track. Notice how Premiere snaps the second clip into position after the first.

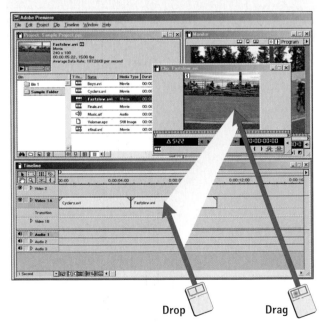

Drop   Drag

➍ Play the Program

To view the program on the **Timeline**, close the **Clip** window, and click the **Play** button on the **Monitor** window (or select the **Timeline** window and press the **Spacebar**). Since the second clip immediately follows the first, the playback shows a simple *cut* from one to the other.

Click

➎ Overlap the Clips

For a more interesting effect, you can add transitions between each pair of clips (see Part 4). Premiere shows this on the **Timeline** with the **Video 1** track split into three *subtrack* rows: **Video 1A**, **Transition**, and **Video 1B**. With this *A/B roll* editing you can overlap each pair of clips and add a transition between them. To stagger a pair of clips in the **Video 1** track, drag the **Fastslow** clip down to the **Video 1B** track, and position it to the left slightly to overlap with the end of the **Cyclers** clip in **Video 1A**.

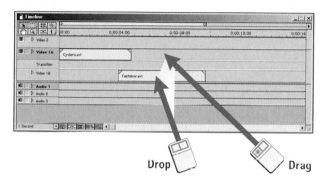

Drop   Drag

➏ Open A Gap

As you assemble clips on the **Timeline** and move them back and forth in time you might introduce gaps in the program. Drag the **Fastslow** to the right beyond the end time of the **Cyclers** clip. If you play the program, the gap will appear as a black screen.

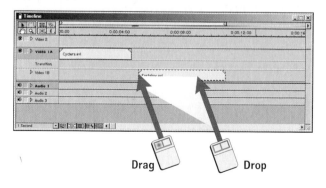

Drag   Drop

How-To Hints

Locating Clips

As you add more and more clips to the **Timeline**, you can start to lose track of which clip came from where. To find the source of a clip in the **Timeline**, select it, and then choose **Locate Clip** from the pop-up context menu. Premiere will display the bin the clip was added from in the **Project** window, and highlight the clip in the bin area.

End

How to Insert and Delete Clips from the Timeline

So far, you have been building the program by adding clips to the end of the Timeline. However, you can also edit a Timeline by inserting new material in between existing clips, or by deleting material from the middle. The other clips will adjust to fit. This is called *ripple* editing, referring to how a change in the program ripples through all the clips as they slide apart to make room from new material, or slide closer together to fill a gap.

1 Insert and Ripple

Drag and hold the **Veloman** still image clip from the **Project** window bin over the front of the **Fastslow** clip in the Timeline. While the cursor is over the **Fastslow** clip, Premiere displays a right arrow icon on the **Fastslow** clip to show that it will be shifted over, and highlights the size of the new clip. Then drop the new clip into place.

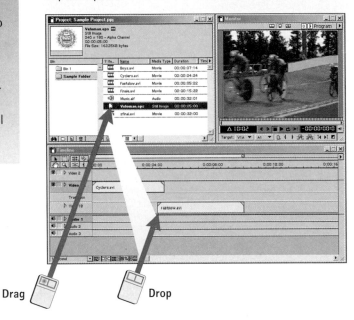

Drag   Drop

2 View Insert

After the ripple insert, the new **Veloman** clip now starts at the time where **Fastslow** used to start, and the **Fastslow** clip has been shifted to the end of the new clip to make room for it.

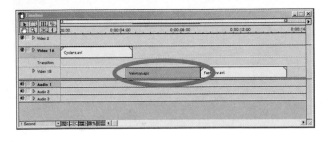

3 Delete a Clip

To delete the **Veloman** clip in place, select the clip and press the **Delete** key, or choose **Clear** from the pop-up context menu.

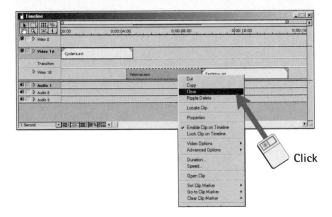

Click

4 View Delete

Simply deleting the clip does not affect the rest of the program, so there is now a gap in the Timeline.

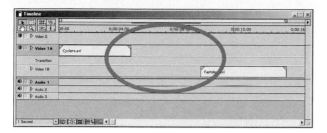

5 Ripple Delete Clip

Pull down the **Edit** menu and choose **Undo** to restore the **Veloman** clip. Now, select **Veloman** clip, and choose **Ripple Delete** from the pop-up context menu.

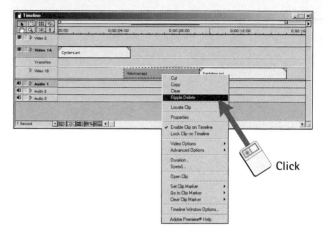

Click

6 View Ripple Delete

After the ripple delete, the end of the program is shifted back to the left to fill the time period of the deleted clip.

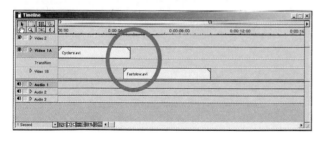

How-To Hints

Advanced Editing

Premiere provides an amazing variety of methods for adding, inserting, and adjusting clips in the Timeline. See Part 10 for more advanced techniques for inserting and deleting clips.

End

How to Add a Group of Clips to the Timeline

Dragging individual clips to the Timeline to assemble a program can quickly become tedious. Instead, you can select and drag a collection or group of clips all at once. The trick is to have Premiere understand what order you want them placed in the Timeline.

Begin

1 Open the Sample Project

Pull down the **File** menu and choose **Open Recent Project**, and then choose the **Sample Project** file. Or, if the Project is already open, pull down the **File** menu and choose **Revert**.

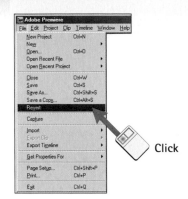

Click

2 Drag a Group of Clips

Select the **Cyclers**, **Fastslow**, and **Finale** clips from the **Sample Folder** bin in the **Project** window by clicking and dragging a selection rectangle over their names. Then to add them all to the Timeline, click and drag with the hand cursor from the icon area to the left of the names to the **Video 1A** track in the **Timeline** window.

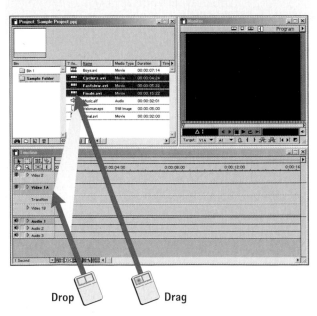

Drop   Drag

3 View Timeline

Premiere then lays out the selected clips in alphabetical order on the destination track. Scroll back in the Timeline to see their order.

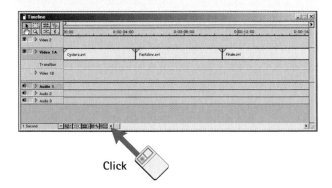

Click

4 Arrange in Icon View

Pull down the **Edit** menu and choose **Undo** to empty the Timeline. For more control over selecting clips, click on the **Icon View** button below the bin area. Then, rearrange the clips in the desired order, left to right and top to bottom.

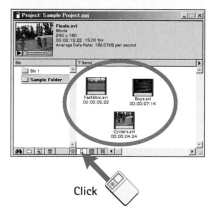

Click

5 Drag from Icon View

Select the three clips by clicking and dragging a selection rectangle around them, and then click and drag them down to the **Video 1A** track in the Timeline.

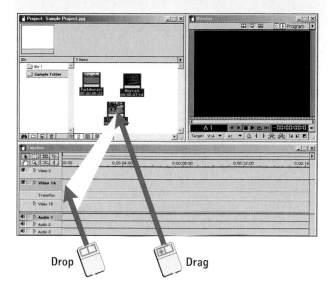

Drop   Drag

6 View Timeline

This time, Premiere lays out the clips in the order that they were organized in the bin.

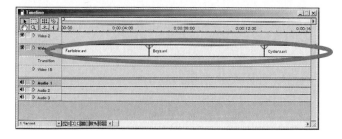

How-To Hints

Multiple Selections

You can select a list of clips in the Premiere windows using the normal selection techniques for your system. To select a set of files grouped together, click and drag a selection rectangle over them. To select a list of non-contiguous files from a larger group, click on the first one, and then use Ctrl+Click (Windows) and Shift+Click (Macintosh) to add or remove items from the multiple selection. For some operations, Premiere uses the order in which you select the clips.

End

How to Automate to the Timeline

To simplify assembling clips on the Timeline, Premiere also provides an Automate to Timeline feature. Automate to Timeline not only adds a group of clips, but also arranges them alternately on the A and B tracks, with a default transition between each pair.

Begin

1 Open the Sample Project

Pull down the **File** menu and choose **Open Recent Project**, and then choose the **Sample Project** file. Or, if the Project is already open, pull down the **File** menu and choose **Revert**.

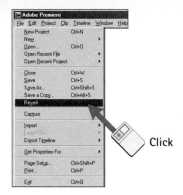

Click

2 Automate to Timeline

Select the **Boys, Cyclers,** and **Fastslow** clips from the **Sample Folder** bin in the **Project** window by clicking and dragging a selection rectangle over their names. Then, pull down the **Project** window menu and choose **Automate to Timeline**, or select it from the **Project** menu.

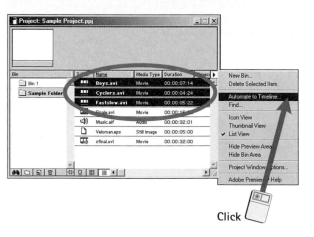

Click

3 Select Contents

Premiere displays the **Automate to Timeline** dialog. In the **Contents** drop-down menu, select **Selected Clips** to add only the clips you want to the Timeline (or select **Whole Bin** to add the entire bin).

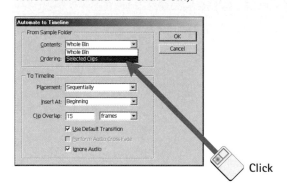

Click

4 Select Insertion Point

In the **Insert At** drop-down menu, select **Beginning** to insert the clips at the front of the Timeline (or select **Edit Line** or **End** to insert them at the current edit line position or at the end).

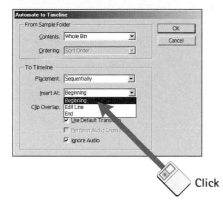

Click

5 Select Clip Overlap

In the **Clip Overlap** drop-down menu, enter the number of **frames** or **seconds** that each clip should overlap the adjacent clips for a transition. Select **Use Default Transition**, and click **OK**.

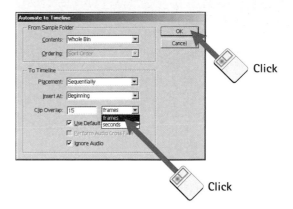

Click

Click

6 View Resulting Timeline

Scroll in the Timeline and look at the **Navigator** window to view the resulting layout. The specified clips have been laid out alternating on the **A** and **B** tracks. The ends have been overlapped, and a default transition has been inserted between them.

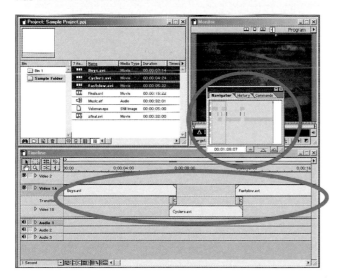

How-To Hints

Rendering Transitions

If you play the automated Timeline layout, you will not see any transition effect; instead, the playback will simply cut whenever an A track clip overlaps a B clip below it. The red colored bar above the *time ruler* at the top of the **Timeline** window warns that this portion of the Timeline still must be *rendered* to create the frames showing the transition effect. See Part 4 for more on previewing and rendering transitions.

End

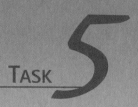

How to Use the Storyboard

An even better way to organize a collection of clips before adding them to the Timeline is to use a storyboard layout to arrange the individual clips in sequence. In addition to the **Project** and **Bin** windows, Premiere also provides a **Storyboard** window for arranging the order of a group of clips into a rough cut.

Begin

1 Open the Sample Project

Pull down the **File** menu and choose **Open Recent Project**, and then choose the **Sample Project** file. Or, if the Project is already open, pull down the **File** menu and choose **Revert**.

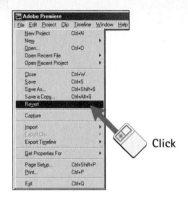

Click

2 Open a Storyboard Window

Pull down the **File** menu and choose **New**, **Storyboard**. Premiere opens a new empty **Storyboard** window.

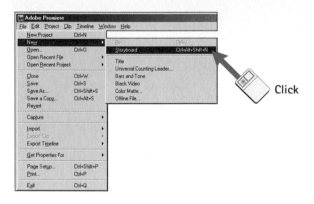

Click

3 Import Clips

To add clips to **Storyboard** window, select and drag the **Sample Folder** from the **Project** window to the **Storyboard** window. You can also drag individual clips, or use the **File** menu or pop-up context menu to choose **Import File** or **Import Folder**.

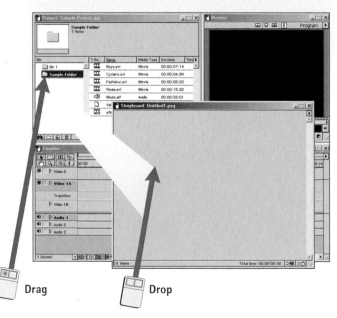

Drag

Drop

4 Delete Clips

The clips are numbered to show their sequence, and also have arrows connecting them to show the flow from one to the next. Each clip is displayed with a thumbnail icon, along with its duration. Select the **zFinal** clip and then press the **Delete** key to delete it from the storyboard.

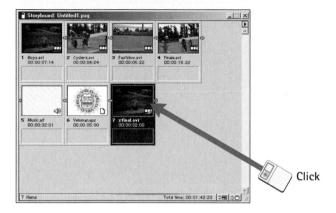

Click

5 Reorder Clips

Drag the **Fastslow** clip earlier in the sequence to insert it in front of the preceding **Boys** clip. Then drag the **Cyclers** clip later in the sequence to insert it after the **Finale** clip.

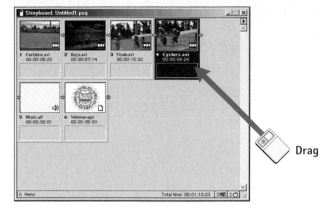

Drag

6 Automate to Timeline

Pull down the **Project** menu and choose **Automate to Timeline**, or choose it from the **Storyboard** window menu or the pop-up context menu, or press the button at the bottom right of the window. Set the Storyboard and Timeline options in the **Automate to Timeline** dialog, and Premiere automatically lays out the clips on the Timeline.

Click

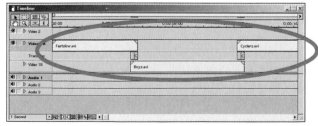

How-To Hints

Icon Sizes

Choose **Storyboard Window Options** from the **Storyboard** window menu or the pop-up context menu to set the size of the clip thumbnail icons in the window.

Save the Storyboard

Once you have organized your clips in a **Storyboard** window, you can save your work for later use. Pull down the **File** menu and choose **Save**. Premiere creates storyboard files in Windows with the extension **.PSQ**.

Print Storyboard

You can also print the **Storyboard** window display for use as a reference. Just pull down the **File** menu and choose **Print**.

End

Task

PART 4

Adding Transitions Between Clips

*A*fter you have organized your clips in the Project window, and laid them out in a sequence in the Timeline window, you can start to think about what happens when you move or transition from clip to clip during the playback of your production. The simplest visual effect is to simply *cut* from one clip to the next, with the last frame of the first clip immediately followed by the first frame of the next clip.

While a cut is often the best and most direct transition, you have arranged the clips to tell a story, and might find that the visual effect of a cut is too abrupt. Instead, you might want to use a visual transition between the clips to help advance the story or set a mood—for example, to suggest the passage of time, or movement in location, or a switch to a different part of the story.

Premiere offers more than 75 transitions, including wipes, dissolves, stretches, zooms, 3D motion, and masks. These provide a wonderful range of creative freedom to your work, as each transition also can be customized in duration, speed, direction, and other ways. In addition, you can use transitions in Premiere to show two clips at the same time with a split-screen or inset. Just don't get too carried away with your creative freedom so that you distract from your story! ●

How to Use Automated Transitions

As we saw in the previous part, Premiere's Automate to Timeline greatly simplifies building a Timeline from a group of clips by automatically laying them out on the Timeline. It also can automatically insert a default transition between each pair of clips, which you can then modify and customize.

Begin

1 Open the Sample Project

Open the **Sample Project** (from Part 1), select the **Sample Folder** bin, and then click and drag a selection rectangle to select the first three clips. From the pop-up **Project** window menu, choose **Automate to Timeline**, or select it from the **Project** menu.

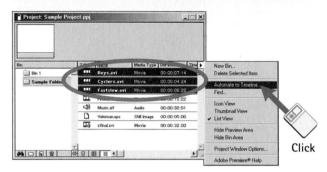

2 Automate to Timeline

In the **Automate to Timeline** dialog, pull down the **Contents** menu and select **Selected Clips**. Verify that **Use Default Transition** is checked, and then click **OK**.

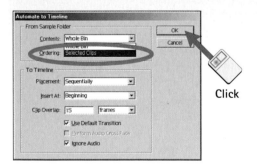

3 Review the Transitions

Premiere then automatically lays out the three clips in the **Timeline** window, alternating between the **Video 1A** and **Video 1B** tracks. Premiere also adds a default transition on the **Transition** track between the video tracks. To view the settings for the first transition (between the **Boys** and **Cyclers** clips), click the transition clip and select **Transition Settings** from the pop-up context menu, or simply double-click the transition.

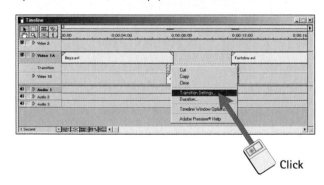

4 View Transition Settings

The title area of the **Transition Settings** dialog shows that this default transition is a **Cross Dissolve**. The animation in the bottom-right corner shows that the transition starts with the **A** track and dissolves to the **B** track.

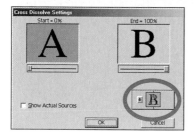

5 Show Actual Sources

Click the **Show Actual Sources** check box to view the actual clips from the Timeline. Drag the **Start/End slider** under the **Start** window to preview the effect of the transition. Then click **Cancel** to prevent any changes to the default transition settings.

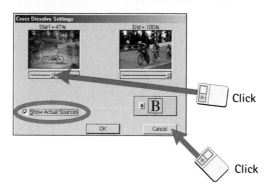

Click

Click

6 View the Second Transition

Double-click the second transition (between the **Cyclers** and **Fastslow** clips) to show its settings. Notice that Premiere has automatically set the transition to dissolve back from the **B** to the **A** track. You can click the **Track selector** arrow button to the left of the animation to reverse the direction of the transition.

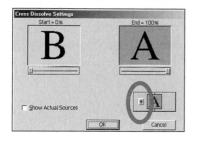

How-To Hints

Clip Overlap

Use the **Clip Overlap** option in the **Automate to Timeline** dialog to adjust the amount of overlap between adjacent clips. You can specify the amount of overlap in frames or seconds, or specify no overlap for simple cut transitions.

End

How to Preview Transitions

Transitions involve combining the information from a sequence of frames in two different clips, according to the options that you have selected. The frames must be distorted or blended together, and the effect also changes during the transition. As a result, in order for you to preview the transition, Premiere must first render it, or generate all the frames for the transition between the two clips.

Begin

1 Play the Program

Select the **Timeline** window, and then press the **Spacebar** to play through the **Timeline** (or click on the play controls in the **Monitor** window). Notice that the transition seems to have no effect; the playback simply cuts directly from the **A** track to the **B** track, and then back again. This is because the transition has not yet been rendered for previewing, as indicated by red bar above the time ruler in the area of the two transitions.

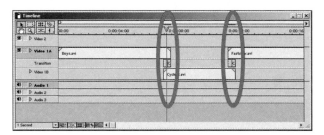

2 Scrub Through the Transition

To check the visual effect of the transition, you can preview the transition by *scrubbing* with the edit line. Press the **Alt** (Windows) or **Option** (Macintosh) key, and then click and drag the edit line in the time ruler. The cursor changes from a triangle to an arrow, and the **Monitor** window shows the transition effect. Scrubbing shows the visual effect of the transition, but not at full playback speed.

3 Select the Work Area

To render an area of the **Timeline** in order to preview a transition, first select a *work area* in the yellow bar above the time ruler. Double-click on the work area bar to select only the currently visible area of the **Timeline** (the right end marker moves into the window), and then drag the two ends of the work area to cover just the first transition.

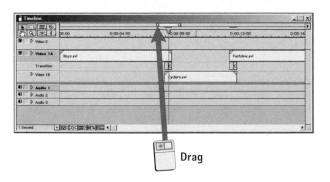

Drag

4 Generate a Preview

To generate a preview of the work area, select **Preview** from the pop-up context menu in the work area (or from the **Timeline** menu), or simply press the **Enter** key.

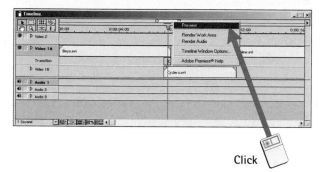

Click

5 Build the Preview

Premiere then displays the **Building Preview** dialog as it computes the frames to preview the transition for the selected work area.

6 Play the Preview

Once the preview has been generated, Premiere then plays the work area. The colored bar above the time line is now colored green to indicate that the preview has been generated. Press **Enter** again to play just the work area, or press the **Spacebar** or use the **Monitor** window controls to play through the Timeline, with the first transition now previewing.

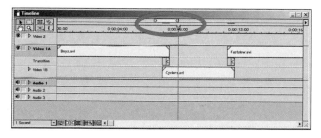

How-To Hints

Using the Work Area

To preview all the transitions, first double-click the work area bar to expand it to cover the entire window, or click and drag the work area bar over the second transition.

Rendering without Playing

You can also have Premiere render the transition without playing the result by using the **Render Work Area** option in the pop-up context menu for the work area, or in the **Timeline** menu.

End

How to Set Transition Durations

You can adjust the length or duration of a transition by adjusting the extent that the clips overlap, and then shrinking or lengthening the transition to match.

Begin

1 Change the Clip Overlap

To increase the overlap of the first two clips, drag the **Cyclers** clip to the left.

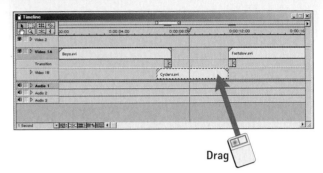

Drag

2 Move the Transition

Drag the transition clip to the left to align with the start of the **Cyclers** clip.

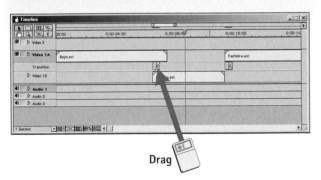

Drag

3 Adjust the Transition Duration

Extend the transition to the end of the **Boys** clip by clicking and dragging the right edge of the transition clip. The cursor changes to a bar with arrows pointing left and right.

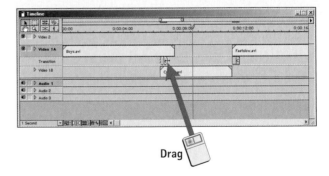

Drag

4 Check the Duration

To set or check the duration length, choose **Duration** from the pop-up context menu (or the **Clip** menu). Premiere displays the **Clip Duration** dialog with the length of time of the transition.

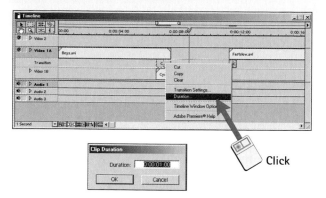

Click

5 Set the Work Area

Double-click the work area bar above the time line to extend the work area to cover the entire visible area in the **Timeline** window.

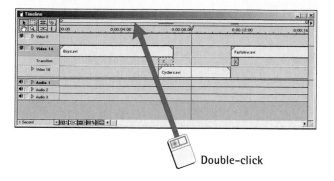

Double-click

6 Preview the Transitions

Finally, press the **Enter** key to render and preview both transitions. Premiere builds a preview for each transition, and then plays through the entire window work area.

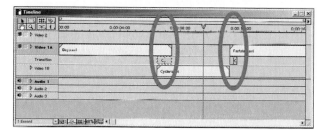

How-To Hints

Fade to Black

You can also use a dissolve transition to create a fade up from black or fade down to black. The second transition in step 6 actually fades up from black because there is no clip in the second track.

Preview Files

When you render a transition and create a preview, Premiere actually saves the frames for the transition in a preview file on the hard disk. You can change the defaults for rendering in the **Project** menu, under **Project Settings, Keyframe and Rendering**.

End

How to Use the Transition Palette

To make it easier to select and modify transitions, Premiere organizes them into the **Transitions** palette. Like other Premiere elements, the **Transitions** palette is organized into a hierarchy of folders, and can be customized to match your work style.

1 Show the Transition Palette

To show the **Transitions** palette, click on the **Transition** tab in the **Palette** window, or pull down the **Window** menu and choose **Show Transitions**.

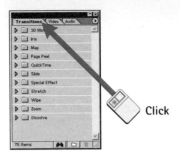

Click

2 Expand the Transition Palette

Click on the triangle to the left of the **Page Peel** folder to expand the folder to show all the included transitions. Scroll though the list of transitions, and pop up the **Transition** palette menu to choose **Expand all Folders** or **Collapse all Folders**.

Click

3 Animate the Transitions

For a visual preview of the effect of the transitions, pop up the **Transition** palette menu and choose **Animate**. Each of the transition icons now animates to show the effect of the transition.

Click

4 View Transition Information

For a brief explanation of each transition, click the transition and then look at the **Info** palette. To show the **Info** palette, click the **Info** tab in the **Palette** window, or pull down the **Window** menu and choose **Show Info**.

5 Set the Default Transition

Double-click on the **Dissolve** folder to show its contents. The **Cross Dissolve** transition is marked with a red outline, to show that it is the current default transition, used by the **Automate to Timeline** command. To change the default transition, select a transition, and then choose **Set Selected as Default** from the pop-up **Palette** window menu.

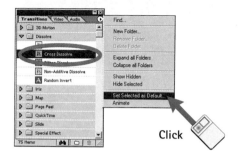

Click

6 Set the Default Properties

Premiere then displays the **Default Effect** dialog, to set the default duration of the default transition and its alignment relative to the cut point. Click **OK** to accept the current settings.

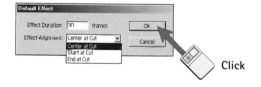

Click

How-To Hints

Customizing the Transitions Palette

You can reorganize and customize the **Transitions** palette by dragging your favorite transitions to the front of the list and using the pop-up palette menu to add new folders and even hide transitions to simplify the list.

Finding Transitions

You can also search for transitions by name; choose **Find** from the pop-up palette menu, or click the **Find** button (binoculars icon) at the bottom of the window.

End

How to Insert and Modify Transitions

Inserting and modifying transitions with Premiere is as easy as working with any other kind of clip. Just drag to move transitions and double-click to change settings.

1 Insert a Push Transition

To replace the default **Cross Dissolve** transition, open the **Slide** folder in the **Transitions** palette, select the **Push** transition, and drag it on top of the first transition in the **Timeline**.

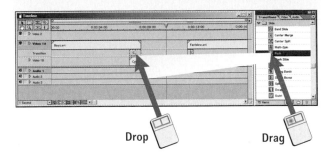

Drop   Drag

2 Set the Edge Direction

Double-click the new **Push** transition clip to display the **Push Settings** dialog. The transition defaults to pushing the old clip out left to right, as shown by the red **Edge Selector** arrow next to the animation in the bottom-right corner of the window. Click on the edge at the top center of the animation to change the transition to push from top to bottom.

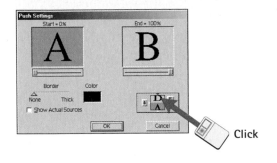

Click

3 Show the Sources

For a better understanding of the visual effect of the transition, click the **Show Actual Sources** check box to display the corresponding frames of the two clips. Drag the **Start** and **End** sliders under the two windows to preview the transition.

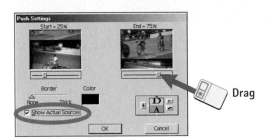

Drag

4 Set the Border

Drag the **Border** slider to add a border between the frames and adjust its thickness. Click on the **Color** rectangle to display the **Color Picker** dialog and select yellow. Then press **Cancel** to close the dialog and experiment with another transition.

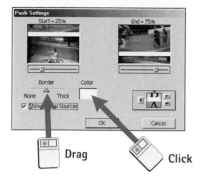

Drag

Click

5 Set the Zoom Transition

Open the **Zoom** folder in the **Transition** palette, and double-click the **Zoom** transition to display the **Zoom Settings** dialog. Click and drag the small rectangle in the **Start** window to change the center point of the zoom effect to the top-left corner of the frame. Drag the **Start** slider to preview the effect.

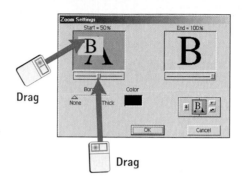

Drag

Drag

6 Set the Play Direction

To change the play direction of the transition from Forward to Reverse, click the small **F** button to the right of the animation. The button marking changes to **R**. The transition now zooms A out to reveal B, instead of zooming B in to cover A.

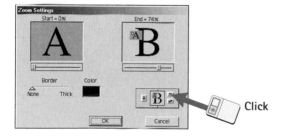

Click

How-To Hints

Anti-Aliasing

Click the **Anti-Aliasing** selector button under the **Forward/Reverse** button to adjust the smoothness of the edges of the transition through three settings: Off, Low, and High (indicated by two square pixels, blocky connected pixels, and a smoother diagonal line).

Local and Global Settings

When you double-click a transition clip in the Timeline and change the **Settings** dialog, you are setting the options only for that specific instance of the transition between two clips. When you change the **Settings** dialog in the **Transition** palette, you are changing the global default settings for that transition each time you use it.

End

How to Choose Transitions

Premiere provides lots of transitions, but also organizes them into categories as folders in the Transitions palette to help you make sense of them. This task provides a brief tour of the different types of transitions.

1 Using Dissolve Transitions

Double-click the **Dissolve** folder in the **Transitions** palette to view the list of dissolve transitions. Then double-click the **Additive Dissolve** transition to view its controls. The dissolve transitions fade one clip into another, so that the first fades away, and the second gradually appears. Press **Cancel** to view the next group of transitions.

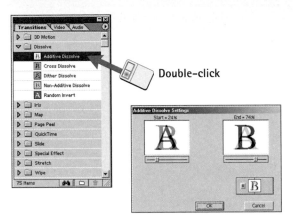

Double-click

2 Using Wipe Transitions

Double-click the **Wipe** folder, and then double-click the **Barn Doors** transition. The wipe transitions push away the first clip to reveal the second, using various geometric patterns. You can control the starting location and direction of the wipe.

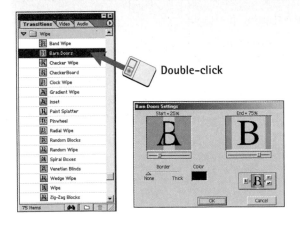

Double-click

3 Using Slide and Stretch Transitions

Double-click the **Slide** and **Stretch** folders, and then double-click the **Funnel** transition. The slide transitions move the second clip in to cover the first, and the stretch transitions distort the clips as they slide in. Some also break the clips into pieces, or rotate the clips as they slide.

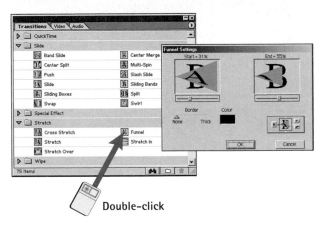

Double-click

4 Using Iris & Page Peel Transitions

Double-click the **Iris** and **Page Peel** folders, and then double-click the **Iris Star** transition. The iris transitions perform wipes in geometric shapes from the center of the display. The page peel transitions curl the first clip away to reveal the second.

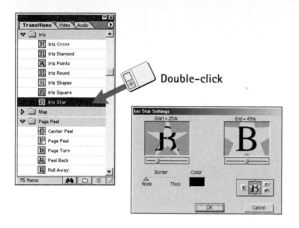

Double-click

5 Using Zoom Transitions

Double-click the **Zoom** folder, and then double-click the **Zoom Trails** transition. The zoom transitions zoom down the first clip and zoom up the second clip into place.

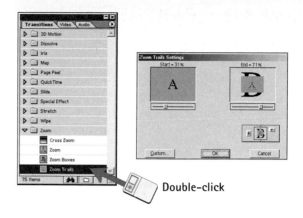

Double-click

6 Using 3D Motion Transitions

Finally, double-click the **3D Motion** folder, and then double-click the **Curtain** transition. The 3D transitions move away the first clip in 3D perspective to reveal the second clip.

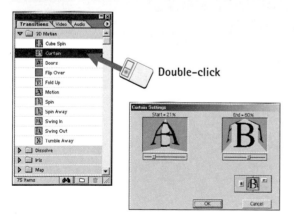

Double-click

How-To Hints

Special Effect Transitions

Check out the **Special Effect** and **Map** transitions for more complex effects. Use **Direct** and **Take** to force the use of the B track even when it is overlapped by an A track. Use **Image Mask** to design your own transition effect based on a user-supplied mask image.

Multiple Transitions

You can also create more complex effects by chaining multiple transitions, one after another, or by applying multiple transitions at the same time, for example, to dissolve a wipe effect.

End

How to Create Split-Screens and Insets

You can also use transitions to create an effect showing two clips playing on the display at the same time, by using a split-screen or inset. The trick is to set the transition at a specific point, and have it not change while the clips are playing.

Begin

1 Align the Clips

Clear the **Timeline** by dropping down the **File** menu and choosing **Revert**. Then select the **Sample Folder** bin and drag the **Boys** and **Fastslow** clips into the **Video 1A** and **Video 1B** tracks so they are aligned at the beginning of the window.

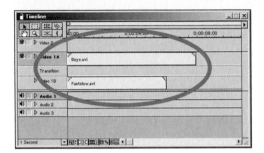

2 Add a Wipe Transition

To create a split-screen effect, open the **Wipe** folder in the **Transitions** palette, and drag the **Wipe** transition to the **Transition** track in the **Timeline** between the two clips. Premiere automatically sets its duration to match the shorter clip.

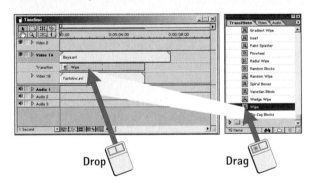

Drop   Drag

3 Set Up the Split-Screen

Double-click the **Wipe** transition to open the **Wipe Settings** dialog. Then, hold down the **Shift** key while moving the **Start** slider to around 50%. This sets the same **Start** and **End** point for the transition, so its effect is frozen as the clips play. Click **Show Actual Sources** to preview the split-screen effect.

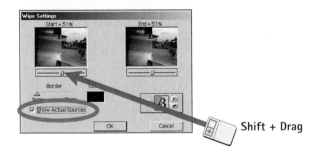

Shift + Drag

4 Add an Inset Transition

Similarly, to create an inset effect, replace the **Wipe** transition by dragging and dropping the **Inset** transition (also in the **Wipe** folder in the palette) over it.

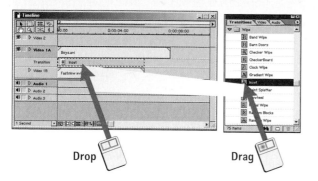

Drop   Drag

5 Set Up an Inset

Double-click the **Inset** transition to open the **Inset Settings** dialog. Again, hold down the **Shift** key while moving the **Start** slider to around 50%. Click **Show Actual Sources** to preview the inset effect.

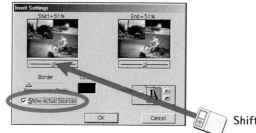

Shift + Drag

6 Get Creative

Click on the edges of the animation to move the **Edge Selection** red triangle and show the inset in another corner. Or get creative by using a different transition such as **Iris Round** (in the **Iris** folder) to create a circular inset, and then drag the center point to a corner.

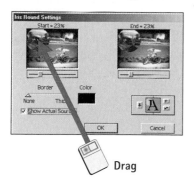

Drag

How-To Hints

More Splits and Insets

You can use a **Stretch** transition to show a split screen with the entire width of both frames squeezed into the display, or a **3D Motion** effect such as **Cube Spin** to show both frames in perspective. You can also use the **Zoom** transition to control the size and position of a rectangular inset in the frame. Look through the **Transition** palette for more ideas.

End

Task

PART 5

Exporting Video Clips

Now that you have imported and organized clips and laid them out in a production on the Timeline, it is time to export your work, saving it to a movie file that you can keep and share with others. Premiere provides built-in support for exporting to common desktop video and audio formats, including Microsoft Video for Windows (.AVI) and Apple QuickTime (.MOV), and for exporting in Web formats (see Part 7, "Creating Internet Media").

Premiere provides a wide range of options for the exported file format, including video and audio compressors, video resolution and frame rate, audio size and sample rate, and other special processing options. To help manage all these options, Premiere includes preset Project Settings to use while editing the clips and Export Settings to define the output format. You can also define and save your own settings. Premiere also provides a Settings Viewer to help ensure that all these different settings are consistent.

In this part, you will apply the Export Settings to save individual clips in a variety of different formats. You can use Premiere in this way to quickly convert clips to new formats, and even trim and resize clips, all without importing them into a project. You will also explore the most useful video and audio compression options for the QuickTime and AVI file formats. In the next part, you will move on to exporting an entire production from the Timeline, and using other video and audio file formats.

For much more information on file formats and compressors, see the Tutorials and other information on the Adobe Web site (www.adobe.com).

How to Export a Video Clip

To start making sense of all of the export options in Premiere, you will first step though the process by exporting a single video clip. For the moment, you will not set any of the export options, so Premiere will export the clip in the default video file format. In the next task, you will then check the results by looking at the clip properties.

Begin

1 Open the Sample Project

Open the **Sample Project** that you saved in Part 1. If you have just launched Premiere, click the **Open** button in the initial **Load Project Settings** dialog, navigate to the **Sample Folder**, and select the **Sample Project** file. Otherwise, pull down the **File** menu and choose **Open** to select the **Sample Project**, or, even easier, pull down the **File** menu and choose **Open Recent Project, Sample Project**.

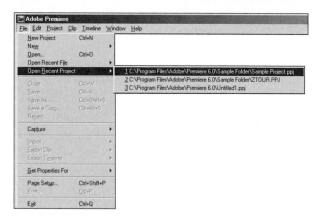

2 View the Cyclers Clip

Click on the **Sample Folder** in the bin to show all the clips, and then double-click the **Cyclers** clip to open a **Clip** window and view the clip.

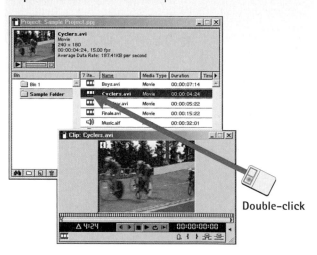

Double-click

3 Export the Clip

To export the clip to a new video file, pull down the **File** menu and choose **Export Clip, Movie**.

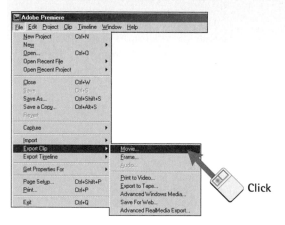

Click

4 Name the Clip

Premiere displays the **Export Movie** dialog. Navigate to the **Sample Folder**, click the **File name** field, type **Cyclers Copy** as the name of the clip, and click **Save**.

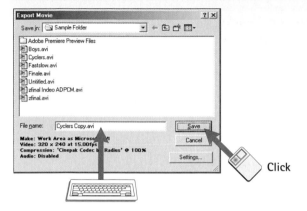

Click

5 Save the Clip

Premiere then displays the **Exporting** dialog as it processes the clip and saves it to disk as a new clip file. The dialog includes a meter to indicate progress as it counts through the frames in a clip. Click **Stop** if desired to abort the export.

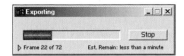

6 View the New Clip

When the export completes, Premiere displays the saved clip in a new **Clip** window. Oddly, the new clip appears to be larger than the original. Go on to the next task to see what happened to it.

How-To Hints

Export Properties

Premiere displays a summary of the current export settings at the bottom of the **Export Movie** dialog so you can review them at a glance. You will check the settings in more detail, and change them, in the following tasks.

Converting Clips

While Premiere is designed for creating and saving entire video productions, you can also use it for simpler tasks such as saving a clip in a different format, or quickly changing the length or resolution of a clip. You can even use the **Open** option in the **File** menu to open and export clips that are not part of a project.

End

How to Check Clip Settings

In Task 1, you saved a copy of the Cyclers clip using the default settings. However, it now appears that the new clip is larger than the original. In this task, you will look at the clip properties to understand what happened.

Begin

1 Resize the Cyclers Clip Window

Premiere automatically shrinks a video clip to fit in a Clip window. Click on the triangular area at the bottom right of the original **Cyclers** clip window. Premiere displays the clip size (240×180) at the top left, and also shows the extent of the full clip as a rectangular outline. Drag the window down and to the right so that the clip expands to full size in the window.

Drag

2 Resize the New Clip Window

Click on the corner of the new **Cyclers Copy** clip window. The copied clip (320×240) is indeed larger than the original. Resize the window to also expand it to full size.

Click and Drag

3 Open the Clip Properties

To find out more about the clips, click on each **Clip** window menu and choose **Properties,** or use the pop-up context menu.

Click

4 View the Clip Properties

Premiere displays the Properties dialog for each clip. Both files have the same **Duration** (4:24, or under five, seconds) and the same **Frame Rate** (15.00 fps). Both are compressed with the same **Compressor** (Cinepak). However, the **Cyclers Copy** clip has a larger resolution or **Frame Size** (320×240 versus the original's 240×180)—and therefore has a larger **File Size** on disk (1.57MB versus 899.60KB).

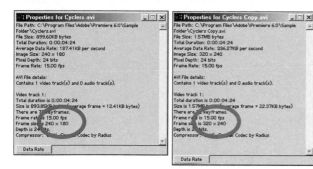

6 View the Project Settings

The **Settings Viewer** is a great way to check that your capture, project, clip, and export settings are consistent. Premiere highlights the **Frame Size** row in red to show the problem: The **Project Settings** and **Export Settings** use a size of 320×240, but the sample clip files imported into the project were created at 240×180. As a result, Premiere expanded the **Cyclers** clip to the larger size before exporting it. Click **OK** to close the dialog.

5 Open the Project Settings Viewer

To understand why the new **Cyclers Copy** clip has a different size, check the default settings for the project. Close the **Clip** windows and **Properties** dialogs, and then pull down the **Project** menu and choose **Settings Viewer** to review the current project settings.

Click

How-To Hints

Clip Properties

You can check the properties for a clip without even opening it. Just pull down the **File** menu and choose **Get Properties for, File**, and select the file.

Project Settings

Typically, you want to capture, process, and export your clips with the same settings to avoid any extra conversions or processing. However, when doing a rough edit, you might want to set the Project settings to a lower resolution to save processing time and storage. And, you might want to use more than one Export setting to export a clip or production in several different output formats.

Changing Settings

Premiere provides several different ways to change settings. You can change **Capture, Project**, and **Export** settings from the **Settings Viewer** dialog; you can change **Project Settings** from the **Project** menu and the initial **Load Project Settings** dialog; and you can change the export settings from the **Export** dialog.

End

How to Use Export Settings

Premiere provides a great deal of flexibility for exporting your clips and productions. You can use the **Export Settings** dialog to customize the file type, video and audio properties, and other special processing to be used. In this and the following tasks you will first step through the options in the **Export Settings** dialog, and then save the clips in several different formats.

Begin

1 Export a Clip

For the next few tasks, you will use the **zfinal** clip from the **Sample Folder** because it is longer than previous sample clips and contains both video and audio. Open the **Sample Project**, and open the **zfinal** clip in the **Sample Folder**. Premiere displays it in a **Clip** window. Then pull down the **File** menu and choose **Export Clip**, **Movie**.

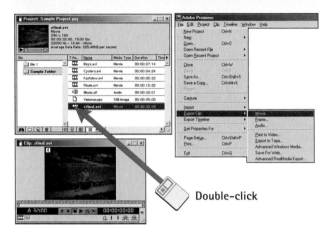

Double-click

2 Open the Export Settings

Premiere displays the **Export Movie** dialog, with the default export settings listed at the bottom left of the window. Click the **Settings** button to review and change the export settings.

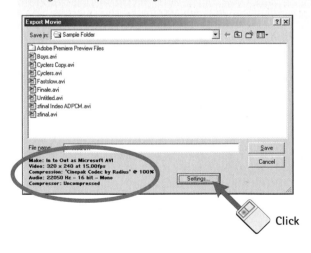

Click

3 Review the Export Settings

Premiere displays the **Export Movie Settings** dialog. It has several different panels to group the export settings, beginning with the **General** panel. Click the drop-down list at top left to switch between the different panels, or click the **Prev** and **Next** buttons at bottom right to cycle through the panels in order.

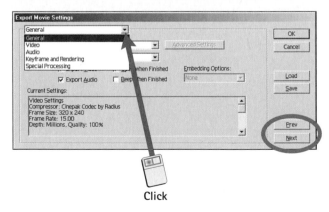

Click

4 Review the General Settings

The **General** panel displays a summary of the current settings. Make sure that both **Export Video** and **Export Audio** are checked, if you want to save a file with both video and audio. Also check **Open When Finished** to have Premiere automatically open the exported clip to play.

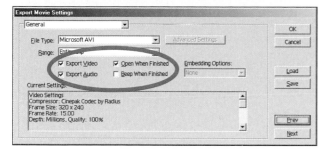

5 Set the Export Range

Click the **Range** drop-down list and choose **Entire Clip** so that the full clip is exported. You can also select **In to Out** to export only a part of the clip.

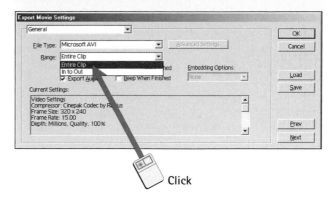

Click

6 Set the File Type

The **File Type** setting in the **General** panel determines the available compression and processing options for the **Video** and **Audio** panels. Premiere can export to the common desktop video formats, **Microsoft AVI** and Apple **QuickTime**, as well as to a sequence of image files. Go on to Task 4 to choose video settings.

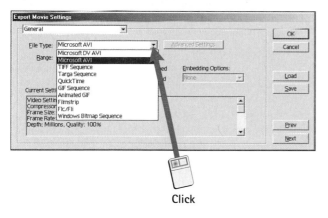

Click

How-To Hints

Choosing the File Type

Select a basic **File Type**, and video and audio compressors, that will be compatible with the systems where the file is to be played. Typically, choose **Microsoft AVI** if the file is to be played on a variety of Windows machines, and **QuickTime** if the file is to be played on Apple Macintosh machines, or on both kinds of machines. If in doubt, check the properties of an existing file that works well, and use the same settings for the files that you export.

Load and Save

Premiere offers **Load** and **Save** options in the **Project** and **Export** settings dialogs. Use these options to save your preferred settings and then reload them when you need them. That way, you won't have to click through all the dialog options to set and verify the settings.

End

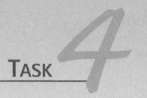

How to Choose Video Settings

The Video panel of the Export Movie Settings dialog provides options to specify the compression format, color depth, frame size, frame rate, and other attributes of the output file. Once you choose the basic file type, these settings determine the file size and visual quality of the file that you export.

Begin

1 Review the Video Settings

In the **General** panel of the **Export Movie Settings** dialog, click the **File Type** drop-down list and choose the **QuickTime** format. Then click **Next** to move to the **Video** panel.

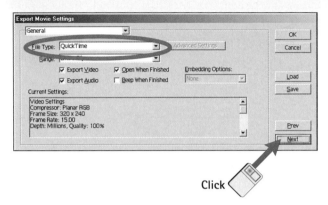

Click

2 Select the Video Compressor

In the **Video** panel, click on the **Compressor** drop-down list and choose **Sorenson Video**. Sorenson Video is a widely used compressor for the QuickTime format.

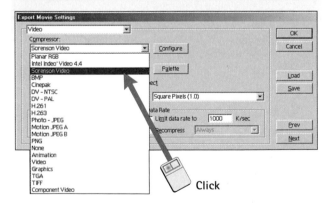

Click

3 Select the Video Depth

The **Depth** option with Sorenson compression defaults to **Millions** for full-color video. Some formats, such as **None**, offer the **Depth** option to specify the amount of color detail.

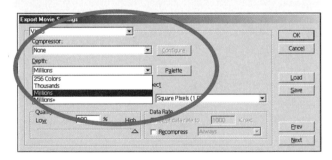

4 Select the Frame Size

Since the clip you are exporting is smaller than the default frame size, click the **Frame Size** field and type the new horizontal size (**h**) as **240**. Notice the vertical size (**v**) is automatically changed to **180**. This is because **4:3 Aspect** is checked to maintain the 4 to 3 ratio between the width and height of the frame.

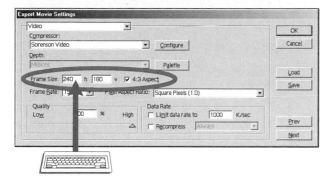

5 Select the Frame Rate

Click the **Frame Rate** drop-down list to review the available frame playback speed. Leave the setting at **15** frames per second (fps) to maintain the setting of the original file.

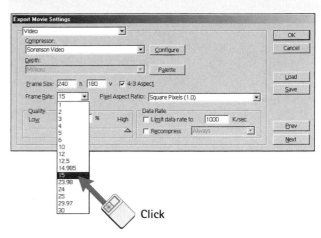

Click

6 Select the Quality

Finally, click and drag the **Quality** slider to 90% to set the desired video quality. (**Low** is 0%, and **High** is 100%.) Depending on the compressor, you can typically reduce the output file size significantly with only a small apparent reduction in quality. Experiment with your specific material to find the right trade-off between file size and visual quality.

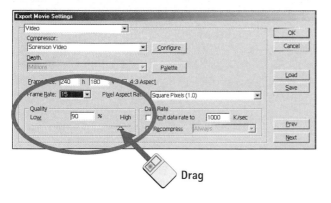

Drag

How-To Hints

Choosing a Compressor

There are lots of video compressors available, and even more compressor-specific options available by clicking the **Configure** button. Unless you have special circumstances, however, it is best to stick with the common settings so that your exported files are playable on the widest variety of systems.

Quality Versus File Size

Compressing video always involves a difficult trade-off between the output file size and the quality of the video frames. The whole purpose of compression is to significantly reduce the file size, but the challenge is to do this without seriously damaging the video quality. For best results, capture video clips in a format with as little compression as possible (that is, None, Motion JPEG, or DV), and also edit them in that format to minimize damage from continually decompressing and then recompressing. Then use heavier compression when the final production is exported to a file for later playback.

End

How to Choose Audio Settings

The **Audio** panel of the **Export Movie Settings** dialog provides options to specify the data rate, format, compressor, and other audio attributes of the output file. Again, you will leave most of the settings from the original file unchanged.

1 Select the Audio Rate

Select the **Audio** panel, and then click the **Rate** drop-down list to select the audio sampling rate. Choose **22050 Hz** (Hertz), which should provide good quality for a background music soundtrack.

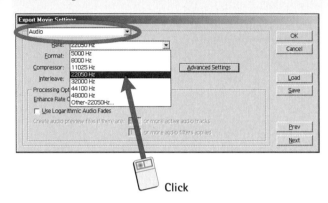

Click

2 Select the Audio Format

Click the **Format** drop-down list and choose **16 Bit – Mono**. Use **Stereo** only if you are working with true stereo clips because it can double the size of the audio data. Some compressors also offer an **8 Bit** format, which can be used to reduce the audio data size, but typically with a noticeable loss of quality.

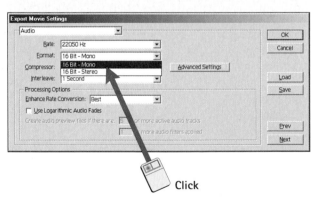

Click

3 Select the Audio Compressor

Click the **Compressor** drop-down list and choose **QDesign Music 2**, a common QuickTime audio compressor for music tracks. While the audio data size is much smaller then the video size in the final exported file, it is still worth compressing the audio. The quality loss from this compression is often imperceptible to human ears, especially when the clip plays on low-end consumer speakers.

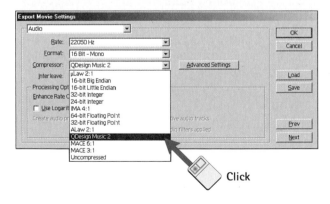

Click

4 Select Advanced Settings

Click the **Advanced Settings** button to display the compressor-specific settings dialog. The **QDesign Music Encoder** dialog provides a **Bitrate** drop-down list to set the target data rate for the compressed audio. Click **Cancel** to use the default rate.

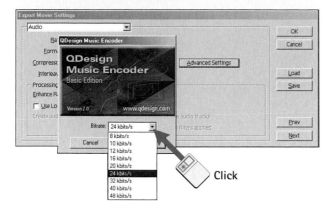

Click

5 Select the Interleave

Click the **Interleave** drop-down list to select how often blocks of audio data are *interleaved*, or inserted among the video frames in the exported file. A setting of **1/2** or **1 Second** is typical, but might need to be increased if audio is breaking up during playback.

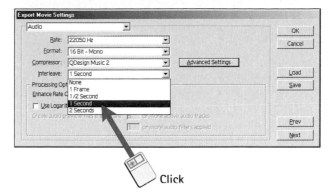

Click

6 Select the Rate Conversion

Click the **Enhance Rate Conversion** drop-down list to select the amount of processing to be used when converting the input clips to a different sample rate for export. Select **Best** for highest quality results, although these come at the expense of additional processing time.

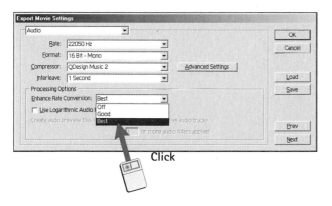

Click

How-To Hints

Controlling the Data Rate

Depending on the compressors, you might be able to set a target data rate for the audio and video data using the **Advanced Settings** in the **Audio** panel and the **Data Rate** settings in the **Video** panel. This limits the amount of bandwidth required to play the file over a network or from a slow disc like an older CD-ROM drive.

End

How to Use Special Processing Settings

Beyond all the editing functions and effects available when working with clips in the Timeline, Premiere also provides Special Processing functions during export that can be applied to the entire clip or production.

1 Review the Special Processing Settings

Select the **Special Processing** panel to review the summary of current processing settings. Then click **Modify** to change the settings.

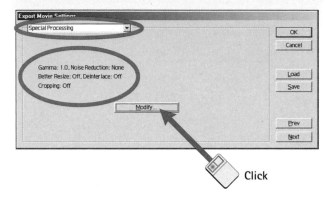

Click

2 Select the Cropping Region

Premiere displays the **Special Processing** dialog. To crop the exported video, drag the corner handles of the cropping rectangle, or type specific values for the **Left**, **Right**, **Top**, and **Bottom** margins. The **Size** readout displays the cropped size of the video. Click and drag within the rectangle to position it over the frame. Use the slider below the video display to preview the cropping for other frames in the movie.

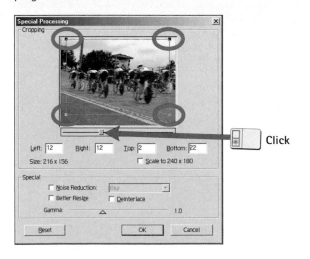

Click

3 Select the Scaling

Click to select **Scale** to have the cropped video enlarged to the original frame size specified in the **Video** panel. Otherwise, the video will be exported at the cropped size.

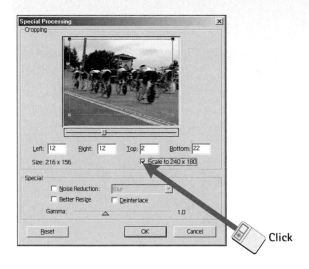

Click

4 Select Noise Reduction

Select **Noise Reduction** to reduce video noise in the movie being exported and improve compression quality. Noise reduction smoothes large changes between pixel values, which can blur images. Select **Blur** for a subtle blur, **Gaussian** for a stronger blur, or **Median** for a blur that keeps edges sharp.

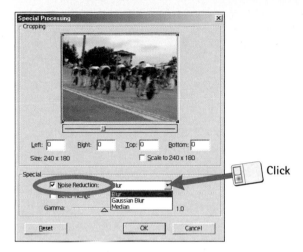

Click

5 Select Better Resize

Check **Better Resize** if you have selected cropping and scaling. Premiere will then use its own high-quality resizing method. Otherwise, the video will be resized by the method built into the selected compressor, which might be faster but produce lower quality.

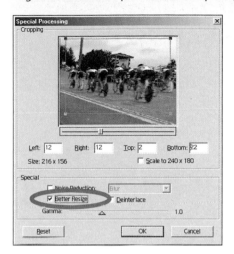

6 Select Deinterlace

Select **Deinterlace** if you are processing *interlaced* television video, in which each frame contains alternating pairs of lines from two separate fields captured at different times. The motion between fields can cause visible tearing when displayed. Deinterlacing uses every other line from one field and interpolates new in-between lines without tearing. Otherwise, the video will be deinterlaced by the method built in to the selected compressor, which might be faster but of lower quality.

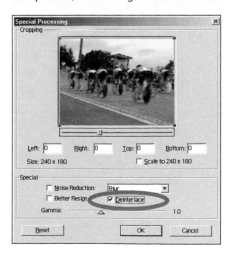

7 Select the Gamma

Click and drag the **Gamma** slider to adjust the brightness of the middle tones of the image while preserving the darker and lighter areas. This adjustment compensates for the differences between various display devices. Set the value to around 0.8 for use across multiple platforms, from PC to Macintosh. Then click **OK** to save the **Special Processing** options.

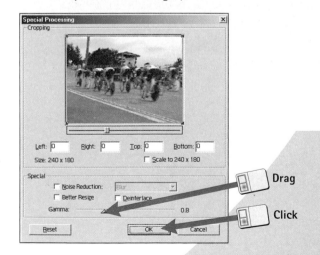

Drag

Click

End

How to Load and Save Export Settings

After going to all this effort to review and change the export settings, it would be nice to be able to save and reuse the settings. Premiere provides Load and Save options on each panel of the Export Movie Settings dialog to save the current settings, and to load new settings. You can also review the built-in preset settings provided with Premiere to use as a starting point for customizing your own settings.

Begin

1 Save the Export Settings

Click back to the **General** panel, and review the settings defined in the previous tasks, as displayed in the **Current Settings** area. Click the **Save** button.

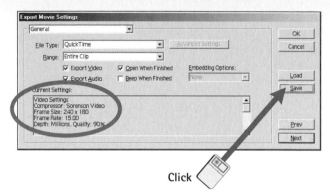

Click

2 Name the Export Settings

Premiere displays the **Save Export Settings** dialog. Type **QuickTime Sorenson QDesign 240x180** as the name for your settings in the **Name** field, and additional information in the **Description** field, if desired. Then click **OK**.

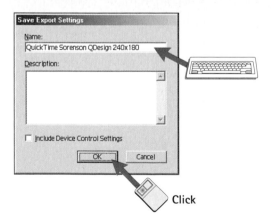

Click

3 Load Export Settings

Click **Load** in the **Export Movie Settings** dialog to review the available settings, including the presets provided with Premiere and additional settings you have saved.

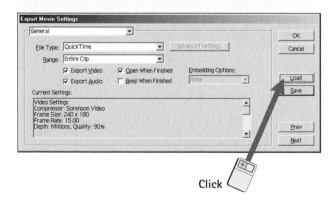

Click

4 View Multimedia QuickTime Settings

Premiere displays the **Load Export Settings** dialog. Your new QuickTime setting now appears at the bottom of the **Available Presets** list, with the corresponding **Description** on the right. Click **Multimedia QuickTime** to review the preset settings for the Apple QuickTime format when used as a cross-platform format for desktop video playback. The video uses Cinepak video compression at 320×240 frame size and 15fps frame rate. The audio uses uncompressed audio at 22,050Hz.

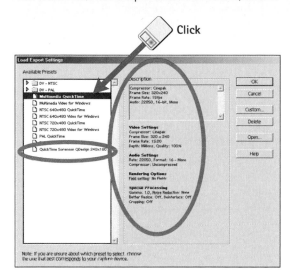

Click

5 View Video for Windows Settings

Click **Multimedia Video for Windows** to review the preset settings for the Microsoft AVI format for desktop video playback. Like the corresponding QuickTime format, the video uses Cinepak video compression at 320×240 frame size and 15fps frame rate, and the audio uses uncompressed audio at 22,050Hz.

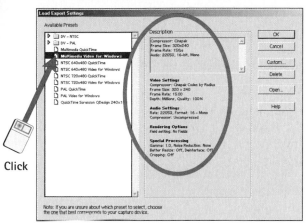

Click

6 View Full-Screen QuickTime Settings

Click **NTSC 640x480 QuickTime** to review the preset settings for the QuickTime format when used for full-size, full-rate video. The video uses Motion JPEG video compression at full 640×480 frame size and full 29.97fps frame rate, and the audio uses uncompressed audio at 44,100Hz.

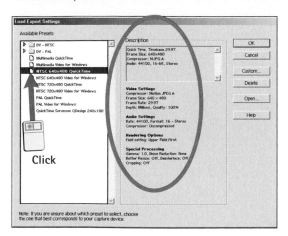

Click

7 View DV Settings

Open the **DV – NTSC** folder, and then click **Standard 32kHz** to review the preset settings for the DV camcorder digital video format. The video uses standard DV video compression at full 720×480 frame size and full 29.97fps frame rate, and the audio uses uncompressed audio at 32,000Hz. When you have finished reviewing the export presets, click **Cancel** to exit the **Export Movie Settings** dialog.

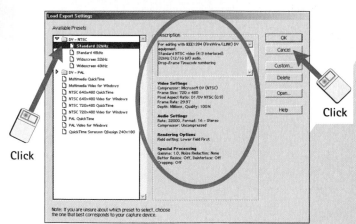

Click

Click

End

TASK 8

How to Export in QuickTime Format

Now that you have defined a preset for exporting the sample clips in QuickTime format, you can export clips in the correct size and format by loading the preset. You will use the zfinal clip from the Sample Folder because it is longer than the previous sample clips and contains both video and audio.

Begin

1 Export the Clip

Open the **Sample Project**, open the **zfinal** clip, and then pull down the **File** menu and choose **Export Clip, Movie**.

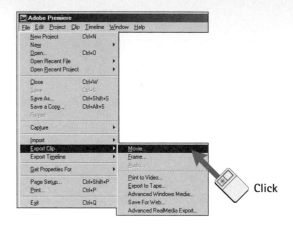

Click

2 Open the Export Settings

Premiere displays the **Export Movie** dialog. Check the current export settings listed at the bottom left. Then click **Settings** to change the settings.

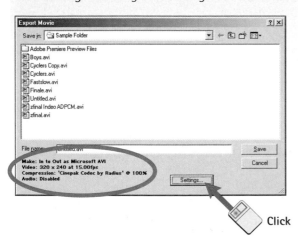

Click

3 Load New Settings

Premiere displays the **Export Movie Settings** dialog. Click **Load** to load the preset you saved earlier.

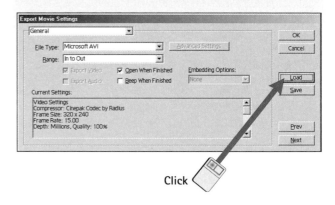

Click

4 Select Export Settings

Premiere displays the **Load Export Settings** dialog. Select the **QuickTime Sorenson QDesign 240x180** preset saved earlier and then click **OK**.

Click

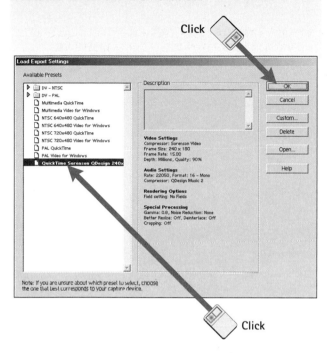

Click

5 Confirm the Export Settings

Premiere returns to the **Export Movie Settings** dialog. Click **OK** to use the preset you just selected.

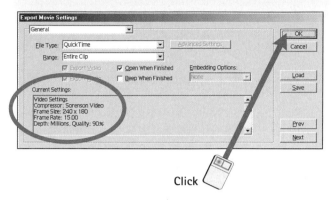

Click

6 Name the Clip

Navigate to the **Sample Folder** installed with Premiere, click the **File name** field, and type **zfinal QuickTime** as the name of the clip to be saved as a QuickTime Movie file (**.MOV** under Windows). Then click **Save** to begin the export.

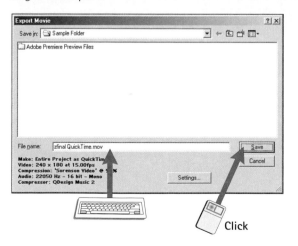

Click

7 View the New Clip

Premiere then displays the **Exporting** dialog as it processes the clip and saves it to disk as a new clip file. This takes longer than the 5-second **Cyclers** clip did because the **zfinal** clip is 32 seconds long. When the export finishes, Premiere displays the saved clip in a new **Clip** window.

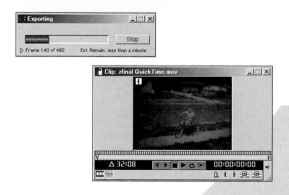

End

How to Export in AVI Format

You can also export the clip in a different format, such as Microsoft AVI for Windows, by using the **Export Settings** dialog to modify an existing preset.

Begin

1 Open the Export Settings

Open the **Sample Project**, open the **zfinal** clip, and then pull down the **File** menu and choose **Export Clip, Movie**. In the **Export Movie** dialog, click **Settings** to change the settings.

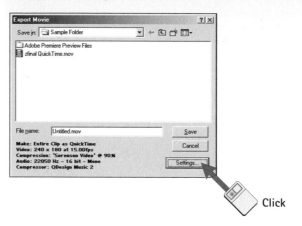

Click

2 Select the General Settings

Premiere displays the **Export Movie Settings** dialog. In the **General** panel, click the **File Type** drop-down list and select **Microsoft AVI**. Scroll the **Current Settings** list to review the export settings. Check that **Export Video** and **Export Audio** are both selected. Click **Next** to display the **Video** panel.

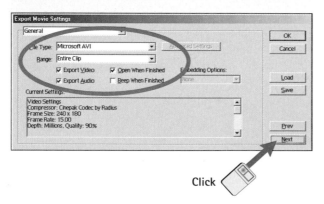

Click

3 Select the Video Settings

In the **Video** panel, click the **Compressor** drop-down list to select **Intel Indeo Video 4.4**. The Intel Indeo compressors are widely available for both the AVI and QuickTime formats. Verify that the **Frame Size** is 240×180, and **Frame Rate** is 15fps. Click **Next** to display the **Audio** panel.

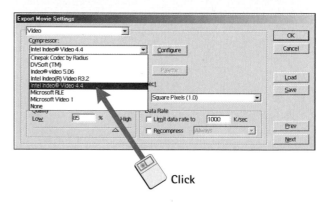

Click

4 Select the Audio Settings

In the **Audio** panel, click the **Compressor** drop-down list to select **Microsoft ADPCM**. Verify that the sample **Rate** is **22050 Hz**. Then click **OK** to keep the settings.

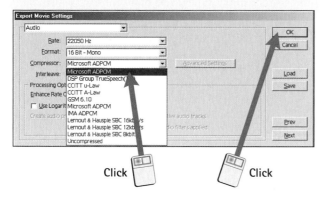

Click   Click

5 Name the Clip

Premiere returns to the **Export Movie** dialog. Navigate to the **Sample Folder**, click the **File name** field and type **zfinal AVI** as the name of the clip to be saved as a Microsoft Video for Windows file (**.AVI** under Windows). Then click **Save** to begin the export.

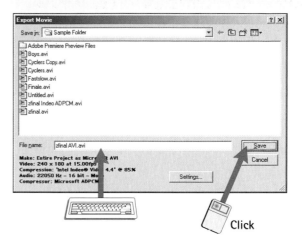

Click

6 View the New Clip

Premiere then displays the **Exporting** dialog as it processes the clip and saves it to disk as a new clip file. When the export finishes, Premiere displays the saved clip in a new **Clip** window.

How-To Hints

Save the Export Settings

You might want to save the export settings that you just used. Repeat the first steps of this task to display the **Export Movie Settings** dialog. Notice that Premiere retains the settings from your last export. Click Save to save the export settings as a new preset, with a name like **AVI Indeo ADPCM 240x180**.

End

Task

PART

Exporting Video and Audio Projects

In Part 5, you saved individual video clips in a variety of formats. You used the Premiere Export Settings to save and reuse the appropriate settings for the video clips in the Sample Folder, including different file format, compressor, and frame size information. You also used the Settings Viewer to check that all these values were consistent for capture, project, clip, and export settings.

In this part, you will go through the process of creating and saving a project from end to end, from importing the clips to editing them on the Timeline and exporting the final edited production. But, first, you will set up the Project Settings to match the input clips.

Premiere also can export video and audio to other formats besides Microsoft AVI and Apple QuickTime multimedia files. Premiere can export video to animated GIF format and as a sequence of still image files. It can export audio to audio-only formats such as AIFF and Windows Wave. It can also export to a variety of Web formats, including MPEG video and MP3 audio, through the Save For Web export option (see the following Part 7, "Creating Internet Media."). ●

How to Set Project Settings

The first step in starting a new project is to set up the appropriate Project Settings to be compatible with the input clips and output export formats. In earlier parts, you have been using the presets for Multimedia QuickTime or Multimedia Video for Windows as your default setting. However, as you saw in the last part, the frame size does not match the clips you are using from the Sample Folder.

Begin

1 Launch Premiere

Close Premiere if it is already running so that you can start from the beginning. Launch Premiere, and it displays the **Load Project Settings** dialog. At this point, you could click **Custom** to set up a new custom project setting. Instead, click **Open** to open the **Sample Project** to review its settings.

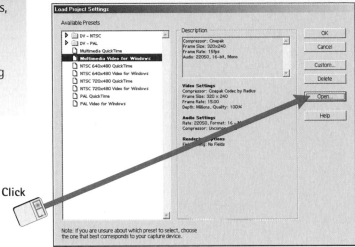

Click

2 Open the Project

Premiere displays the **Open** dialog. Navigate to the **Sample Folder** installed with Premiere, click to select the **Sample Project** (**.PPJ** under Windows), and then click **Open**.

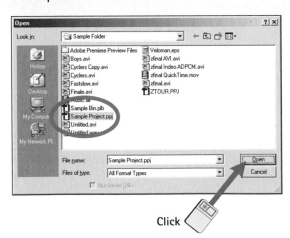

Click

3 Open the Settings Viewer

Premiere opens the saved project. To check the current settings, pull down the **Project** menu and choose **Settings Viewer**.

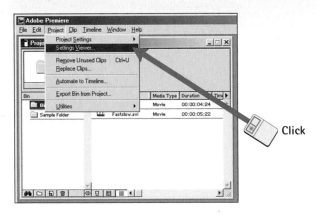

Click

4 Open the Project Settings

Premiere displays the **Settings Viewer** dialog. The **Frame Size** row is highlighted in red to show that the **Project Settings** are inconsistent with the clip and **Export Settings**. Click **Project Settings** to change them.

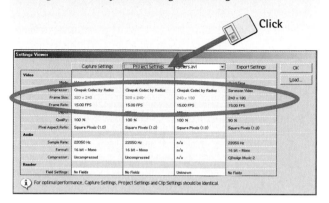

Click

5 Review the General Settings

In the **Project Settings** dialog, scroll the **Current Settings** area to review them. Click **Next** to display the Video pane.

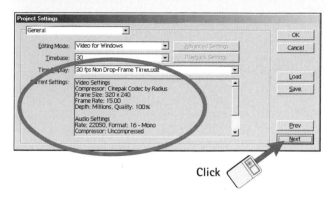

Click

6 Change the Video Settings

In the **Video** pane, click the **Frame Size** field and type the new horizontal size (h) as **240**. The vertical size (v) automatically changes to **180** because **4:3 Aspect** is checked to maintain the 4 to 3 ratio between the width and height. Click **Save**.

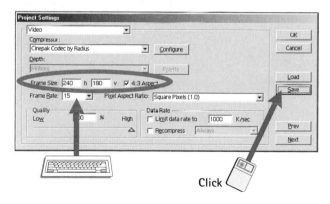

Click

7 Save the Project Settings

Premiere displays the **Save Project Settings** dialog. Click the **Name** field and type **Multimedia AVI 240x180** (or **QuickTime** for Macintosh) as the new project preset name. Click **OK** to save the settings. Premiere returns to the **Project Settings** dialog. Click **OK** to apply these settings to the current project.

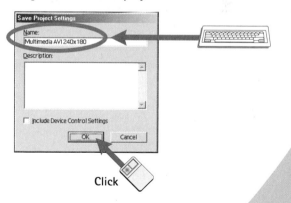

Click

Continues

8 Review the Project Settings

In the **Settings Viewer** dialog, the **Frame Size** row is still highlighted in red to warn you that the Capture Settings are not consistent. But the frame size for the Project, clip, and Export settings now all match. Click **OK** to close the dialog.

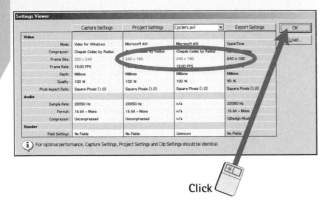

Click

9 Change the Project Settings

While you are working on your project, you can access the **Project Settings** dialog to change individual project settings and capture settings. If needed, click on the **Project** menu and choose **Project Settings** to select one of the panes of the **Project Settings** dialog.

Click

10 Save the Project

To save the project with its new settings, click on the **Project** window to select it, and then pull down the **File** menu and choose **Save**.

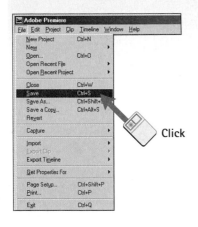

Click

11 Name the Project

Premiere displays the **Save File** dialog. Navigate to the **Sample Folder**, click the **File name** field, and type **Sample Project 240x180** as the new project name. Then click **Save**.

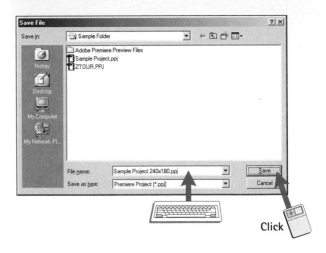

Click

𝒵2 Open the Project Presets

Now check the new project settings. Pull down the **File** menu and choose **New Project**.

Click

𝒵3 Review the Project Presets

Premiere displays the **Load Project Settings** dialog again. Click on the new preset that you saved, **Multimedia AVI 240x180** (or **QuickTime**), to verify that it is set up properly.

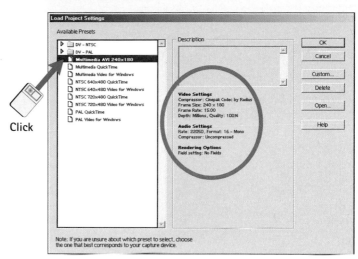

Click

How-To Hints

Project Settings

Premiere uses the project settings for previewing your production from the Timeline. Typically, settings are determined by the format of the video and audio that you are editing, either from clips on disk or input from a video capture card. However, it can be useful to change them, for example, to temporarily reduce the frame size or frame rate so that your edits and previews can be processed faster.

Export Settings

The export settings are independent of the project settings, so you can edit a project once, and then export it in a variety of different formats. You can set the export settings from the **Settings Viewer** dialog at any time, or from the **Export Movie** dialog when you export.

End

How to Export a Project

In this task, you will step through the entire process of importing, editing, and exporting a project. You will use the new sample project that you saved in Task 1, and the export settings you saved in Part 5. These are compatible with the clips in the Sample Folder installed with Premiere.

Begin

1 Launch Premiere

Close Premiere if it is already running so that you can start from the beginning. Launch Premiere, and it displays the **Load Project Settings** dialog. Click **Open** to open the new **Sample Project** to review its settings.

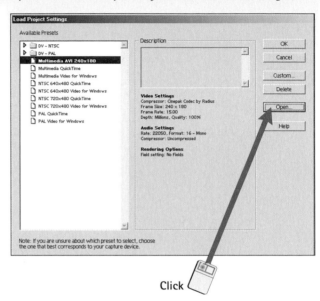

Click

2 Open the Saved Project

Premiere displays the **Open** dialog. Navigate to the **Sample Folder** installed with Premiere, click to select the new **Sample Project 240x180** that you saved in the previous task, and then click **Open**.

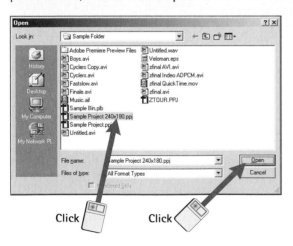

Click   Click

3 Open the Settings Viewer

Premiere opens the saved project. To check the current settings, pull down the **Project** menu and choose **Settings Viewer**.

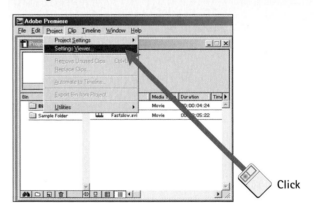

Click

4 Review the Project Settings

Premiere displays the **Settings Viewer** dialog. The **Frame Size** row is highlighted in red to warn you that the capture settings are still not consistent. But the frame size for the Project, clip, and Export settings now match. Click **OK** to close the dialog.

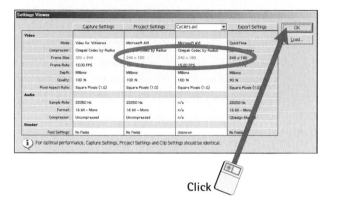

Click

5 Automate to Timeline

Select the **Sample Folder** in the **Bin** area of the **Project** window, and then select the first four clips (**Boys**, **Cyclers**, **FastSlow**, and **Finale**) by clicking and dragging a selection rectangle over them. Click the **Project** window menu and choose **Automate to Timeline**.

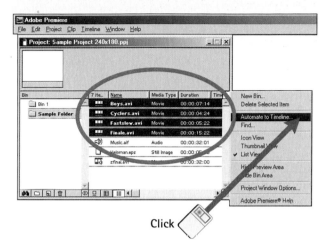

Click

6 Select Automation Settings

Premiere displays the **Automate to Timeline** dialog. Click the **Contents** drop-down list and choose **Selected Clips** (and not **Whole Bin**). Use the default transition settings, and then click **OK**.

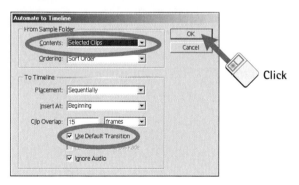

Click

7 Zoom the Timeline

Premiere automatically lays out the four clips on the **Timeline** window, with default transitions between them. Click the **Time Zoom Level** pop-up menu in the bottom-left corner to change the zoom to **2 Seconds**, so the entire production is visible.

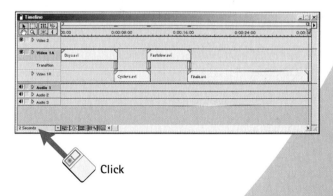

Click

Continues

8 Add Background Music

Click and drag the **Music** clip from the **Sample Folder** bin to the **Audio 1** track in the Timeline.

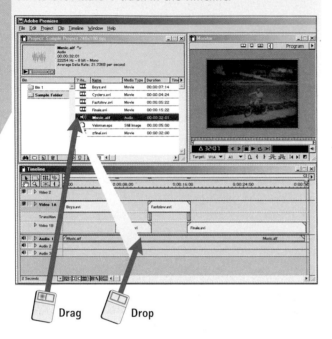

Drag   Drop

9 Export the Production

You now have a full video and audio production on the Timeline. To export the production, click the **File** menu and choose **Export Timeline, Movie**.

Premiere displays the **Export Movie** dialog. You can accept the current settings displayed in the bottom left of the dialog. Instead, click **Settings** to change the settings or load a new preset.

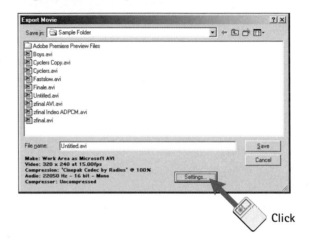

Click

10 Review the Export Settings

Premiere displays the **Export Movie Settings** dialog. As in Part 5, you can review and change the settings to make sure they are correct. Instead, click **Load** to load a preset.

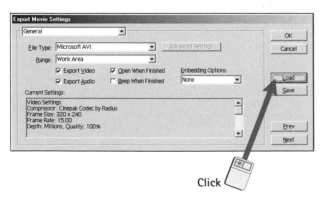

Click

11 Load the Preset Settings

Premiere displays the **Load Export Settings** dialog. Click to select the **QuickTime Sorenson QDesign 240x180** preset you saved in Part 5, or choose similar settings. Then click **OK**.

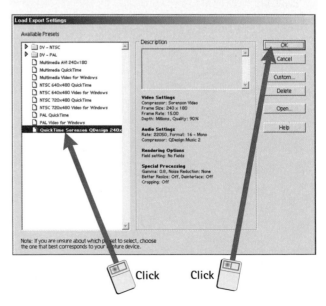

Click   Click

12 Review the Settings

Premiere returns to the **Export Movie Settings** dialog. Review the settings in the **Current Settings** scroll box, and then click **OK**.

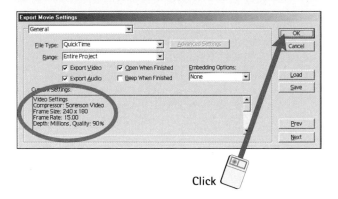

Click

13 Name and Save the Clip

Premiere returns to the **Export Movie** dialog. Navigate to the **Sample Folder**, click the **File name** field and type **zfinal QuickTime** as the name of the clip to be saved as a QuickTime Movie file (**.MOV** in Windows). Then click **Save** to begin the export.

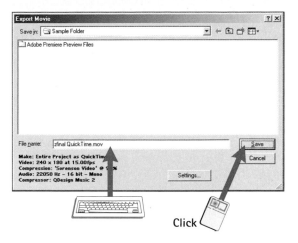

Click

14 Review the New Clip

Premiere displays the **Exporting** dialog as it processes the clip and saves it to disk as a new clip file. When the export completes, Premiere displays the saved clip in a new **Clip** window. Choose **Properties** from the **Clip** window pop-up context menu to view the clip properties (or pull down the **Clip** menu and choose **Properties**).

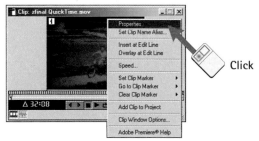

Click

15 Review the Clip Properties

Premiere displays the **Properties** window for the clip. Verify that the clip contains both video and audio tracks, compressed with the Sorenson Video and QDesign Music compressors, with a 240×180 frame size.

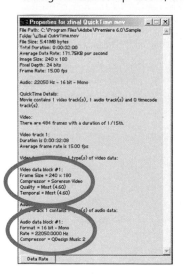

End

How to Export to Audio Formats

Premiere can export audio to other formats besides Microsoft AVI and Apple QuickTime multimedia files. Under Windows, Premiere can export audio-only files to the Windows Wave audio format (**.WAV**). On the Macintosh, Premiere can export audio-only files to the AIFF audio format.

Begin

1 Open an Audio Clip

To open an audio clip, pull down the **File** menu and choose **Open**. Premiere displays the **Open** dialog. Navigate to the **Sample Folder** installed with Premiere, click to select the **Music** clip file, and click **Open**.

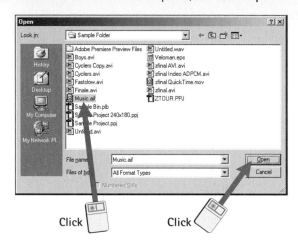

2 Export the Clip

Premiere opens a new **Clip** window to play the clip. Pull down the **File** menu and choose **Export Clip, Audio**.

3 Open the Export Settings

Premiere displays the **Export Audio** dialog. Click on **Settings** to change the export settings.

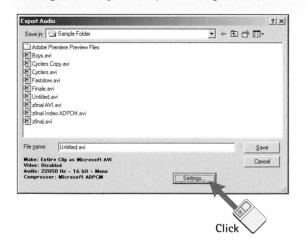

4 Select the Audio Format

Premiere displays the **Export Audio Settings** dialog. Click the **File Type** drop-down list and select **Windows Waveform** (or AIFF on the Macintosh). Verify the audio settings in the **Current Settings** field. (Use **Rate 22050** and **Format 16 - Mono**, and ignore the **Compressor** setting.) Then click **OK**.

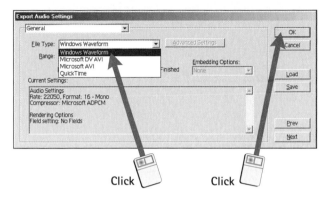

Click   Click

5 Name and Save the Clip

Premiere returns to the **Export Audio** dialog. Navigate to the **Sample Folder**, click the **File name** field, and type **Music Wave** (or **Music AIFF**) as the name of the new file. Then click **Save**.

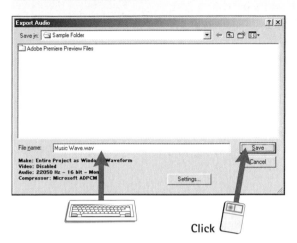

Click

6 Play the New Clip

Premiere then displays the **Exporting** dialog as it processes the clip and saves it to disk as a new clip file. When the export completes, Premiere displays the saved clip in a new **Clip** window. Choose **Properties** from the **Clip** window pop-up context menu to view the clip properties (or pull down the **Clip** menu and choose **Properties**).

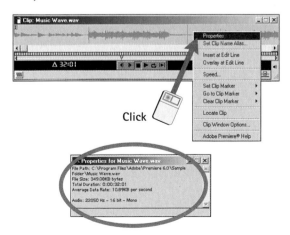

Click

How-To Hints

Audio-Only Files

You can save audio-only clips and productions in the Microsoft AVI and Apple QuickTime multimedia file formats. Even if your clip project includes video, you can export only the audio portion by pulling down the **File** menu and choosing **Export Clip** (or **Export Movie**), and then **Audio**.

MP3 Audio

You can also use Premiere to export audio clips in the MP3 compressed-audio format with the **Save For Web** option (see the next task, and Part 7).

End

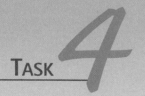

TASK 4

How to Export Image and Web Formats

Premiere can export video sequences to other formats besides Microsoft AVI and Apple QuickTime multimedia files. Premiere can export to a sequence of image files as well as a variety of Web formats.

Begin

1 Open a Clip

To review the other export options for a video clip, pull down the **File** menu and choose **Open**. Premiere displays the **Open** dialog. Navigate to the **Sample Folder** installed with Premiere, click to select the **zfinal** clip file, and click **Open**.

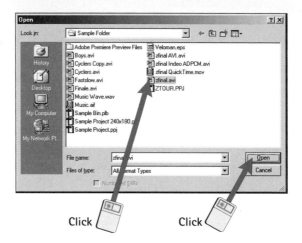

Click   Click

2 Export the Clip

Premiere displays the **Clip** window. To open the export settings, pull down the **File** menu and choose **Export Clip, Movie**. Premiere then displays the **Export Movie** dialog. Click **Settings**.

Click

3 Export a Still Image Sequence

Click the **File Type** drop-down list to view the available export file types. You can export a video sequence as a series of still image files in several different formats, including **TIFF**, **Targa**, **GIF**, and **Windows Bitmap** sequences.

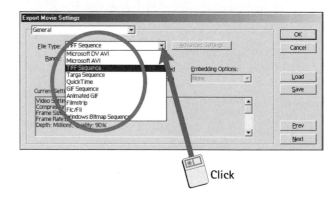

Click

94   PART 6: EXPORTING VIDEO AND AUDIO PROJECTS

4 Export an Animated GIF

Or click the **File Type** drop-down list and select **Animated GIF** to export an animated GIF file containing the video sequence as an animation.

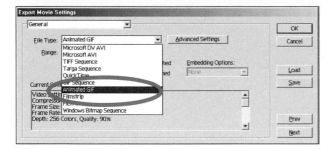

5 Export in Web Formats

To view the Premiere Web export options, click **Cancel** to close the **Export** dialogs, and then pull down the **File** menu and choose **Export Clip, Save For Web**.

Click

6 Review the Save for Web Options

Premiere displays the **Save for Web** dialog for the Cleaner EZ export plug-in. Click the **Settings** field to display the drop-down list of available export formats. Cleaner EZ can export to the standard Web streaming media options, **QuickTime**, **Real**, and **Windows Media** (see Part 7). Like Premiere, Cleaner EZ can also export to AVI and **QuickTime** desktop multimedia formats, as well as **Still Image** sequences, MPEG standard, and MP3 audio. Click **Cancel** to close the dialog.

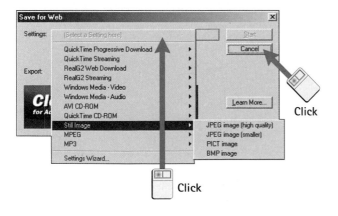

Click

Click

End

Task

Creating Internet Media

*O*ne of the best ways to share your video productions, whether for business or with friends and family, is to convert them to Internet media formats and post them on a Web site where they can be accessed from around the globe.

However, there are many different Web formats that you might use, depending on your requirements and the type of video players that your users have available. You can export files in formats intended for *downloading*, to be stored and played back later, and for *streaming*, to be played live over the Internet.

However, good streaming performance and playback quality over the Internet is extremely dependent on optimizing your files to the type of your audio and video material and to the expected bandwidth that your users will have available when connecting to the Internet.

Premiere has built-in support for exporting in a variety of Web formats, including Microsoft Windows Media, RealNetworks RealMedia, and Apple QuickTime. Each of these formats support a range of compression options, tuned to the type of material (that is, talking-head or fast-motion video, and voice or music audio). They also are designed to encode the material to specific target bandwidths (from 28K and 56K modems to ISDN to broadband and LANs).

Premiere provides three different Web export options. The Advanced Windows Media (Windows only) and Advanced RealMedia Export provide presets and options for the Microsoft Windows Media and RealNetworks RealMedia formats. In addition, the Save For Web option uses the Terran Media Cleaner EZ plug-in to export in a variety of formats, including QuickTime, RealMedia, Windows Media, MPEG-1, MP3 audio, and Still Image. ●

How to Export to Internet Formats

Premiere provides several different ways to export your material to Internet formats. This task provides an overview of these different approaches. The following tasks provide more detail on exporting in specific formats.

Begin

1 Export a Timeline

Once you have created your video production in Premiere, you can export the timeline into a file optimized for Internet viewing. From an open project, pull down the **File** menu and choose **Export Timeline** to select one of the three export options (see below).

2 Export a Clip

You also can export a single clip directly to Internet formats. In the **Timeline** window, select a clip on the timeline and then pull down the **File** menu and choose **Export Clip** to select one of the three export options (summarized in each of the steps below).

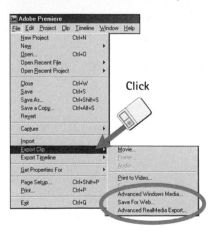

3 Advanced Windows Media

Use **Advanced Windows Media** (Windows only) to create a Windows Media file that can be played using the Microsoft Windows Media Player application. See Task 2 to use the **Advanced Windows Media** dialog.

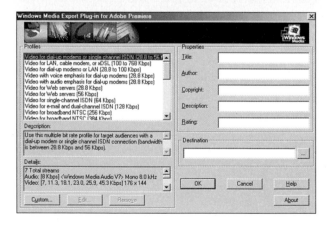

4 Advanced RealMedia Export

Use **Advanced RealMedia Export** to create a RealMedia file that can be played using the RealNetworks RealPlayer application. See Task 3 to use the **Advanced RealMedia Export** dialog.

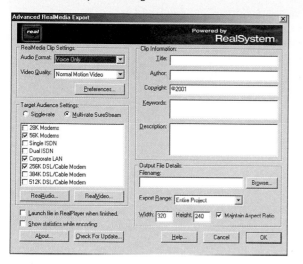

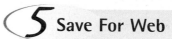 ## 5 Save For Web

Use **Save For Web** to use the **Terran Media Cleaner EZ** plug-in to export in a variety of formats, including Apple QuickTime. Use the **Export** drop-down list to select the **Entire Project** or the currently **Selected Work Area**.

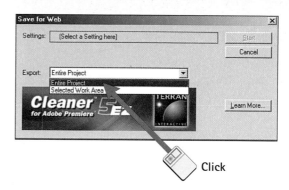

Click

6 Save For Web Settings

Use the **Settings** drop-down list in the **Save for Web** dialog to select the desired format (QuickTime, RealMedia, Windows Media, MPEG-1, MP3 audio, and Still Image). See Task 4 to export using Apple **QuickTime** format. See Task 5 to use the **Settings Wizard** to have Media Cleaner EZ help you select an appropriate setting.

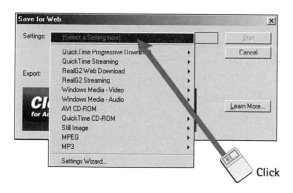

Click

How-To Hints

Cleaner EZ Settings

You can use Cleaner EZ to export in a wide variety of formats, both streaming formats for playing across the Web and other file formats for Web download or playing from a local disk.

Codec Central

Terran Interactive, the developer of the Cleaner EZ plug-in, provides a Web site with extensive information about video and audio compression formats. In the **Save for Web** dialog, click the **Learn More** button to access the Cleaner online documentation. Also visit www.terran.com/CodecCentral for information about a wide variety of compression formats (codecs).

End

How to Use Advanced Windows Media

Use the Advanced Windows Media export option (Windows only) to export your movie in Microsoft Windows Media format (**.WM**). The movie must contain audio. Windows Media files can be played back from a local file or over the Web using the Windows Media Player application, available as a free download from www.microsoft.com/windows/windowsmedia.

Begin

1 Export to Windows Media

To display the **Windows Media Export** dialog, pull down the **File** menu and choose **Export Timeline**, **Advanced Windows Media**. Or, to export a single clip, select the clip in the Timeline and then pull down the **File** menu and choose **Export Clip**, **Advanced Windows Media**.

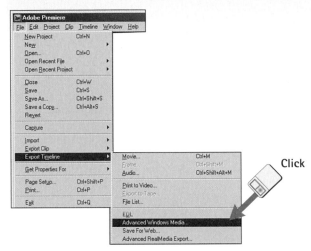

Click

2 Select the Target Profiles

From the **Profiles** list, select the standard profile that best matches the type of content being streamed and your target bandwidth. Click **Video for Web servers (56 Kbps)** to encode your movie for streaming over low-speed, dial-up modems. Review the **Description** and **Details** information below your selection.

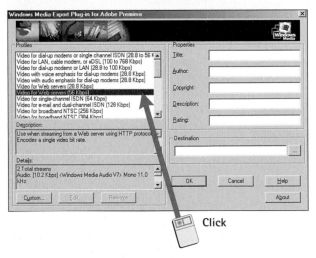

Click

3 Enter Output File Properties

If desired, you can also enter optional descriptive information about your movie in the **Properties** section. This information is displayed in Windows Media Player when the file is viewed.

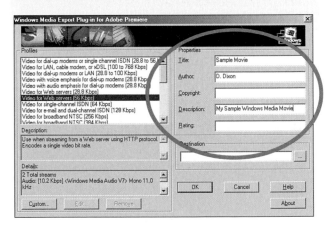

4 Select the Destination

From the **Destination** section, click the **"..."** button to display the **Save As** dialog to enter the Windows Media filename for export (with a `.wma`, `.wmv`, or `.asf` extension).

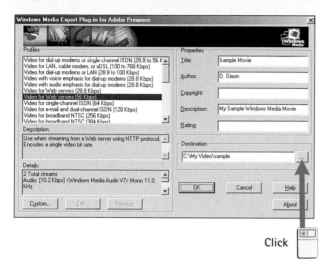

Click

5 Start the Compression

After reviewing your settings, click **OK** to start the export process.

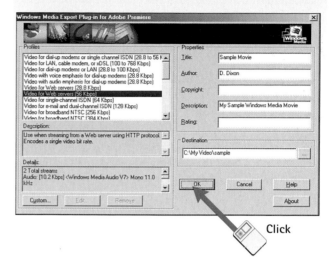

Click

6 View Your Movie

The **Exporting** dialog is then displayed as your movie is encoded to Windows Media format. After the process is complete, you can run the Windows Media Player to view your exported movie.

How-To Hints

Encoding Options

For more control over the encoding options, use the **Custom** button to create and save custom profiles. You can then specify specific target audience bandwidths, the audio and video codecs and formats, and the frame rates for each video stream.

Multiple Bit Rate Video

You can support a wider audience and a better experience when the network gets congested by compressing using one of the **Multiple Bit Rate** profiles to include several different rates in a single file. However, unlike single-rate files that can play from any Web site, multi-rate requires using a Microsoft Windows Media server (consult your Web site administrator for more information).

End

How to Use Advanced RealMedia Export

Use the Advanced RealMedia Export option to export your movie in RealMedia Media format (.RM). RealMedia files can be played back from a local file or over the Web using the RealPlayer application, available as a free download from www.real.com.

Begin

1 Export to RealMedia

To display the **Advanced RealMedia Export** dialog, pull down the **File** menu and choose **Export Timeline**, **Advanced RealMedia Export**. Or, to export a single clip, select the clip on the timeline and then pull down the **File** menu and choose **Export Clip**, **Advanced RealMedia Export**.

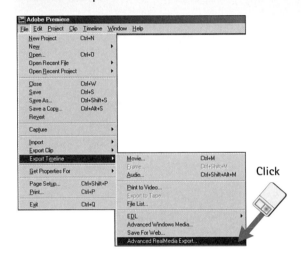

Click

2 Select the Clip Settings

From the **Clip Settings** section, use the **Audio Format** drop-down list to select the quality that best matches your movie's audio content and the **Video Quality** drop-down to select the quality that best matches the amount of motion in your movie.

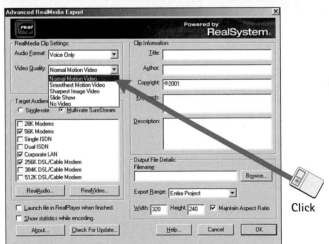

Click

3 Select the Target Audience

From the **Target Audience** section, click the **Single-rate** radio button and then click **56K Modems** to encode your movie for streaming over dial-up modems.

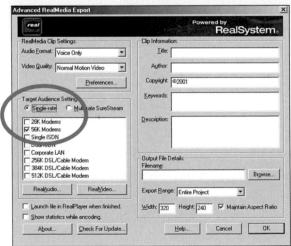

4 Enter Output File Details

If desired, you can enter optional descriptive information about your movie in the **Clip Information** section. From the **Output File Details** section, click the **Browse** button to display an **Export** file dialog to enter the RealMedia filename for export (with a `.rm` extension). You also can adjust the output pixel resolution in the **Width** and **Height** fields.

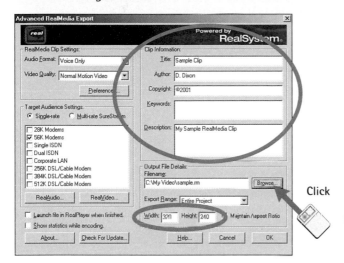

Click

5 Start the Compression

From the **Export Range** drop-down list, choose how much of your current project you want to export: the **Entire Project** (or **Entire Clip**), or the current **Work Area** (or **In Point to Out Point**). Click **Launch file in RealPlayer** to automatically play the file after the export is finished. Then click **OK** to start the export process.

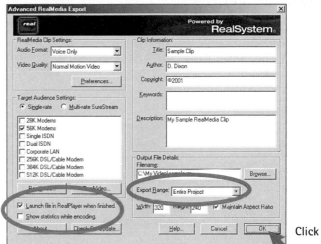

Click

6 View Your Movie in RealPlaycr

The **Exporting** dialog is then displayed as your movie is encoded to RealMedia format. After the process completes, Premiere will automatically launch the RealPlayer to play your movie.

How-To Hints

Encoding Options

Use **Preferences** under **Clip Settings** to specify advanced compatibility and compression settings, and **RealAudio** and **RealVideo** under **Target Audience** to specify compression rates.

Multi-Rate SureStream

You can support a wider audience by compressing for several different rates with the **Multi-Rate SureStream** option. Unlike single-rate files that can play from any Web site, multi-rate requires using a RealNetworks RealServer.

Compression Statistics

Click **Show statistics when encoding** (Windows only) to display a statistics window with performance data for your file.

End

How to Export to QuickTime

Use the Save For Web option to use the Terran Media Cleaner EZ plug-in to export your movie in QuickTime Web format (.MOV). QuickTime files can be played back from a local file or over the Web using the Apple QuickTime Player application, which is preinstalled on Macintosh systems or available as a free download for Windows from www.apple.com/quicktime. See Task 5 to use Cleaner EZ to export in other formats.

Begin

1 Open the Save For Web Dialog

To display the **Save For Web** dialog, pull down the **File** menu and choose **Export Timeline, Save For Web**. Or, to export a single clip, select the clip on the timeline and then pull down the **File** menu and choose **Export Clip, Save For Web**.

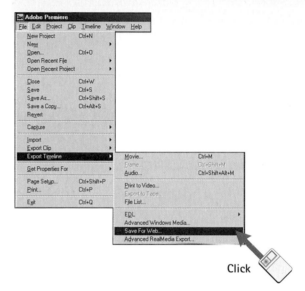

Click

2 Select a QuickTime Format

Use the **Settings** drop-down list to select **QuickTime Progressive Download, Small movie (best for modem viewers)**.

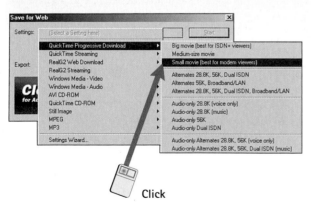

Click

3 Start the Export

Use the **Export** drop-down list to select the **Entire Project** or the currently **Selected Work Area**. Then click **Start** to launch the **Cleaner EZ** plug-in.

Click

_4_ Specify the Output File

Premiere starts the **Cleaner EZ** plug-in. In the **Save As** dialog box, navigate to the desired directory and enter the filename for the output QuickTime file. Then click **Save**.

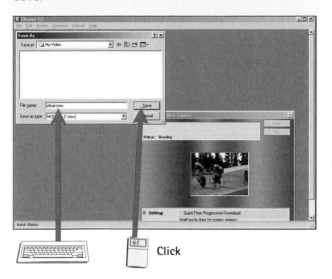

Click

_5_ Encoding

Cleaner EZ then encodes your movie to QuickTime format. The **Output** dialog displays the elapsed time and average total data rate for your movie.

_6_ View Your Movie in QuickTime Player

After the process completes, you can run the **Apple QuickTime Player** to view your exported movie.

How-To Hints

Progressive Download

Choose **Progressive Download** so that your movie can be played from any Web site, and not require a special real-time streaming Web server.

Alternates

Use the **Alternates** options to create multiple versions of your movie at different data rates. You can then set up your server so that QuickTime can chose the best available version for each viewer that plays it.

End

How to Use Cleaner EZ

Use the **Save For Web** option to export your movie in a wide variety of formats with the Terran Media Cleaner EZ plug-in. Cleaner EZ can create both streaming formats for playing across the Internet (QuickTime, RealMedia, and Windows Media), and other file formats for Web download or playing from a local disk (AVI, QuickTime, MPEG-1 video, MP3 audio, and Still Image sequences).

Begin

1 Open the Save For Web Dialog

To display the Save for Web dialog, pull down the **File** menu and choose **Export Timeline**, **Save For Web**. Or, to export a single clip, select the clip on the timeline and then pull down the **File** menu and choose **Export Clip**, **Save For Web**.

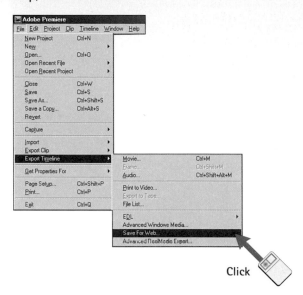

Click

2 Select a Format

You can use the **Settings** drop-down list in the **Save for Web** dialog to select a specific format (QuickTime, RealMedia, Windows Media, MPEG-1, MP3 audio, and Still Image sequence).

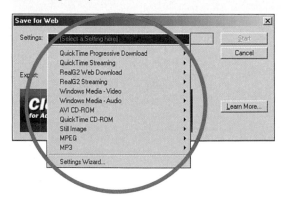

3 Select the Settings Wizard

Click the **Settings** drop-down list and select **Settings Wizard** to have **Media Cleaner EZ** help you select an appropriate setting.

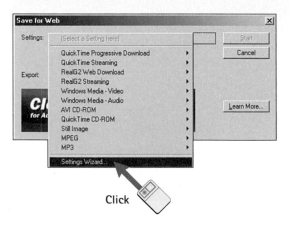

Click

4 Start the Export

Use the **Export** drop-down list to select the **Entire Project** or the currently **Selected Work Area**. Then click **Start** to launch the **Cleaner EZ** plug-in and **Settings Wizard**.

Click

5 Select Delivery Medium

The **Cleaner EZ Settings Wizard** then steps though a series of screens to help you select the proper settings for exporting your movie. In the first **Delivery Medium** dialog, select **WWW** for Internet formats. Use the **Continue** and **Go Back** buttons to explore the various media formats and conversion options available in the Cleaner EZ Wizard.

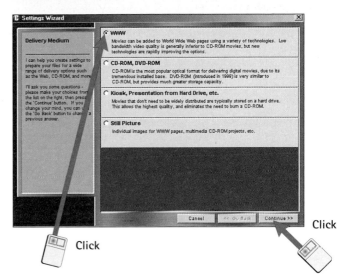

Click

Click

6 Select Quality Options

Depending on your choice of **Delivery Medium**, **Cleaner EZ Settings Wizard** then steps though a series of screens to select more specific format and processing options. But **Cleaner EZ** does more than convert movies to different formats. It also provides the **Options** dialog to enhance the quality of your movie, including cleaning up the audio with volume normalization and noise reduction.

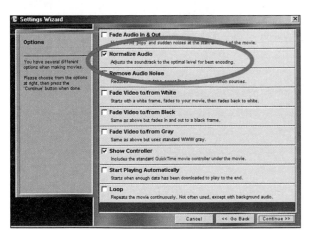

How-To Hints

Soundtrack Options

When exporting for the Web, use the **Soundtrack** screen in the **Settings Wizard** to best describe the characteristics of your audio (speech, music, or mixed), and whether the video or audio should have higher priority when bandwidth is limited.

Optimize for the Web

Use the **Optimize** screen in the **Settings Wizard** to define your priorities for the video (higher video quality, smoother motion, larger image size, or dropping down to a slide show for very slow connections).

End

Task

PART 8

Capturing and Using DV

*T*he advent of the DV (Digital Video) format has brought dramatic improvements in the ability to conveniently edit good-quality video on personal computers:

- DV is "real" video, high-quality, full-resolution, full-rate video and audio.
- DV is a digital format, so copies are exactly the same as the original, and no longer suffer the losses of converting back and forth to analog.
- DV is compressed in hardware in the camcorder, so there is no need for additional special-purpose processing on a capture board.
- DV is compressed lightly, so it is reduced enough in size to be feasible to transfer and store on personal computers, but still high enough quality to edit and manipulate without damage.
- DV camcorders use the IEEE-1394 digital interface (also called FireWire by Apple and i.Link by Sony), so devices like camcorders can communicate with your computer using a single, consistent interface.
- The DV/1394 interface is two-way, so not only can you capture video from your camcorder to Premiere, but you can also export your clips and productions back out to the camcorder.
- DV and the 1394 interface also supports *device control*, so you can operate your DV camcorder directly from Premiere, and even schedule automated capture and recording.
- DV supports both audio and video, so both are captured together and stay in sync with each other.
- DV keeps a timecode with the recorded video, so you can organize clips on a tape with their exact timecode, and keep the timecode with the captured clips in Premiere.

Premiere provides strong built-in support for DV, with presets for specific camcorder models and capture and editing presets for the DV format. You can use the Movie Capture window to control your camcorder from your computer, and then capture clips into your project. You also can log a list of clips for automated capture using the Batch Capture window. And when you have finished editing your production, you can export it back to DV tape to save and share.

Of course, if you do not have a DV camcorder, Premiere also can capture audio and video clips using analog capture boards. ●

How to Connect Your DV Camcorder

The first step in setting up your computer to work with your DV camcorder is to connect the two with an IEEE 1394 cable, and then configure Premiere to work with DV video. Premiere depends on the DV support in your operating system (Windows or Macintosh) to connect to and control your DV camcorder. It also depends on the IEEE 1394/FireWire hardware in your system to interface to your camcorder, which must be compliant with the OHCI specification.

2 Connect Your DV Camcorder

Connect your DV camcorder to your computer using an IEEE 1394 cable, as described in the documentation for your camcorder and 1394 interface. Plug the smaller 4-pin connector on the 1394 cable into the DV interface on your DV camcorder (typically marked **DV IN/OUT** or **IEEE 1394**). Plug the larger 6-pin connector to the IEEE 1394 connector on your computer. Next, plug your camcorder into its power adapter, turn it on, and set it to **VCR** or **VTR** mode (tape player), not camera mode.

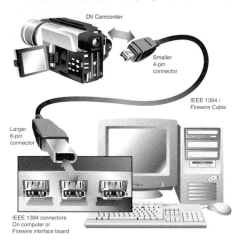

Begin

1 Check Your DV Capture Board

If you have a DV-enabled Macintosh system, then DV support is built in. On Windows PCs, an add-in board typically provides the 1394 interface. To check your hardware, open the **Start** menu and choose **Settings**, **Control Panel**, and then open the **System** control panel. Click the **Device Manager** tab, and open the **1394 Bus Controller** entry to check that your hardware is described as "OHCI Compliant."

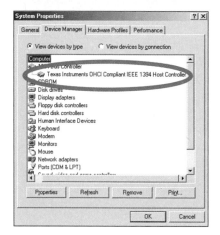

3 Select DV Preset

After the camcorder is connected and turned on, then launch Premiere. On the initial **Load Project Settings** dialog, select **DV-NTSC** (or **DV-PAL**), and choose the **32kHz** or **48kHz** audio preset, depending on the video and audio formats provided by your camcorder. Click the **OK** button.

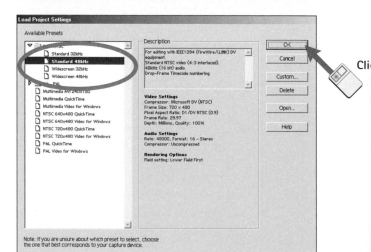

4 Open Project Settings

Premiere opens a new project. Pull down the **Project** menu and choose **Project Settings, General** to verify the playback settings.

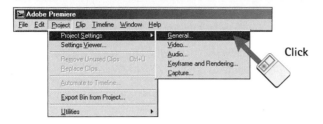

Click

5 Open Playback Settings

Premiere displays the **Project Settings** dialog, with the **General** options. With the DV preset, the editing mode is set to **DV Playback** for Windows and **QuickTime Playback** for Macintosh. Click the **Playback Settings** button.

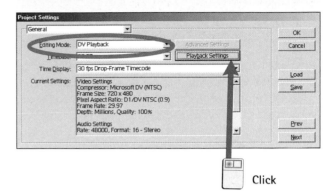

Click

6 Set Playback Settings

In the **DV Playback Options** dialog, use the **Output** settings to specify whether video is played back on the camcorder, on the desktop in the Monitor and Clip windows, or on both. Use the **Render Scrub** settings to specify whether Timeline previews are displayed on the camcorder or desktop. Press **OK** when done, and then press **OK** again to close the **Project Settings** dialog.

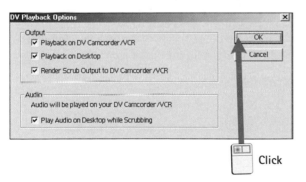

Click

How-To Hints

Capturing Analog Video as DV

If your DV camcorder supports analog input, you can use it to *dub* (copy) your old analog videotapes to digital format on a DV tape. You can also use some DV camcorders to convert analog video input into digital 1394 format.

Display Quality

Remember that television video, including DV, is interlaced, with alternating fields of odd and even lines captured at slightly different times, so individual frames can appear ripped or blurred on your computer monitor. The video also might not be decompressed at the highest quality in order to save processing time. However, the original DV video still will look fine on a television screen.

End

How to Select Your DV Device

The next step in setting up Premiere to work with DV is to configure Premiere for your specific DV camcorder, and then test the connection to verify that Premiere can communicate with, and control, your camcorder.

Begin

1 Open the Device Control Preferences

To configure Premiere for your DV camcorder, pull down the **Edit** menu and choose **Preferences, Scratch Disks and Device Control**.

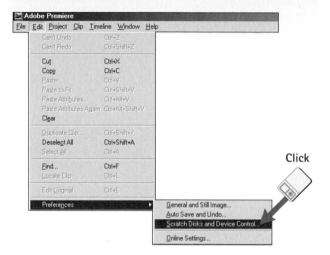

Click

2 Open Device Control Options

Premiere displays the **Preferences** dialog with the **Scratch Disks and Device Control** options. In the **Device Control** section, make sure that **Device** is set to **DV Device Control 2.0**, and then click **Options**.

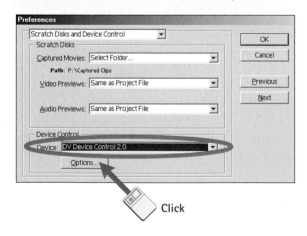

Click

3 Set the DV Device

Premiere displays the **DV Device Control Options** dialog. Click the **Device Brand** drop-down list and select the brand name of your camcorder. Then click the **Device Model** drop-down list and select your camera model. If your model is not listed, check the Adobe Premiere Web site for a profile of your device.

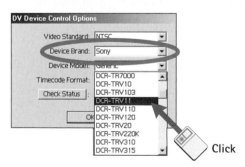

Click

4 Check the Connection Status

Click the **Check Status** button to have Premiere attempt to verify the connection with your camcorder.

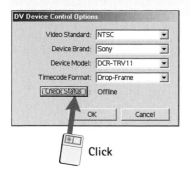

Click

5 Verify the Connection Status

Premiere reports the device control status. **Offline** status means that Premiere cannot communicate with your camcorder; check the connections and settings and verify that the camera is turned on in **VCR** or **VTR** mode. **Detected** status means that Premiere can communicate with your camcorder, but cannot control the tape; check that a tape is inserted. **Online** status means Premiere can communicate with your camcorder and can control the tape. Click **OK** to close the dialog.

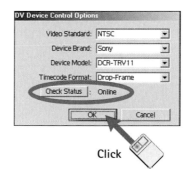

Click

6 Set Scratch Disks

Premiere returns to the **Preferences** dialog with the **Scratch Disks and Device Control** options. In the **Scratch Disks** section, select the disk and folders to be used for **Captured Movies**, **Video Previews**, and **Audio Previews**. Ideally, use a separate, fast disk for capture and for preview files. This should not be just a partition on the same disk, use a physically separate disk. Click **OK** to close the dialog.

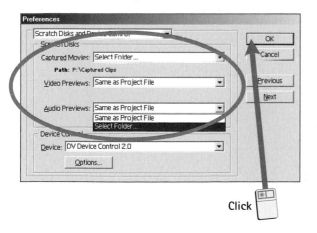

Click

How-To Hints

Device Control

Although you can capture from a DV device even if Premiere cannot control it, having a full connection with device control is much better. Instead of stopping and starting the camcorder manually, you can use the VCR-like controls on the Premiere display, and even automatically capture a group of clips.

Low Disk Space Warning

Premiere can warn you when scratch disk space is running low. Pull down the **Edit** menu and choose **Preferences**, **General and Still Image** to set the **Low Disk Space Warning Level**.

End

How to Set Up Movie Captures

The next step in capturing from a DV camcorder is to open the Movie Capture dialog and set up the final settings for capturing. The Movie Capture dialog is used to control the whole capture process, from previewing the video to controlling individual and batch captures.

Begin

1 Open the Movie Capture Window

Pull down the File menu and choose Capture, Movie Capture.

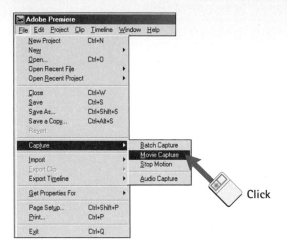

Click

2 Open the Capture Settings

Premiere displays the Movie Capture dialog. If the control panel is not visible, pull open the Movie Panel window menu and choose Expand Window. Click the Settings tab to display the current Capture Settings and Preferences. Open the Movie Panel window menu and choose Capture Settings, or click the Edit button under the Capture Settings (or pull down the Project menu and choose Project Settings, Capture).

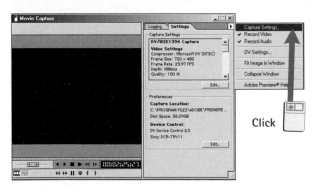

Click

3 Set the Capture Format

Premiere opens the Project Settings dialog to the Capture settings. The Capture Format should be set to DV/IEEE 1394 Capture. Click the DV Settings button.

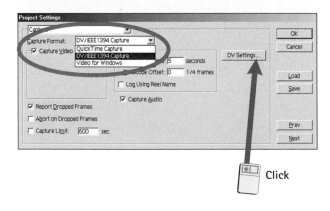

Click

4 Review the DV Capture Options

Premiere displays the **DV Capture Options** dialog. Leave the **Preview Video** and **Preview Audio** boxes checked to view the DV input on the computer display, while previewing and capturing from the camcorder. If this causes too much processor load on your system, uncheck the boxes in order to view the video only on your camcorder display. Click **OK**.

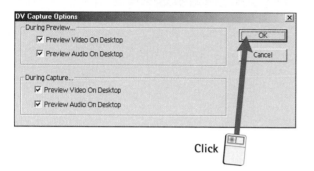

Click

5 Set the Capture Settings

Premiere returns to the **Capture** settings in the **Project Settings** dialog. Click the **Preroll Time** field and type a value of 5 seconds, so Premiere will back up the tape and roll up to full speed before starting capture. Leave the **Report Dropped Frames** box checked to display a warning if not all the input frames were captured successfully. Check the **Capture Limit** box, if desired, to specify the maximum number of seconds to record. Click **OK** when done.

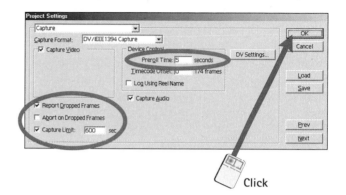

Click

6 Set the Capture Options

Premiere returns to the **Movie Capture** dialog. If you need to change the settings for video and audio display during preview and capture, you can open the **Movie Panel** window menu and choose **DV Settings** to display the **DV Capture Options** dialog (from step 4). You are now ready to capture from your DV camcorder.

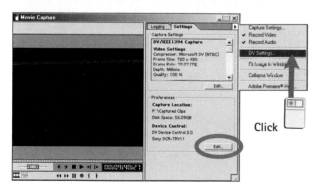

Click

How-To Hints

File Size Limits

The Premiere Timeline can contain up to three hours of video. However, older versions of the Windows and Macintosh operating systems limit file sizes to no larger than 2GB. In some cases, Premiere will need to divide a long project into a collection of separate files, each smaller than the file size limit.

See the Premiere documentation for more details.

Close the Movie Capture Window

Close the Motion Capture window whenever you are done with it. While it is open, it has primary focus within Premiere, and any other operations might be slowed accordingly.

End

How to Use DV Device Control

Besides being able to capture full digital video, another bonus feature of using a DV camcorder with the IEEE 1394/FireWire interface is that you also can control your camcorder directly from within Premiere. This is a wonderful advance if you have ever tried to coordinate capturing on a computer while at the same time fumbling with the little buttons on a miniature camcorder. With Premiere, if device control is available for your camcorder, you can just click the VCR-style controls under the Movie Capture window.

Begin

1 Open the Movie Capture Window

Start a new capture. Pull down the File menu and choose Capture, Movie Capture (as in Task 3).

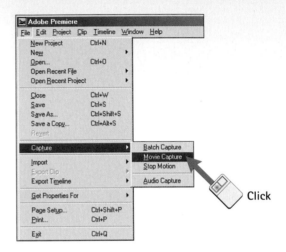

Click

2 Play the Tape

Premiere displays the Movie Capture dialog. Use the VCR device control buttons along the bottom of the window to move through the tape. Click Play to start playback, Pause to pause the tape, and Stop to stop the tape. Or press the Spacebar to start and pause play.

3 Step Through the Tape

To step slowly through the tape, click the Frame Back or Frame Forward buttons (to the left of Stop) to move a frame at a time (or press the Left or Right cursor control arrows). Or click the Reverse Slow Play or Slow Play buttons (to the right of Play) to play at slow speed. The Timecode display to the right of the controls displays the timecode for the current frame, as hours, minutes, seconds, and frames.

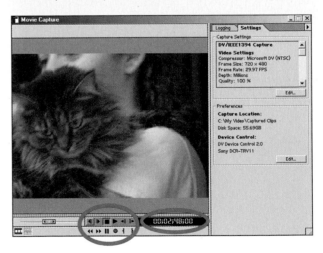

4 Rewind and Fast Forward

To move more quickly through the tape, click the **Rewind** or **Fast Forward** buttons (or press the **R** or **F** key, respectively). If the tape is stopped, these move the tape at full speed. If the tape is playing, these act as a fast scan, and will still display the video as the tape is moving.

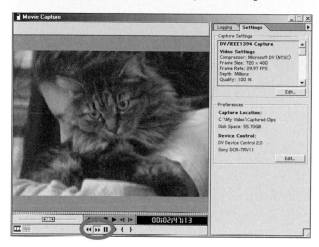

5 Jog Through the Tape

To move frame by frame through the tape, click and drag the **Jog** control bar (the dashed line above the controls). As you move it one step to the left or right, it will rewind or advance the tape a single frame at a time.

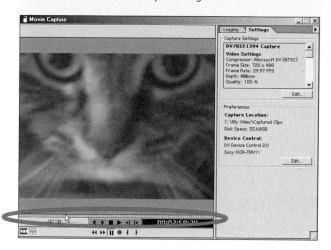

6 Shuttle Through the Tape

To move rapidly through the tape, click and drag the **Shuttle** control (to the left of the VCR controls), with the speed of movement proportional to the distance of the control from the center point.

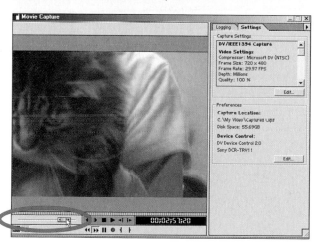

How-To Hints

Window Size

By default, Premiere displays the Movie Capture window in a reduced size in a corner of the display. But the input DV format video is full-size video, with a 720×480 frame size. You can drag the lower-right corner of the window to resize it and see your input video in much more detail.

Continuous Timecode

It is really helpful to have unbroken timecode throughout your entire DV tape. Unlike consumer VCRs that display an estimate of the elapsed time, the DV timecode is actually recorded on the tape. But, if you record the tape with gaps, you will end up with multiple segments with the same timecode. Avoid gaps when you shoot by always recording for a few extra seconds at the end of each clip, and then later, restart recording after backing up into this "scratch area." Even better, *stripe* each new tape by prerecording timecode onto it—simply record through the entire tape with the lens cap on.

End

How to Capture with Device Control

The device control capabilities of Premiere make scanning though your DV tapes easy and convenient. Even better, you can use device control to simplify the process of capturing a clip by marking the **In** and **Out** points, the beginning and end, of the clip that you want to capture. Premiere will then automatically control the tape to capture the clip, and even can automate the batch capture of a list of clips (see Task 6).

Begin

1 Set the In Point

As in Task 4, pull down the **File** menu and choose **Capture, Movie Capture**. Then click the **Logging** tab on the right side of the **Movie Capture** window. As you play through the clip, use the device control buttons to move to the starting point of the clip. Click the **Set In** button under the display or in the **Logging** area (or press the **I** key) to mark the first frame of the clip that you want to capture.

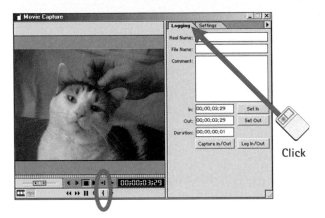

Click

2 Set the Out Point

Use the device control buttons to move to the end of the clip. Click the **Set Out** button under the display or in the **Logging** area (or press the **O** key) to mark the last frame of the clip that you want to capture.

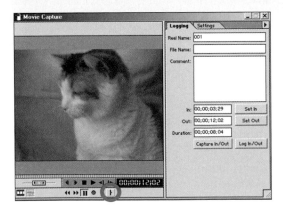

3 Play the Marked Clip

Press the **Alt** (Windows) or **Option** (Macintosh) key and click the **Set In** button to move the tape back to the **In** point. Click **Play** (or press the **Spacebar**) to play the clip. Press the **Alt** (Windows) or **Option** (Macintosh) key and click the **Set Out** button to move the tape to the **Out** point.

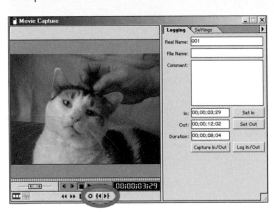

4 Start Capture

To capture the marked clip, click **Capture In/Out** in the **Logging** area, or press the **Alt** (Windows) or **Option** (Macintosh) key and click the red **Record** button.

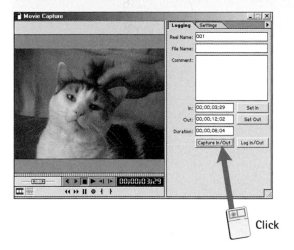

Click

5 Monitor the Capture

Premiere moves to the preroll position before the **In** point, starts playing the tape, starts capturing at the **In** point, and stops capturing at the **Out** point. The current capture status is displayed in the top-left corner of the window. Press the **Escape** (Esc) key at any time to abort the capture.

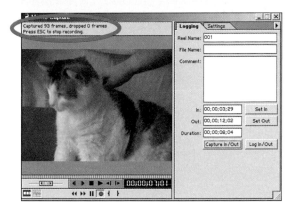

6 Name the File

When capture is complete, Premiere displays the **File Name** dialog. Type the name of the file to be saved and click **OK**. The file is saved in the **Captured Movies** folder specified in the **Preferences** dialog under the **Scratch Disks and Device Control** options. Premiere adds the clip to the current **Project** window, if one is open. Otherwise, Premiere opens a new **Clip** window to display the captured file.

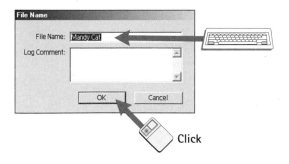

Click

How-To Hints

Manual Capture

As with other Premiere controls, you can enter a timecode directly by clicking the **In**, **Out**, or **Duration** fields and typing a new time. You can also capture from the current position in the tape at any time; just click the **Record** button (or press the **R** key).

Capturing Without Device Control

If device control is not available for your camcorder, then Premiere displays simplified controls in the **Movie Capture** window with a **Record** button. You can then use the VCR controls on your camcorder to queue the tape for capture.

Capture Video or Audio

Use the **Capture Video** and **Capture Audio** buttons in the bottom-left of the **Movie Capture** window (or the corresponding boxes in the **Capture** settings of the **Project Settings** dialog) to capture only video or audio.

End

How to Create a Batch Capture List

You can use device control not only to simplify the capture of a single clip, but also to create a timecode log so that Premiere can perform an automated capture of an entire collection of clips. The Batch Capture window contains a list of clips, with the timecode value for each **In** and **Out** point.

Begin

1 Open the Movie Capture Window

Pull down the **File** menu and choose **Capture, Movie Capture**. Premiere opens the **Movie Capture** window. Click the **Logging** tab, click the **Reel Name** field, and type a name to be used to identify this tape and when capturing clips.

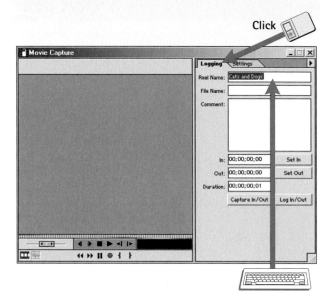

Click

2 Set In and Out Points

As in Task 5, use the device controls to position the tape and click the **Set In** and **Set Out** buttons to mark the beginning and end of the clip you would like to capture. Then click **Log In/Out** under the **Logging** tab.

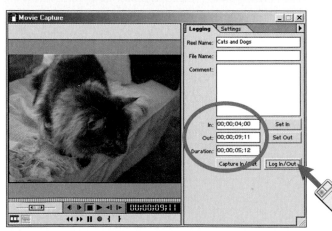

Click

3 Enter the Filename

Premiere displays the **File Name** dialog. Type the name to be used for the clip file, and then click **OK**.

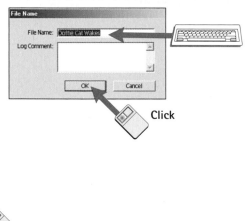

Click

4 Add More Clips

Premiere displays the **Batch Capture** window with an entry for the clip. Now, add more clips to the batch list by setting each **In** and **Out** point, and then clicking **Log In/Out** in the **Movie Capture** window.

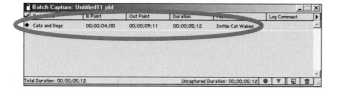

5 Save the Batch List

After adding all the clips that you want to capture to the batch list with their timecode settings, you can save the list. Click the **Batch Capture** window to select it, and then pull down the **File** menu and choose **Save**.

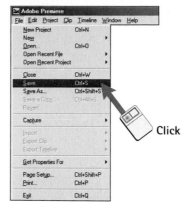

6 Name the Batch List

Premiere displays the **Save File** dialog. Click in the **File Name** field and type a filename for the batch list file (.PBL under Windows). Then click **Save**.

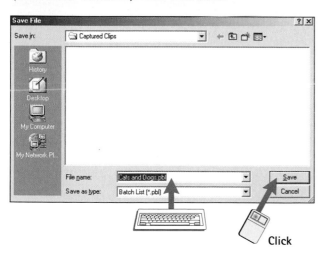

How-To Hints

Enter the Batch List Manually

You can also enter a batch list manually. Pull down the **File** menu and choose **Capture, Batch Capture**. Then click the **Add New Item** button at the bottom right of the window to enter timecode values for the **In** and **Out** points.

Export the Batch List

The batch list can also be exported as a plain text file, for your records, or to import into another application. Open the **Batch Capture** window menu and choose **Import/Export Settings, Export to Text File**.

End

How to Capture with a Batch List

Once you have created (and saved) a batch list with the clips you want to capture, you can use Premiere to automatically record the clips from your DV camcorder.

Begin

1 Open the Handles

Open the **Batch Capture** window menu (from Task 6), and choose **Handles**.

Click

2 Set the Capture Handles

Premiere displays the **Capture Handles** dialog. Type the number of frames to be used as handles, which are captured before the In point and after the Out point of each clip to provide extra frames to use during editing. Click **OK**.

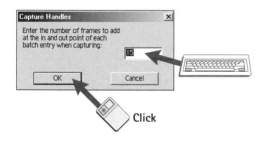

Click

3 Capture a Single Entry

To capture a single entry from the batch list, click the row in the list and then pull open the **Batch Capture** window menu and choose **Send In/Out to Movie Capture**. Premiere sets the **Movie Capture** window with the **In** and **Out** points from the selected clip, so you can record the clip by clicking **Capture In/Out** (see Task 5).

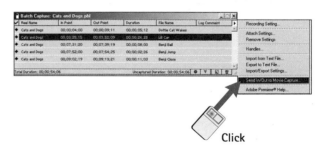

Click

4 Capture Multiple Entries

To capture multiple entries from the batch list, first select the clips to be captured by clicking the diamond symbol in the leftmost column of the entries. Or click the check box in the heading to select or unselect all the entries. When you have selected the desired clips, click the **Record** button to start the batch capture.

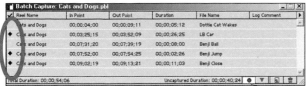

Click

5 Watch the Batch Capture

Premiere displays the capture progress for each clip in the **Movie Capture** window. Click the mouse, press the **Escape** (Esc) key, or press **Command-period** (Macintosh) to abort the capture when the camcorder is not seeking.

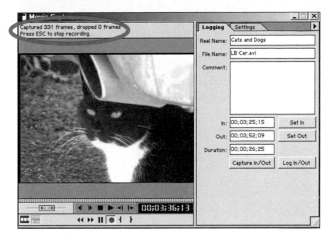

6 View the Clips

Premiere adds the captured clips to the current **Project** window, if one is currently open. The clips are now available for you to play, or to import into your projects.

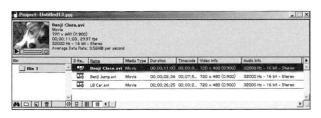

How-To Hints

Edit Batch List Entries

You can edit an individual entry in a batch list by double-clicking it to open the **Clip Capture Parameters** dialog, or by using **Send In/Out to Movie Capture** to change the settings in the **Movie Capture** window, and then clicking **Log In/Out** to add the new settings back to the batch list (under a new name).

Redigitizing

With batch lists, you can save processing time and disk space by capturing and editing low-resolution clips, and then recapture only the clips you need for the final edit at full resolution. Once you have finished editing the low-res clips, pull down the **Project** menu and choose **Utilities, Project Trimmer** to create a trimmed batch list.

End

How to Export to a DV Camcorder

DV camcorders not only provide a wonderfully convenient source for capturing high-quality digital video, but you also can record your clips and productions back out to your camcorder to save and share with others.

Begin

1 Connect Your DV Device

Turn on your DV camcorder and set it to **VCR/VTR** mode (not camera), connect your DV camcorder, and check that it is set up properly for device control (see Tasks 1 and 2). If needed, check the status of the connection using the **DV Device Control Options** dialog, accessed from the **Scratch Disks and Device Control** options in the **Preferences** dialog.

2 Open Playback Settings

Pull down the **Project** menu and choose **Project Settings, General**. Premiere displays the **Project Settings** dialog. Since you are editing a project using DV clips, the **Editing Mode** should be **DV Playback** (Windows) or **QuickTime** (Macintosh). Click **Playback Settings** to use the **DV Playback Options** dialog; there, you can set the output and audio to display on the DV camcorder or desktop. Click **OK** to close each dialog.

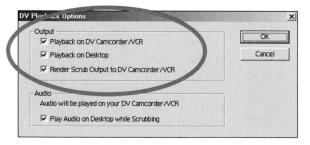

3 Open a Clip

Open the clip to be exported in a **Clip** window, or click the **Timeline** and select the portion to export. If needed, generate the preview file so it ready to play.

4 Export to Tape

Make sure that the proper tape is loaded, and that it is positioned where you want to start recording, with pre-recorded timecode on the tape (see Task 4). Pull down the **File** menu and choose **Export Clip** (or **Export Timeline**), **Export to Tape**.

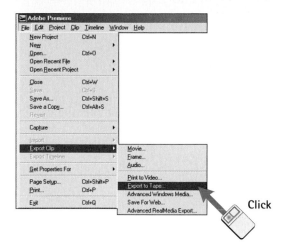

Click

5 Select Export Settings

Premiere displays the **Export to Tape Settings** dialog. Check **Activate recording deck** to let Premiere control the DV camcorder. Check **Assemble at time code** to enter an **In** point for the capture; otherwise, recording begins at the current tape location. Set **Preroll** to around 150 frames (5 seconds) so that Premiere will back up the tape and roll up to full speed before starting to record. Click **Record** to begin exporting.

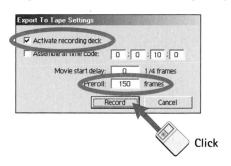

Click

6 Watch the Export

Premiere then starts the tape rolling and exports the clip back to the DV camcorder. Watch the camcorder display to see the video and hear the audio being recorded. Depending on the **Playback Settings**, the video is also shown on the computer display, but the playback might be jumpy if too much processing is required to feed the digital output to the camcorder.

How-To Hints

Movie Start Delay

Use the **Movie Start Delay** option in the **Export to Tape Settings** dialog if needed to allow a slight delay before the camcorder starts recording.

Other Export Options

See the Premiere documentation for several other ways to export video, with and without device control or a DV device. You can export a portion of the Timeline to a DV camcorder directly from the **Monitor** window. Also, under the **File** menu, use **Export Timeline**, **Print to Video** to play back full-screen video to record.

End

How to Capture Analog Video and Audio

Beyond capturing digital video from DV camcorders, Premiere can also capture analog video and audio, and use digital audio files from audio CD. However, these forms of capture are more dependent on your computer and operating system (Windows or Macintosh), and on the specific capture hardware and associated software drivers installed on your machine. See the Premiere documentation for more information.

Begin

1 Analog Video Capture

Premiere can capture analog video and audio from analog devices such as 8mm camcorders and VHS video recorders. Your copy of Premiere might have been bundled with a video capture card, or you might have added one to your computer. You typically connect your video input device to the capture card with a composite or an S-video cable. Then pull down the **Project** menu and choose **Project Settings**, **Capture**.

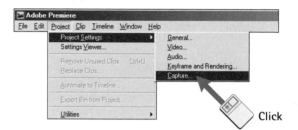
Click

2 Analog Capture Format

In the **Project Settings** dialog, click the **Capture Format** drop-down list and select **Video for Windows** (Windows) or **QuickTime Capture** (Macintosh), as supported by your capture device. Click **VfW Settings** to display Windows capture settings.

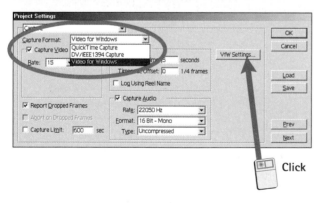
Click

3 Windows Analog Capture Settings

Premiere displays the **Video for Windows Capture Options** dialog. On newer machines, click **Video Overlay** for a higher-quality preview during capture. Use the **Driver Settings** buttons to set detailed video capture format options. Click **OK** to close each dialog.

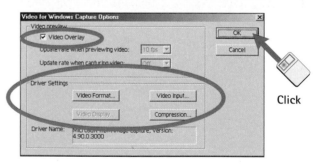
Click

4 Analog Video Capture

Pull down the **File** menu and choose **Capture, Movie Capture** to open the **Movie Capture** window, and click the **Settings** tab. If your capture device does not support device control, click the **Edit** button in the Preferences section to disable it and display a simplified **Movie Capture** window. When ready, click the large **Record** button to start recording.

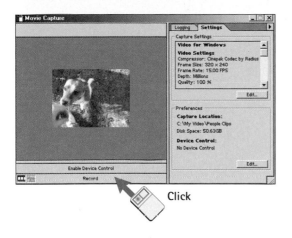

Click

5 Import Digital Audio from CD

You can also use digital audio files imported from audio CD. Under Windows, use a third-party CD "ripper" tool to extract the audio clips from the CD and save them as Windows Wave (.WAV) files to import into Premiere. On the Macintosh, use the CD import converter built in to QuickTime: Pull down the **File** menu and choose **Open**, and then select and import the desired track.

How-To Hints

Analog Audio Capture

While Premiere does provides a separate Audio Capture option, it is designed to interface to the audio capture tools provided with your operating system or by third parties. Instead, you can simply use the same Movie Capture window used for video, but only enable audio capture (by disabling the **Capture Video** button at bottom left).

Video Capture Devices

Video capture is available in a multitude of formats these days, from internal capture cards and PCMCI cards for laptops to external capture devices connected though a USB (Universal Serial Bus) or other cable. The capture devices also vary in the quality, resolution, and frame rate they can support, from lower-rate Web capture and TV tuner cards for TV in a window to full-rate, full-resolution video and audio. The capture card manufacturers provide drivers and Premiere presets to interface with and control their devices.

Check the Adobe Premiere Web site (http://www.adobe.com/premiere) for a list of compatible capture cards.

Video Capture Checkout

Before trying to capture directly from Premiere, or to resolve problems with capture, check out your capture device, and the connections from your analog video source, using the capture utility software that was provided with your capture hardware. When you are sure the device is working, set up Premiere to work with it.

End

Task

PART 9

Trimming and Editing Clips

*I*n Part 3, "Assembling Clips Using the Storyboard and Timeline," you took the clips you had organized in bins in the Project window and laid them out into a production in the Timeline window. However, by using the files provided in the Premiere Sample Folder, you took a shortcut in the editing process because the sample files were already segmented and trimmed, with each scene separated into its own individual clip file.

Usually, however, especially when working with captured material, there is an additional editing step in organizing your material in bins. If you have captured several scenes to one media file, then you need to go though the file to mark and trim the individual clips that you will want to use on the Timeline. And, even if you have used batch capture with a DV camcorder to capture each scene to an individual clip file, it is a good idea to capture the clips with handles, extra frames at each end. You can then trim the edges at the handles as precisely as needed.

Premiere provides tools in the Clip window to mark and trim individual clips. You can even make duplicate copies of clips with different trim settings that can be applied multiple times. Once the clips are laid out on the Timeline window, Premiere also provides an extensive collection of tools for editing and adjusting the clips relative to each other and the overall production, as described in Part 10, "Editing in the Timeline." ●

How to Trim Clips

The Bin folders in the Project window can be used not only to organize clip files, but also to segment and trim the clips before they are laid out in the Timeline window. To do this, you set *markers* and *In* and *Out* points associated with the clip in the Premiere Clip window. Even better, you can make duplicate copies of a clip with different trim settings to play in multiple places on the Timeline.

Begin

1 Open the Sample Project

Pull down the **File** menu and choose **Open Recent Project**, and select the **Sample Project** file (.**PPJ** in Windows) that you created in Part 1. Or start a new project and import the **Sample Folder**.

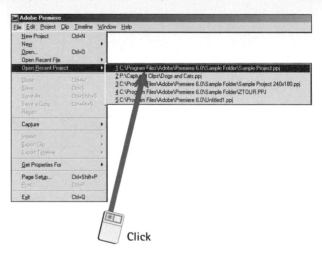

Click

2 Open the zfinal Clip

Premiere opens the **Project** window and **Timeline** window for the project. Click the **Sample Folder** bin and double-click the **zfinal** clip to open it. You will work with this clip because it is the final result of editing together the other clips—it contains multiple scenes and includes both video and audio.

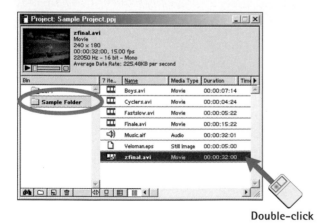

Double-click

3 Find the Cyclers Scene

Premiere opens a **Clip** window with the **zfinal** clip. You will mark the second scene in the **zfinal** clip, from **5:18** to the dissolve at **11:18**, for a total duration of about 6 seconds. Click and drag the **Set Location** blue triangular slider to shuttle through the clip. Click and drag in the **Frame Jog** striped tread area to jog though the frames.

4 Set the In Point

Move to the beginning of the clip at a timecode of **5:18**, as shown in the timecode display. Play and step through the clip with the VCR controls, or press the **Spacebar** to alternately play and stop. Or press the **Left** or **Right** cursor control arrow keys to step frame by frame through the clip. Then click the **Mark In** button ("{") below the timecode display, or press the **I** key.

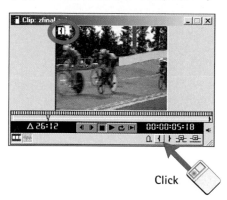

Click

5 Set the Out Point

Premiere sets the **In** point icon in the slider area under the video. Now move to the end of the sequence. Click in the timecode area, type **11:18**, and press **Enter** (Windows) or **Return** (Macintosh) to jump directly to a specific time. Then set the **Out** point to the current time. Press the **Mark Out** button ("}"), press the **O** key, or click and drag the **Out** icon to the desired time.

Click

6 Play from In to Out

Premiere sets the **Out** point icon in the slider area under the video. It also displays **In** and **Out** icons in the upper corners of the video at the associated frames. Click the **Play In to Out** button at the right of the VCR controls to play through the trimmed sequence.

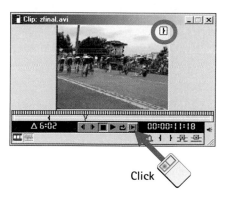

Click

How-To Hints

Playing the Trimmed Clip

Press the **Loop** button next to **Play In to Out** to play the trimmed clip continuously.

Press the **Alt** (Windows) or **Option** (Macintosh) key and click **Play** to play from the current position to the **Out** point.

Entering a Timecode

To jump directly to a timecode in the **Clip** window, type the number on the numeric keypad and press **Enter** (Windows) or **Return** (Macintosh). You can type the time without punctuation. Simply type 518 instead of 5:18.

End

How to Mark Clips

You can mark a clip with In and Out points to keep track of a scene, to trim off the ends, or to trim one scene out of a larger clip. However, when an imported media file contains many different scenes, Premiere also provides the ability to set additional markers to help you quickly jump to specific scenes and easily extract individual clips.

Begin

1 Go to the Next Scene

Continuing from the previous task, move to the next scene in the **zfinal** clip in the **Clip** window. Click and drag the slider, click the VCR controls, or type on the numeric keypad to move to timecode **15:12**.

2 Mark the Next Scene

Pull down the **Marker** menu at the bottom of the window and choose **Mark, 3** to set marker **3** to the beginning of the third scene after the start of the clip (or pull down the **Clip** menu and choose **Set Clip Marker, 3**).

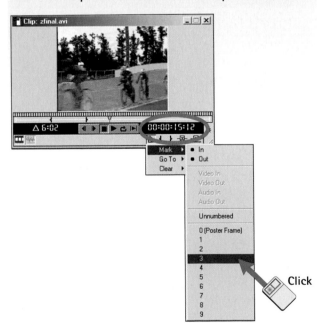

Click

3 Mark the Remaining Scenes

In the **Marker** menu, mark the remaining scenes at **17:14**, **19:16**, and **24:24** as scenes 4, 5, and 6, respectively. Premiere displays the marker number at the top center of the video at the associated frame. You might also want to mark the first two scenes, in addition to using **In** and **Out** points for them.

4 Go to a Marker

Now that the markers are set, you can skip directly to any scene. Press the **Marker** menu button and choose **Go To, In** to jump back to the **In** point. Premiere indicates a marker has been set by a dot to its left in the menus. This is a good point to save your project and the markers for this clip.

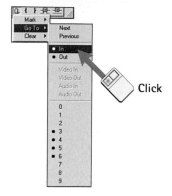

Click

5 Move to Markers

Pull down the **Clip** menu and choose **Go to Clip Marker** to jump directly to any defined marker. Hold down the **Control** (Windows) or **Command** (Macintosh) key and press the **Left** and **Right** arrow keys to jump to the previous and next markers, press the **Up** and **Down** keys to jump to the **In** and **Out** points, or press a number key to jump to a numeric marker.

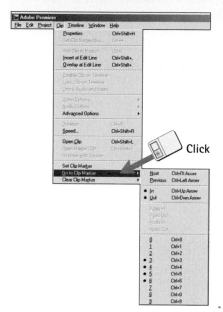

Click

6 Clear Markers

Pull down the **Marker** menu and choose **Clear** (or pull down the **Clip** menu and choose **Clear Clip Marker**). You can clear the current marker, a specific marker, both the **In** and **Out** markers, or all markers at the same time.

Click

How-To Hints

Unnumbered Markers

Besides the **In** and **Out** points and the numbered markers from 0 to 9, Premiere also supports up to 999 unnumbered markers for each clip and on the Timeline. Pull down the **Marker** menu and choose **Mark, Unnumbered** to set an unnumbered marker. Use the **Previous** and **Next** commands to jump to unnumbered markers.

Timeline Markers

Besides setting markers in individual clips, you can also set markers on the Timeline for important time points that affect multiple clips, such as edit points to synchronize video and audio.

End

How to Reuse Clips

In Task 1, you set In and Out points for one scene in the zfinal clip. But the clip contains multiple scenes that you might like to play at different points in the Timeline, each with different trim settings. Premiere can help you keep track of multiple copies of a clip by creating duplicate *instances* of a *master* clip.

Begin

1 Drag the Clip to Timeline

Drag the **zfinal** clip that you trimmed in the first task from the **Clip** window to the **Video 1A** track in the **Timeline**. Premiere also places the associated audio clip in the **Audio 1** track. To show all the clips you are going to use, open the **Zoom** menu in the bottom left corner of the **Timeline** window and set the Timeline display to **2 seconds**.

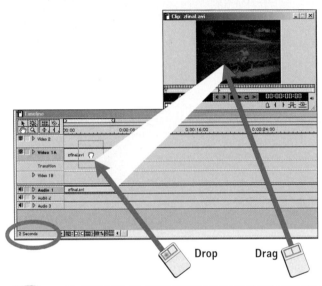

Drop   Drag

2 Change the Trim

Change the trim settings in the **Clip** window. Slide in both the **In** and **Out** markers to trim the beginning and end of the clip, so it runs from **6:18** to **10:18**.

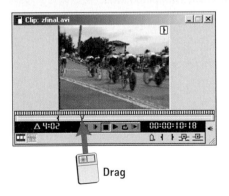

Drag

3 Add a Second Instance

Drag the **zfinal** clip from the **Clip** window to the **Video 1B** track as a second instance of the clip with a shorter duration. The original instance is still the same, retaining the settings from when it was added to the Timeline.

Drag

Drop

4 Add a Third Instance

Close the **Clip** window and drag a third instance of the **zfinal** clip to the **Video 1A** track, this time from the **Sample Folder** bin. The clip copied from the **bin** retains the most recent trim settings.

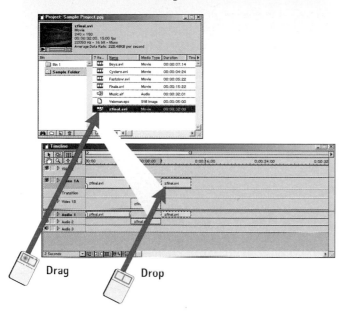

Drag

Drop

5 Open the Clip from the Project

Double-click the zfinal clip in the **Project** window to reopen it. In the **Marker** menu, jump to the **In** point. The **Clip** window shows that the clip retains the most recent trim settings and markers.

6 Open the Clips from the Timeline

Double-click the first and second instances of the **zfinal** clip in the Timeline to open them. The **Clip** windows do not show the entire master clip with trim settings; instead, they show only the trimmed section of the clip, with the trimmed duration. They retain the timecode from the original master clip.

How-To Hints

Anonymous Instances

Premiere supports trimming and using a clip multiple times, but you can end up with a confusing situation in which the same clip appears on the Timeline in multiple anonymous instances, with very different settings. A better solution is make explicit, named duplicates of clips so you can keep track of them, as described in Task 4.

End

How to Duplicate Clips

Even though Premiere can track multiple instances of the same clip on the Timeline, this can become confusing. Instead, you can create duplicate instances of the clip in the Bin window, so you can keep track of each trim setting individually.

Begin

1 Duplicate a Clip

Reopen the **Sample Project**, or pull down the **File** menu and choose **Revert**. Open the **Sample Folder** bin, click the **zfinal** clip to select it, and then choose **Duplicate Clip** from the pop-up context menu (or pull down the **Edit** menu and choose **Duplicate Clip**).

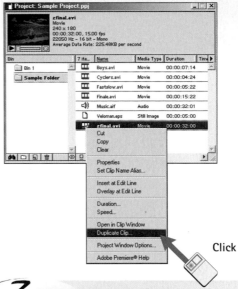

Click

2 Enter the Clip Name

Premiere displays the **Duplicate Clip** dialog. If desired, click in the **Name** field to type a new name for this clip instance. You can also choose a different project from the **Location** drop-down, if desired. Then click **OK**.

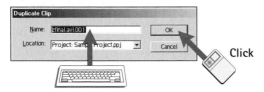

Click

3 View the Duplicate

Premiere creates a duplicate copy of the clip in the **Sample Folder** bin, with the duration set to the trimmed **In** and **Out** points in the master clip.

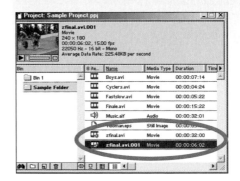

4 Add to the Timeline

Drag the master **zfinal** clip to the Timeline, and then the duplicate **001** clip. These two clips with different settings are easier to keep track of because they also have different names.

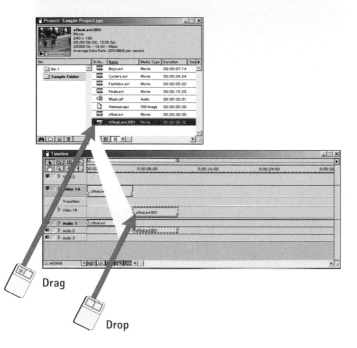

Drag

Drop

5 Locating Clips

Premiere can also help you keep track of which clip is which on the Timeline. Click the original **zfinal** clip in the Timeline to select it, and then choose **Locate Clip** from the pop-up context menu (or pull down the **Edit** menu and choose **Locate Clip**).

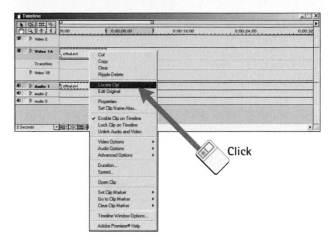

Click

6 View Clip in Bin

Premiere displays the **Project** window and highlights the zfinal clip in the **Sample Folder** bin as the source for the trimmed clip in the Timeline.

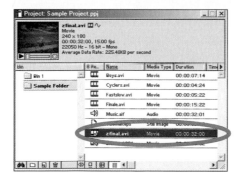

How-To Hints

Clip Name Aliases

You can rename your clips in the Bin and Project windows to help keep track of how you are using them. Click on the clip to select it, and then choose **Set Clip Name Alias** from the pop-up context menu (or select it from the **Clip** menu).

Copy and Paste

You can also make copies of clips by using traditional **Copy** and **Paste** commands. However, explicitly duplicating clips gives you the opportunity to rename them. Copying and pasting in the **Project** or **Bin** windows creates a duplicate clip. Copying and pasting in the **Timeline** creates another instance of the clip.

End

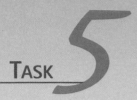

How to Trim Clips in the Timeline

In the previous tasks, you trimmed clips in the Clip window, made duplicates, and added them to the Timeline window. When you then opened the resulting clips from the Timeline, you saw that Premiere displayed them in their trimmed form, with the remainder of the clip no longer accessible. If you now decide that you want to adjust the trim of these clips, you can still do so, by trimming them in the Timeline.

Begin

1 Duplicate the Clip

Reopen the **Sample Project** and duplicate the **zfinal** clip. Give the duplicate a new name. (I added a **002** to the end of the name.)

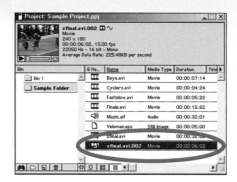

2 Add the Clip to the Timeline

Drag the **002** clip to the Timeline, part-way into the Video 1A track. Double-click the **002** clip in the Timeline to open the **Clip** window.

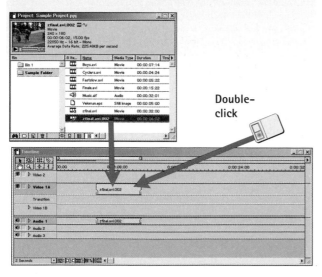

Double-click

3 Check the Timecode and Duration

The duplicated clip was trimmed to have a start time of **5:18** and a duration of **6:02**. Premiere displays both an **In** point icon and any additional markers at the top of the clip.

4 Trim the Clip Shorter

Make sure the **Selection** tool (arrow icon) is selected in the top-left corner of the Timeline. Hold the cursor over the start of the clip in the Timeline, and it changes to the red trim tool (square red bracket with double-sided arrow). Click and drag the start of the clip to the right to set the **In** point later. Premiere also updates the **Clip** window to show the shorter duration.

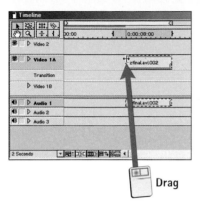

Drag

5 Trim the Clip Longer

Since this clip is actually an instance of a longer clip, you can also lengthen the clip to include more of the original material. Click and drag the start of the clip to the left to set the **In** point earlier. Premiere shows the numeric marker that you set in the original clip at the original **In** point.

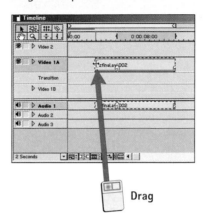

Drag

6 Trim the End of the Clip

Click and drag the end of the clip to extend the **Out** point further into the original clip. Premiere shows the numeric markers that you set in the original clip at other scene changes.

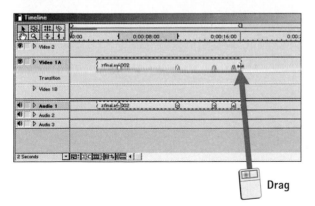

Drag

How-To Hints

Setting Duration

You can also set the duration of a clip directly.

Click the clip in the Project or Timeline window to select it, and then choose **Duration** from the pop-up context menu (or pull down the **Clip** menu and choose **Duration**). Then enter the exact duration time in the **Clip Duration** dialog.

End

Task

PART 10

Editing in the Timeline

*I*n the early parts of this book, you worked with individual clips of the Premiere Timeline window, inserting and deleting clips on the video and audio tracks.

In Part 9, "Trimming and Editing Clips," you prepared clips in the Project window by trimming them before copying them to the Timeline, duplicated them to reuse in the Timeline, and performed simple trims on clips.

In this part, you will explore the Premiere tools for editing clips and tracks on the Timeline, operating on groups of clips, and making independent adjustments to the video and audio tracks of a clip. The tasks in this part roughly follow the order of the Premiere tool buttons in the Timeline window.

Premiere provides a tremendous variety of tools for editing on the Timeline. As a result, it accommodates a range of different editing styles and different levels of precision in editing, from drag-and-drop with the mouse to keyboard shortcuts, from simple edits of individual clips to operations across adjacent clips, from edits on a single track to multiple tracks. See Part 11, "Editing in the Monitor Window," for another more professionally oriented editing approach.

The easiest way to experiment with the Premiere editing commands is to set up the Timeline with a collection of clips, save the setup as a new Project file, and then try the commands. While you are experimenting, use the Undo command or the History Palette to back out changes, or the Revert command to return to the original layout. •

How to Use the Timeline Window

The Premiere Timeline window provides a cornucopia of display and editing options and features. These are accessed from various menus, dialogs, tool buttons, toggle buttons, keyboard selections, and other edit controls across your clips and tracks. This task provides a quick tour of the components of the Timeline window, before the more detailed tasks that follow.

Begin

1 Using the Time Ruler

The **Time Ruler** area at the top of the **Timeline** window displays the current time position in your production, as well as any **In** and **Out** points or other markers. Click the **Hand Tool** (or press H) and then click and drag the cursor to move to a different section of the Timeline (or use the scrollbar). The **Edit Line Marker** shows the current position in the Timeline, or you can click and drag it to scrub through the clips.

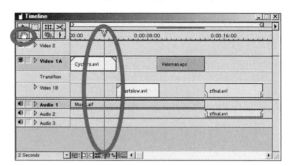

2 Navigating in the Timeline

Pull open the **Time Zoom Level** menu in the lower left of the Timeline to change the time period for the display, and zoom in and out. Select the **Zoom Tool** (or press Z) and click to zoom in on the Timeline view, or press **Alt** (Windows) or **Option** (Macintosh) and click to zoom out. You can also use the **Navigator** palette for an overview of the currently displayed window and time in the Timeline, and to move and zoom the display.

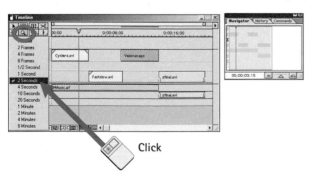

Click

3 Set the Work Area

The **Preview Indicator Area** above the **Time Ruler** shows whether a preview needs to be generated or already exists. The yellow **Work Area Band** above it shows the current working areas for previews. Drag the triangular **Work Area Markers** to adjust the work area, or double-click the bar to set the work area to the currently visible region.

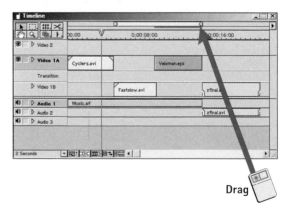

Drag

4 Set the Track Options

The **Track Heading** area on the left side of the Timeline shows the names and status of the available tracks. Open the **Timeline** window menu and choose **Track Options**, or click the **Track Options Dialog** button, to display the **Track Options** dialog where you can add, rename, or delete tracks (see Task 3).

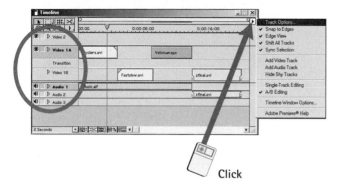

Click

5 Set the Track Display

Use the triangular **Collapse/Expand Track** control and track display buttons to control how the track contents are displayed.

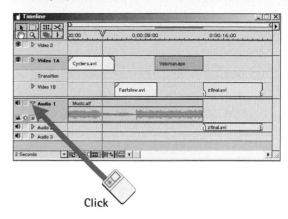

Click

6 Select a Timeline Tool

Click one of the **Timeline Tools** in the upper left of the Timeline window to control editing operations in the Timeline. You can also select a tool by typing a single letter abbreviation. Some tool buttons provide access to several related tools, indicated by a small triangle in the bottom-left corner. Click and hold one of these buttons to select an alternate tool.

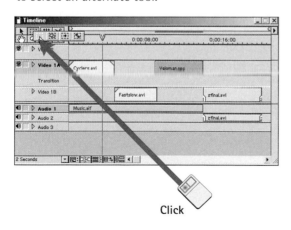

Click

7 Select a Timeline Toggle

Click the **Timeline Toggle** buttons in the bottom left of the window to toggle display and editing operations in the Timeline. These toggles, as well as Timeline and Track options, also can be selected from the **Timeline** window menu and the **Timeline** menu.

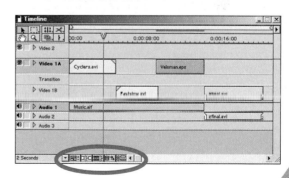

End

How to Customize the Timeline Window

The Timeline Window Options dialog provides options for controlling the overall Timeline display. Depending on the number of tracks in the Timeline, you can increase the size of the clip icons and display frames from the clips.

Begin

1 Open the Timeline Window Options

Open the **Timeline** window menu and choose **Timeline Window Options**.

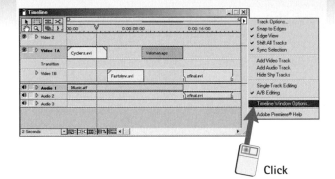

Click

2 The Timeline Window Options Dialog

Premiere displays the **Timeline Window Options** dialog. Use these options to adjust the Timeline display to the current window, adding more information when there are only a few clips in a large window, or removing detail when you have many clips in the Timeline.

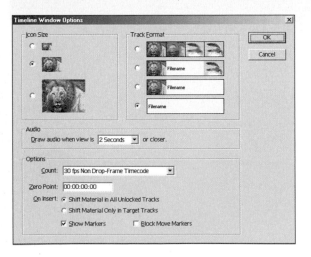

3 Set the Icon Size

In the **Icon Size** section, select the size of the clip icon you want to use in the Timeline. Select a smaller size when working with a larger number of tracks.

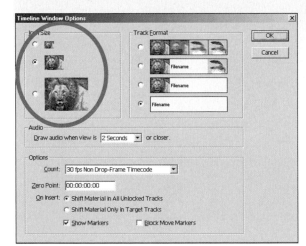

4 Set the Track Format

In the **Track Format** section, select the display format to be used for clip icons in the Timeline. The options include displaying the filename, the poster and ending frame, and intermediate frames. The Timeline updates fastest when displaying only the filename.

5 Set the Audio Display

In the **Audio** section, select the zoom level at which to start displaying the audio waveform graph when you expand the clip in the Timeline.

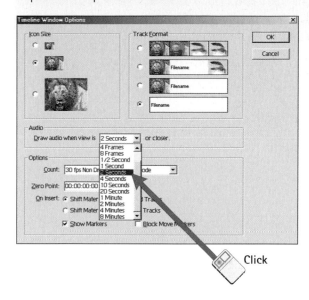

Click

6 Set the Insert Options

In the **Options** section, set the **On Insert** option to specify which tracks are affected by an insert. Select **Shift Material Only in Target Tracks** to specify that adding new clips will cause only the destination tracks to be shifted to make room for the insertion, or **Shift Material in All Unlocked Tracks** to adjust all tracks. This option can also be set using the **Toggle Shift Tracks Options** button at the bottom of the Timeline window, or the **Shift All Tracks** command in the **Timeline** window menu.

7 Set the Marker Options

In the **Options** section, select **Show Markers** to display clip and Timeline markers. Click **OK** to close the dialog.

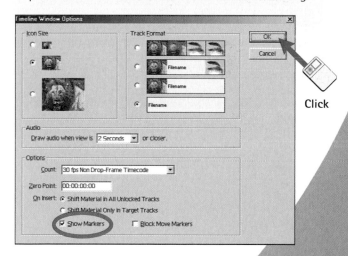

Click

End

How to Add and Lock Clips and Tracks

The Track Heading area on the left side of the Timeline shows the names and status of the available tracks. Use the Track Options dialog to add, rename, or delete tracks.

Begin

1 Open the Track Options

Pull open the **Timeline** window menu and choose **Track Options**, or click the **Track Options Dialog** button.

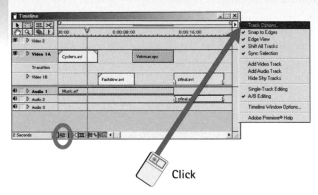

Click

2 Change the Track Options

Premiere displays the **Track Options** dialog. Select an existing track to rename or delete it. Click **Add** to add a new track.

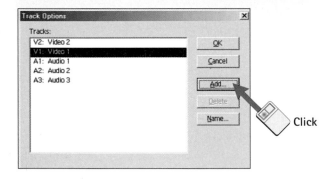

Click

3 Add a Track

Premiere displays the **Add Tracks** dialog. Enter the number of **Video** or **Audio** tracks to add. Click **OK** to exit each dialog and add the new tracks.

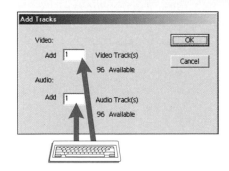

_4_ Lock a Track

Premiere adds two new tracks to the Timeline: **Video 3** and **Audio 4**. Click the **lock** icon area next to the track name to lock an entire track, so that clips in the track cannot be accidentally selected or edited. The cursor changes to a lock symbol when over a locked track.

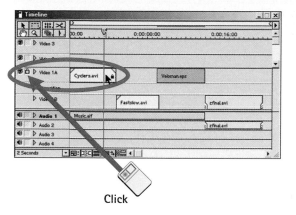

Click

_5_ Lock a Clip

Select one or more clips on the Timeline, and then choose **Lock Clip on Timeline** from the pop-up context menu, or from the **Clip** menu.

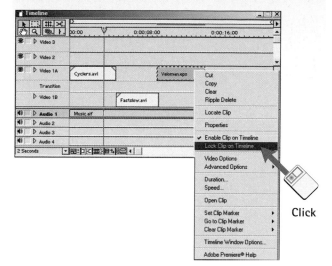

Click

_6_ View a Locked Clip

Premiere marks the locked clips with a hatch pattern of gray slashes, and a check mark next to the command in the menus. Choose the **Lock Clip on Timeline** command again to unlock the clip.

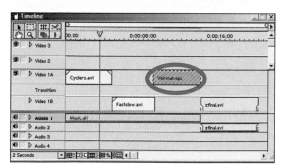

How-To Hints

Adding Tracks When Inserting Clips

You can also add a track when inserting clips in the Timeline by dragging and dropping a clip on the bottom of the Timeline window.

Preventing Mistakes

As you complete work on sections of the Timeline, it is useful to lock the individual clips and even entire tracks to prevent accidental changes. Although the **History Palette** and **AutoSave** option can help you recover from mistakes (see Part 2), locking portions of the Timeline is a better way to prevent unanticipated effects.

End

How to Disable and Hide Clips and Tracks

Premiere provides several approaches for focusing your work on a part of a larger production. You can temporarily disable individual clips and even exclude entire tracks, so that they will be ignored when playing through the Timeline and exporting to a video file. You can also hide tracks from the Timeline display to reduce the clutter in the window.

Begin

1 Disable a Clip

Select one or more clips on the Timeline, and then deselect **Enable Clip on Timeline** from the pop-up context menu, or from the **Clip** menu. Premiere marks enabled clips with a check mark next to the command in the menus.

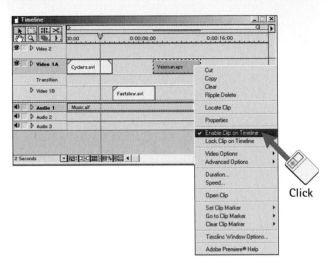

Click

2 View a Disabled Clip

Premiere marks the disabled clips with a hatch pattern of gray backslashes. Choose the **Enable Clip on Timeline** command again to enable the clip.

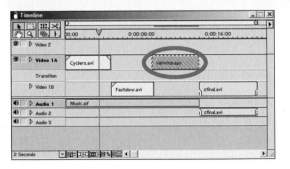

3 Exclude a Track

Click the **eye** (video) or **speaker** (audio) icon at the far left of the **Track Heading** area to mark a track as excluded. The icon disappears, indicating that the entire track will be ignored when previewing the Timeline or exporting to a file. Click again to include the track.

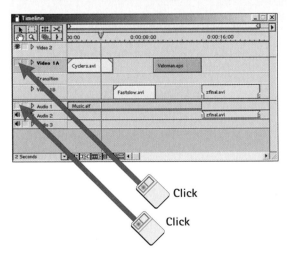

Click

Click

4 Mark a Track as Shy

Press **Control** (Windows) or **Command** (Macintosh) while clicking on the **eye** or **speaker** icon to mark a track as shy. *Shy tracks* are still included when playing or exporting the Timeline, but they can be hidden from view.

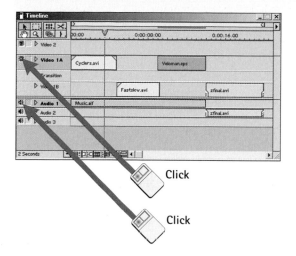

Click

Click

5 Hide the Shy Tracks

Premiere displays the eye icons as outlines to mark the shy tracks. Pull open the **Timeline** window menu and choose **Hide Shy Tracks**, or select it from the **Timeline** menu, to temporarily simplify the Timeline display by hiding the shy tracks.

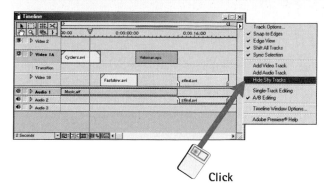

Click

6 Show the Shy Tracks

Premiere hides all the shy tracks from view in the **Timeline** window. Choose **Show Shy Tracks** to display them again.

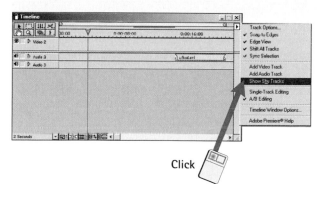

Click

How-To Hints

Locking Hidden Tracks

Disabled clips, and shy and hidden tracks, can still be edited just like any other entry on the Timeline. Use the lock option to prevent editing changes to a track, especially a hidden track (see Task 3).

Hiding All Tracks

Press **Control** and **Alt** (Windows) or **Command** and **Option** (Macintosh) while clicking an **eye** or **speaker** icon to mark all superimposed video tracks (except **Video 1**), or all audio tracks, as shy.

End

TASK **5**

How to Select Clips and Tracks

As your productions become larger and more ambitious, the Timeline becomes correspondingly more complex, with many clips, transitions, and effects. Premiere provides a variety of tools for selecting groups of tracks and clips so they can be moved or edited together.

Begin

1 Select a Clip

Click the **Selection Tool** button (or type **V**) to select individual clips with the mouse in the Timeline window. The cursor changes to an arrow icon. Click on a clip to select it. Press **Control** (Windows) or **Command** (Macintosh) as you click to add or remove additional individual clips to the current selection, or press **Shift** as you click to add a range of clips.

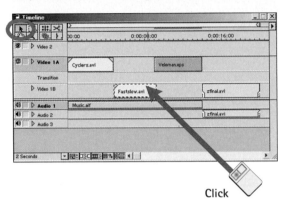

Click

2 Select All Clips

Pull down the **Edit** menu and choose **Select All** to select all the clips in the Timeline, or **Deselect All** to remove all selections.

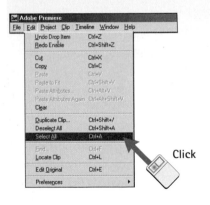

Click

3 Select a Range of Clips

Click and hold the **Selection** tool button and choose the first tool (**Range Select Tool**—or press **M** to select the current tool). The cursor changes to a dashed rectangle icon. Click and drag a rectangle over a group of clips to select them. Press **Shift** as you click to add additional clips to the current selection.

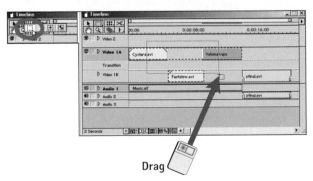

Drag

4 Select a Track

Click and hold the **Selection** tool button and choose the third tool (**Track Select Tool**). The cursor changes to a single right arrow icon. Click a clip to select all the clips in that track from that time forward. Press **Shift** as you click to add additional tracks to the current selection.

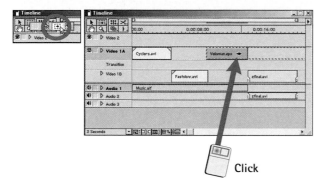

Click

5 Select Multiple Tracks

Click and hold the **Selection** tool button and choose the fourth tool (**Multitrack Select Tool**). The cursor changes to a double right arrow icon. Click a clip to select all the clips that occur in all tracks from that time or later.

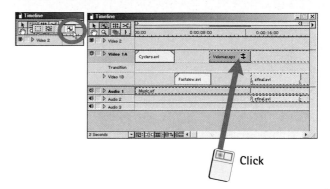

Click

6 Select Video and Audio

Click the **Toggle Sync Mode** button at the bottom of the Timeline to determine whether linked video and audio clips are selected together or independently (or use the **Sync Selection** command in the **Timeline** window and **Timeline** menus). If sync mode is enabled, a link icon is visible on the button, and clicking either the video or audio track of a linked clip will select both portions. Click to disable sync mode, and then click to select the video portion of a clip independently from the audio portion.

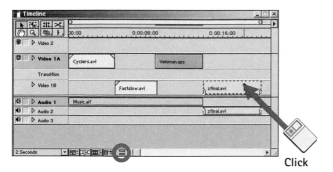

Click

How-To Hints

Block Select Tool

Use the second **Selection** tool (**Block Select Tool**) button to select and duplicate portions of the Timeline to reuse as a *virtual clip* in other portions of the Timeline. See the Premiere documentation for more information on virtual clips.

End

How to Trim Adjacent Clips

As you saw at the end of Part 9, you can trim an individual clip in the Timeline by simply clicking and dragging its ends, or by setting its duration. You can insert or delete a clip from an otherwise empty track without affecting the rest of the production, or you can perform a ripple edit to slide over the adjacent clips to make room for an insertion or to fill the gap from a deletion (see Part 3).

However, things get more complicated when dealing with a group of adjacent clips on the same or neighboring tracks. Premiere provides additional Timeline editing tools to provide even more control over editing operations on adjacent clips.

2 Trim in a Clip Window

Double-click a clip in the Timeline to display it in a **Clip** window. Set the **In** and **Out** points as desired (see Part 9). Then click the **Apply** button at the bottom of the window to apply the changes to the clip in the Timeline.

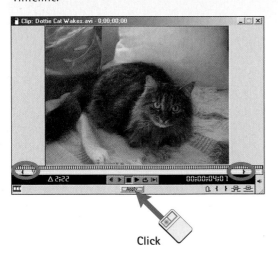

Click

Begin

1 Set Up the Timeline

To experiment with trimming adjacent clips on the Timeline, add a series of clips to the Timeline, with at least three clips side by side on the same track, and additional clips on other tracks. Also, trim the ends of the three adjacent clips to reduce their duration and provide some extra material to work with.

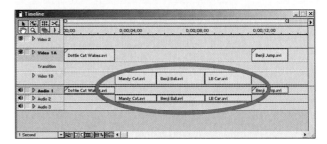

3 Perform a Rolling Edit

Click and hold the **Edit** tool and choose the first **Rolling Edit Tool** (or press **P** to select the current tool). The cursor changes to a red **Rolling Edit** icon, showing that the edit will trim both clips. In a *rolling edit*, as you drag the edge between the two clips, the overall program duration stays the same. The **Out** point of the first clip is adjusted in tandem with the **In** point of the second clip so that, as one increases in duration, the other decreases to match it. As you drag the clip boundary, the **Monitor** window displays a split screen of the frames from the two adjacent clips.

Drag

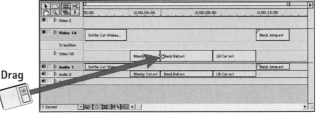

4 Perform a Ripple Edit

Choose the second **Ripple Edit Tool**. The cursor changes to a red **Ripple Edit** icon, showing that the edit will trim only one clip. In a *ripple edit*, as you drag the edge between the two clips, the trimmed clip changes duration, and the rest of the program on the Timeline moves to accommodate the new size.

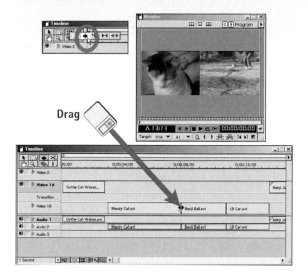

Drag

5 Perform a Slip Edit

Choose the fourth **Slip Tool**. The cursor changes to a black **Slip Edit** icon, showing that the edit will trim only within the one clip. Drag to the left or right to slip the **In** and **Out** points within that clip earlier or later in the clip. As you slip the clip, the **Monitor** window shows the new **In** and **Out** Points. In a *slip edit*, the duration of the clip remains the same, and only the position of the **In** and **Out** points are moved. The rest of the program on the Timeline is unchanged.

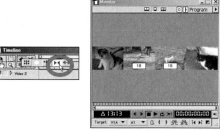

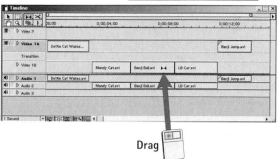

Drag

6 Perform a Slide Edit

Choose the fourth **Slide Tool**. The cursor changes to a black **Slide Edit** icon. Click and drag left or right to slide the clip earlier or later in the program by changing the **In** and **Out** points of the neighboring clips. In a *slide edit*, the clip remains unchanged, and its movement trims the adjacent clips. The rest of the program on the Timeline is unchanged.

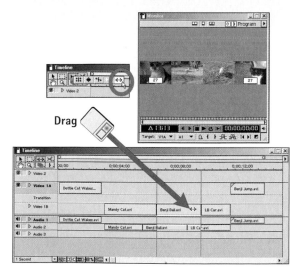

Drag

How-To Hints

Rate Stretch Tool

Use the third **Rate Stretch Tool** to change the playback speed of the clip. See the Premiere documentation for much more on changing clip and program frame rates

Video and Audio Sync Mode

When performing a rolling or ripple edit, use the **Toggle Sync Mode** button at the bottom of the Timeline to determine whether linked video and audio clips are moved together or independently (or use the **Sync Selection** command in the Timeline window and Timeline menus).

End

How to Copy and Paste Clips

In Part 9, you used the same clip multiple times on the Timeline, and made duplicate copies of clips so you could track them as you reused them with different trim settings.

Premiere also provides a razor tool to slit a clip in the Timeline into two parts.

You can also cut, copy, and paste clips directly on the Timeline, and control how they are adjusted to fit into the available space on a track. You can even copy and paste the attributes of a clip to replicate them across other clips.

Begin

1 Split a Clip

To split a clip, position the **Edit Line** to mark the point where you want to split it. Click and hold the **Razor** tool and choose the first **Razor Tool,** or press **C** to select the current Razor tool. Move the cursor over a clip, and it changes to a razor blade icon. Click on the clip at the point where you want to split it.

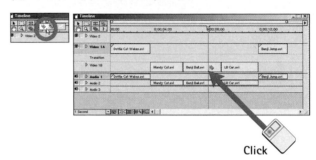

Click

2 View the Split Clip

Premiere splits the clip into two independent instances, with the **Out** point of the first and the **In** point of the second adjusted to match each other. All linked clips are also split.

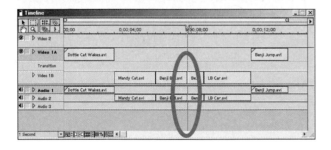

3 Split All Tracks at Once

To split all tracks at a single point in time, position the **Edit Line** there to mark the split point. Choose the second **Multiple Razor Tool**. Move the cursor over a clip in any track, and it changes to a Multiple Razor icon. Click on the clip at the point where you want to split the tracks.

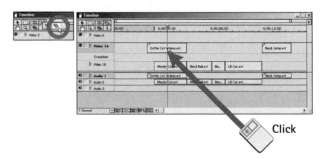

Click

4 View the Split in all Tracks

Premiere splits all the clips at that point on all unlocked tracks.

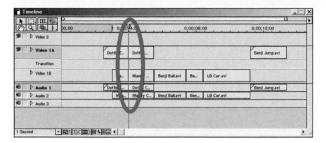

5 Open a Gap

Click a clip to select it. Press **Delete** to remove a short clip from the Timeline to make a gap between clips to paste into. Then click a long clip to select it.

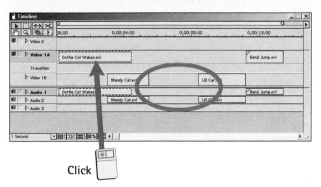

Click

6 Copy a Clip

Pull down the **Edit** menu and choose **Copy**.

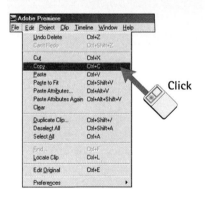

Click

7 Paste the Clip

Click the gap between clips to select it as the destination. Pull down the **Edit** menu and choose **Paste**.

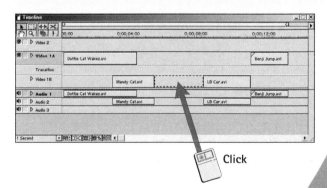

Click

Continues

8 View the Timeline

Premiere inserts the clip at the selected location in the Timeline, and trims the clip, if needed, by adjusting the **Out** point to fit the available space in the Timeline. You can also paste over an existing clip to replace it.

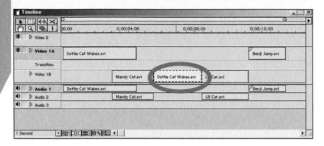

9 Copy the Clip

Copy the long clip again, and then click on another clip to select it. Then pull down the **Edit** menu and choose **Paste to Fit**.

Click

10 Specify the Fit

Premiere displays the **Fit Clip** dialog. You can click **Change Speed** to slow down or speed up the clip to fit the available space. Click **Trim Source** to trim the clip to fit the available space by adjusting the **Out** point.

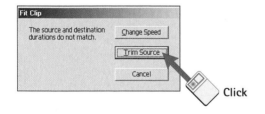

Click

11 View the Timeline

Premiere inserts the clip at the selected location in the Timeline, and adjusts the clip to fit as specified.

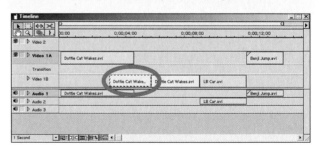

12 Paste Clip Attributes

Copy a clip, click a different clip to select it, and then pull down the **Edit** menu and choose **Paste Attributes**.

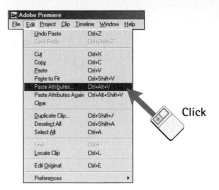

Click

13 Specify Content Attributes

Premiere displays the **Paste Attributes** dialog. Select **Content** to paste the source clip into the selected destination, and choose the type of adjustment to be made to fit the clip into the Timeline. The Content section also shows an animation of the effect of the selected option.

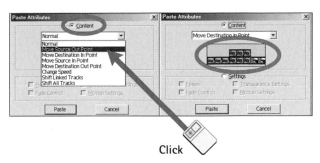

Click

14 Specify Settings Attributes

Select **Settings** to transfer filter, fade control, transparency, or motion settings from one clip to another. Click **Paste** to perform the operation.

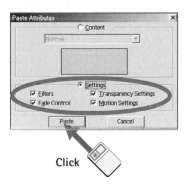

Click

How-To Hints

Paste Attributes Again

Use **Paste Attributes Again** in the **Edit** menu to repeat a **Paste Attributes** operation for multiple clips.

Changing Multiple Clips

You can also select multiple clips, and then use **Paste Attributes** to apply filters or other settings to all of them at once.

End

How to Unlink and Unsync Clips

As you have seen in previous tasks, Premiere displays clips with both video and audio on the Timeline in two pieces, on a video track and an audio track. Premiere keeps track of the two parts, keeping them *linked*—so that they move together—and *synced*—so that they play at the same time. Premiere also provides tools to unlink and unsync the clips, so you can edit them independently, or link other pairs of clips so that they will move together.

Begin

1 View the Timeline

Open the **Sample Project** (from Part 1) and add different kinds of clips to the timeline: **Fastslow** (video only), **Music** (audio only), **Veloman** (still image), and **zfinal** (video and audio). Premiere uses different colors for the different types of clips, and shows both parts of the **zfinal** clip in light green to show that they are linked.

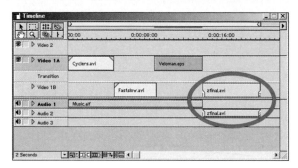

2 Unsync Linked Clips

Click the **Toggle Sync Mode** button at the bottom of the Timeline to determine if linked video and audio clips are selected together or independently (or use the **Sync Selection** command in the **Timeline** window and **Timeline** menus). If sync mode is enabled, a link appears in the button. Click the button so the toggle is unlinked. Click the **Selection Tool** button (arrow) in the top left of the **Timeline** window, and then click and drag the audio portion of the **zfinal** clip out of sync.

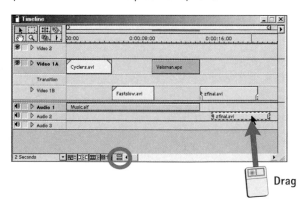

Drag

3 Resync Linked Clips

When linked clips are moved out of sync, Premiere marks each clip with a red triangle. Click the cursor on the red triangle to display the amount of time that the two tracks of the clip are out of sync. Click and drag the cursor into the time value and then release it to snap the two portions of the clip back into sync.

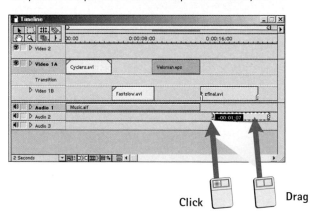

Click   Drag

4 Unlink Video and Audio

Click the **Toggle Sync Mode** button so the clip tracks are in sync again. Click one of the linked tracks to select both and then pull down the **Clip** menu and choose **Unlink Audio and Video**.

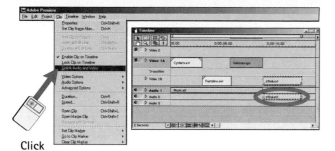

Click

5 Realign Unlinked Clips

Premiere recolors the clips to show that they are no longer linked, and displays each clip with a white marker. To realign unlinked clips after they have been moved independently, click the **Selection Tool** button and click and drag the marker from one clip to the marker in the other clip.

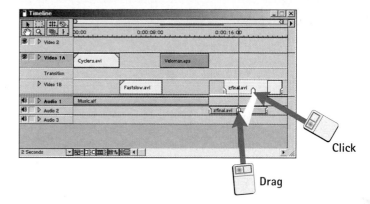

Click

Drag

6 Link Video and Audio

Click on the **Link/Unlink Tool** button (chains) to select it. To link a video and audio clip, or to unlink a linked pair of clips, click the first clip to select it. Move the cursor over the second clip, so it changes to the Link/Unlink icon, and then click on the second clip. Premiere recolors the clips to show the new link status.

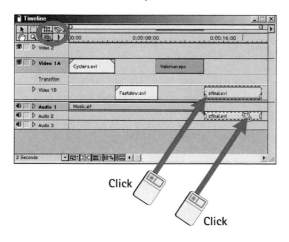

Click

Click

How-To Hints

Toggle Sync Mode

Use the **Toggle Sync Mode** button to temporarily unsync the video and audio tracks of a clip so they can be edited independently. Then click the button again to restore Sync mode.

End

Task

11

Editing in the Monitor Window

Up to this point, you have been editing in the Timeline window with a convenient drag-and-drop method, using the mouse to move, insert, and delete clips. You also have been operating on entire clips, or groups of clips. But Premiere supports an alternative editing method with the Monitor window. Familiar to professional video editors, this approach provides for precise placement of clips.

With this approach, you expand the Monitor window to trim your source clips, specify destination times in the Timeline window, and then make edits using efficient push-button (or keyboard) controls. This approach also permits you to easily edit at arbitrary points in the program, including within and spanning multiple clips.

You can mix and match editing styles at any time, dragging clips to arrange them, and then using the Monitor window controls for precise adjustments. Premiere also simplifies window organization and layout with the Workspace menu options, so as you become more familiar with Premiere, you can switch from the A/B Editing organization that is used throughout this book to this Single-Track Editing organization style used by video professionals. •

How to Use the Monitor Display

In the A/B Editing workspace layout, the Monitor window displays the Program view, so that you can view the current layout assembled in the Timeline window. You can play through the entire program on the Timeline using all the same controls and keyboard commands that are used in Clip windows. You can also display overlaid safe margins on the Monitor window to avoid working too close to the edges of the frames.

Begin

1 Open a Project

Start Premiere and open a project with some clips on the Timeline. To restore the windows and palettes to the default layout, pull down the **Window** menu and choose **Workspace, A/B Editing**.

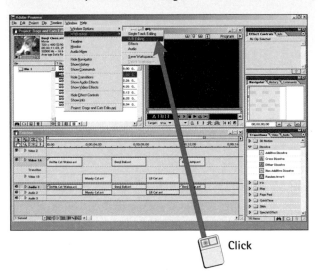

Click

2 View the Monitor Window

The **Monitor** window is labeled **Program** at the top right because it is displaying the entire program currently laid out on the Timeline. As in the **Clip** window, use the VCR controls to play through the Timeline, or use the cursor control keys or keyboard shortcuts (see Part 9, "Trimming and Editing Clips").

3 Show the Safe Margins

Open the **Monitor** window menu (from the triangle next to window name, in this case, **Program**) and select **Safe Margins for Program Side**.

Click

4 View the Safe Margins

Premiere displays a *safe zone* overlay on the **Monitor** window. Television sets typically do not display the entire video image, but instead tend to *overscan* the display to cut off the edges at the edge of the screen. The outer rectangle marks the safe area for action in the scene, and the inner rectangle marks the safe area for displaying titles on overscanned displays.

5 Open the Monitor Window Options

Open the **Monitor** window menu and select **Monitor Window Options**.

Click

6 Set the Safe Margins

Premiere displays the **Monitor Window Options** dialog. Use the **Safe Margins** section to resize the safe margins overlay, reflecting the type of display on which you expect your production to be viewed. Click **OK** when done.

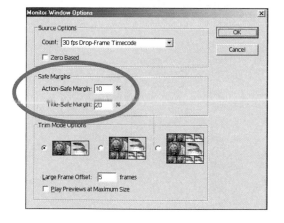

How-To Hints

Safe Margins

Use the safe margins as guidelines for editing your material, especially if you expect it to be viewed on overscanned television displays. To be sure your viewers see what you intend, keep the important action in the scene within the outer rectangle, and keep text overlays within the inner region. If you are editing for viewing only on computers or on the Web, then overscan is not an issue, and you can use the whole frame.

End

How to Set Up the Dual View Display

The Monitor window has a second part. In the dual view display, you can view and trim source clips in the Source view, instead of needing to open separate Clip windows. And, to fit the Monitor window's editing style, you can also set the Premiere workspace for Single-Track Editing.

Begin

1 Select Dual View

Open the **Monitor** window menu and select **Dual View**, or click the **Dual View** button at the top center of the Monitor window.

Click

2 Adjust the Monitor Window

Premiere expands the **Monitor** window to dual view, with the **Program** area on the right and a **Source** area on the left for viewing and trimming source clips. (Move or close any palettes that are open over the expanded window.)

3 Load a Source Clip

Click a clip in the **Project** window and drag it to the **Source** section of the **Monitor** window.

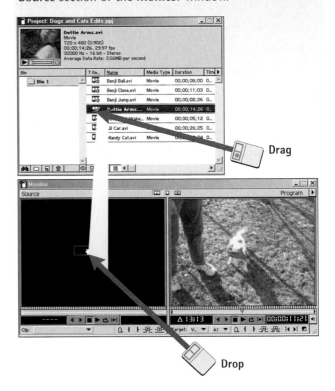

Drag

Drop

4 View the Source Clip

Premiere loads the clip into the **Source** view, and displays its name in the **Select Source Clip** menu at the bottom left of the window. Use the VCR controls to play part way into the clip.

5 Select the Single-Track Editing Workspace

Pull down the **Window** menu and choose **Workspace, Single-Track Editing**.

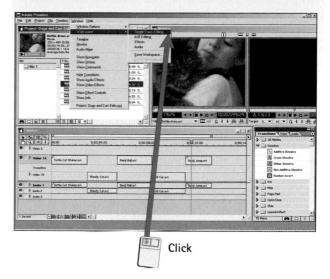

Click

6 View the Single-Track Editing Workspace

Premiere adjusts the window layout to accommodate the dual-view **Monitor** window. It also collapses the **Timeline** window for single-track editing, showing a single row per track, without a separate transition track.

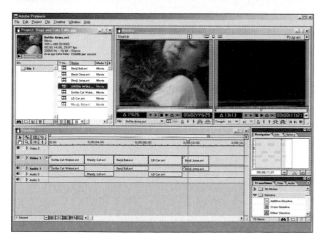

How-To Hints

Dual-View Editing

The **Monitor** window can be used in dual-view editing to quickly switch between and trim source clips. Instead of opening each clip in its own large **Clip** window that overlays the rest of the display, you can view and trim the clips in the **Source** view before adding them to the Timeline.

Single-Track Editing

The single-track editing workspace fits the style of professional video editors. It provides precise and efficient control of editing operations by setting source and destination points and then clicking single-button commands (or using the keyboard equivalents).

Click on the **Track Mode** icon to the right of the track name to expand the **Video 1** track.

End

How to Use the Monitor Source View

With the dual-view Monitor window, you can view and trim clips directly in the Source view, and switch quickly from one to another. You can prepare clips from bins in the Project window, and edit clips already added to the Timeline window. Premiere also provides the option to view individual clips at full size in a Clip window.

Begin

1 Open the General Preferences

Pull down the **Edit** menu and choose **Preferences, General and Still Image**.

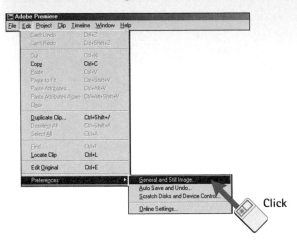

Click

2 Set the Open Movies Option

Premiere displays the **General and Still Image** section of the **Preferences** dialog. Uncheck **Open Movies in Clip Window** to have clips open in the **Source** view of the **Monitor** window, and not in an individual **Clip** window (as in the **A/B Editing** workspace).

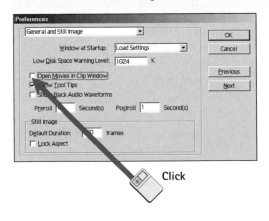

Click

3 Open a Project Clip

Double-click a new clip in the **Project** window.

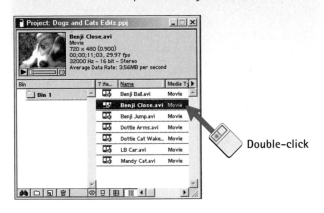

Double-click

4 View the Source Clip

Premiere opens the clip in the **Source** view of the **Monitor** window, and not in a new **Clip** window.

5 Open a Timeline Clip

Double-click a clip on the Timeline to open it, or click a clip and then choose **Open Clip** from the pop-up context menu (or from the **Clip** menu).

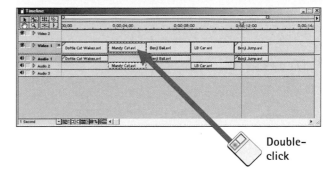

Double-click

6 View the Timeline Clip

Premiere loads the clip into the **Source** view of the **Monitor** window, with its timecode in the **Select Source Clip** menu at the bottom left of the **Source** view. Premiere also shows the extent of the clip within the entire program in the jog tread area at the bottom of the **Program** view.

How-To Hints

Viewing Source Clips

You can override the current **Open Movies in Clip Window** option by pressing **Alt** (Windows) or **Option** (Macintosh) while you double-click. You can also choose how to view a clip in the **Project** window by selecting the clip, and then choosing **Open in Source Monitor** or **Open in Clip Window** from the pop-up context menu.

Multiple Source Clips

You can add a group of clips to the **Select Source Clip** menu by selecting them in the **Project** window and double-clicking or dragging them into the **Source** view.

End

How to Trim in the Monitor Window

The Source view of the Monitor window has the same kinds of trim controls and menu options that you have seen in the Clip window. You can create instances of clips with different trim settings to add to the Timeline, and change the trim settings of clips already on the Timeline.

1 View a Project Clip

Double-click a clip in the **Project** window to load it into the **Source** view of the **Monitor** window, or click the **Select Source Clip** menu at the bottom left of the **Source** view to switch between clips that you have loaded recently.

Click

2 Trim the Source Clip

Use the **Source** view VCR controls to play the clip, and the trim controls to set the source trim points to a very short duration (that is, around **1:00**). You can Set, Go to, and Clear markers in the **Source** view by using the **Marker**, **In**, and **Out** button controls, respectively, or by using the **Clip Marker** commands in the pop-up context menus or **Clip** menu.

3 Add the Clip to the Timeline

Drag the trimmed clip to the Timeline and add it to the current program.

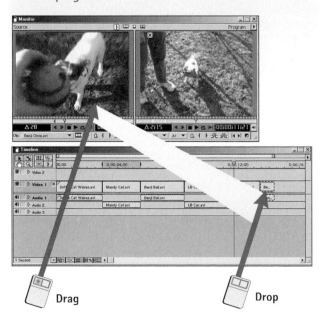

Drag

Drop

4 View the Clip from the Timeline

Double-click the clip in the Timeline to view it in the **Source** view. Premiere displays just the trimmed section of the clip in the **Source** view. The clip name is displayed in the **Select Source Clip** menu with the associated starting timecode in the Timeline.

5 Trim the Clip on the Timeline

Use the trim controls in the **Source** view to set new **In** and **Out** points.

6 Apply the Trim

Press the **Apply** button at the top of the **Source** view of the **Monitor** window to apply the new trim points to the clip on the Timeline.

Click

How-To Hints

Master Clip

Premiere keeps track of multiple instances of the same master clip as you trim and edit a clip, and reuse the same clip with different settings. As a result, instances of the same clip name can occur several times in the **Select Source Clip** menu.

To view the original master clip, choose **Open Master Clip** from the pop-up context menu (or the Clip menu).

End

How to Edit with the Monitor Window

Besides viewing and trimming clips, the full power of the dual-view Monitor window comes from the ability to precisely control how clips are inserted and deleted in the Timeline. By selecting source and destination trim and edit points, you can use the Premiere edit control to insert and delete, overlay and ripple delete, not just individual clips but also within clips and across multiple clips on the Timeline.

Begin

1 Trim the Source Clip

Restart Premiere to clear any history of the previous tasks, open a project with clips on the Timeline, and then load a clip from the **Project** window into the **Source** view of the **Monitor** window. Trim the clip to a short duration (that is, around **1:00**). You can use the **Take Video** or **Take Audio** buttons at the bottom of the **Source** view to specify the source tracks. Premiere draws a red diagonal line through the buttons if the corresponding tracks are disabled.

2 Set the Insertion Point

Position the **Edit Line** in the **Timeline** window to specify the insertion point for the clip. If needed, use the controls in the **Program** view of the **Monitor** window to move to an exact timecode. The insertion point can be at any place in the Timeline, including the middle of another clip.

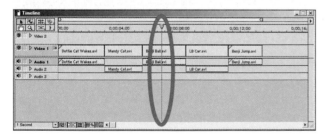

3 Set the Destination Tracks

Click the **Video 1** and **Audio 2** video and audio track names in the Timeline to select the destination tracks. Premiere highlights the selected tracks with the names in bold and the header region grayed.

4 Set the Destination Targets

Alternatively, you can pull down the **Select Video Target** and **Select Audio Target** menus in the **Monitor** window to specify the destination tracks. Choose **None** to disable the corresponding tracks. Premiere also highlights the selected tracks in the Timeline.

5 Insert at the Edit Line

Click the **Insert** button under the **Source** view to insert the clip at the current **Edit Line** position. (You can also type a comma (,) or choose **Insert at Edit Line** from the pop-up context menu or **Clip** menu.)

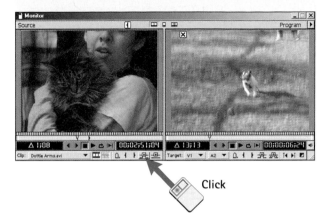

Click

6 View the Insertion

Premiere inserts the specified tracks of the source clip into the destination tracks, and shifts over the existing contents of the Timeline. If the insertion point is in the middle of a clip, that clip is cut into two pieces.

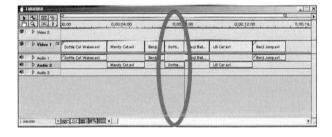

7 Overlay at the Edit Line

Undo the insert operation and then click the **Overlay** button under the **Source** view to overlay the clip at the current **Edit Line** position. (You can also type a period (.) or choose **Overlay at Edit Line** from the pop-up context menu or **Clip** menu.)

Click

Continues

8 View the Overlay

Premiere overlays the specified source tracks onto the destination tracks, on top of the existing contests of the Timeline. If the insert point is in the middle of a clip, portions of that clip will be replaced.

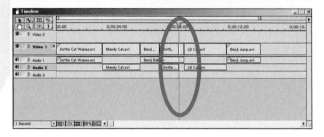

9 Set an Insertion Marker

Undo the overlay operation and then set an **In** point marker in the **Timeline** window to select the destination. You can **Set**, **Go to**, and **Clear** markers in the Timeline by using the **Marker**, **In**, and **Out** buttons under the **Program** view of the **Monitor** window, or by using the **Timeline Marker** commands in the pop-up menus or **Timeline** menu, or by pressing the **I** and **O** keys.

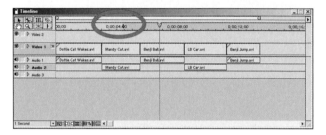

10 Insert at the Marker

Premiere displays the current **In** point under the **Program** view of the **Monitor** window. Click the **Insert** (or **Overlay**) button under the **Source** view. Premiere inserts (or overlays) the source clip in the Timeline, aligned to the specified **In** (or **Out**) point in the Timeline.

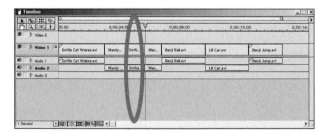

11 Set the Delete Region

Undo the insert operation and then set both an **In** and an **Out** point in the Timeline.

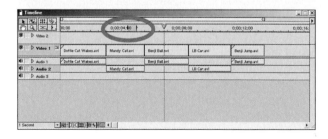

12 Lift Delete

Premiere displays the current trim region under the **Program** view of the **Monitor** window. Click the **Lift** button under the **Program** view.

Click

14 Extract Delete

Undo the delete operation and then click the **Extract** button (to the right of **Lift**) under the **Program** view of the **Monitor** window. Premiere ripple deletes the specified frames from the Timeline between the **In** and **Out** point, and shifts over the rest of the program to fill the gap.

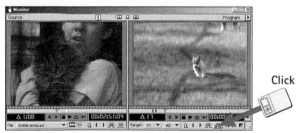

Click

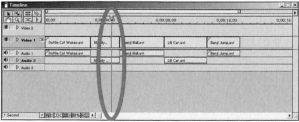

13 View the Deletion

Premiere deletes the specified frames from the Timeline between the **In** and **Out** point, and leaves the rest of the program unchanged with a gap in it.

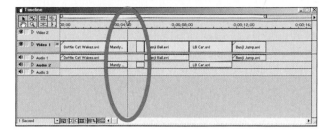

How-To Hints

Timeline Markers

You can use markers in the Timeline window for much more than setting **In** and **Out** points for insertions and deletions. You can mark important edit points and add comments to them.

You even can create Web Links that can be embedded in some exported movie formats, such as QuickTime, and can cause an automatic jump to a Web address when the movies are played in a Web page.

Three- and Four-Point Edits

By setting **In** and **Out** points in the **Source** and **Program** views, you can use the **Monitor** window controls to precisely determine where and how frames are inserted into the Timeline. In a *three-point edit*, you set any three markers; Premiere determines the fourth to match the duration. In a *four-point edit*, you set all four markers; Premiere displays a warning if the durations do not match.

Track Settings

The effect of these **Monitor** window editing operations on the destination tracks and the entire program are controlled by a number of settings. The **On Insert** section in the **Timeline Window Options** dialog specifies whether an insertion affects the target tracks, or all the tracks in the Timeline.

End

Task

PART 12

Adding Titles

While a picture can be worth a thousand words, and moving pictures can be worth even more, there still are times when words can be useful in your production. For example, you can use text for a title screen at the beginning of your production, for subtitles superimposed over the video, and for rolling credits at the end.

Premiere provides a Title window for preparing title screens for video productions. It is actually a specialized text and graphics editor for creating and laying out titles. A title is essentially a still image intended to be used as a title screen, either by itself, or overlaid with transparency on video clips.

You can create text and graphic objects with colors, gradient fills, graduated transparency, and shadows. You can also create titles with text in motion, for rolling or crawling credits.

You can then save and use titles like any other clip in your projects. You can also import other graphic images from applications such as Adobe Photoshop and Illustrator to use in the same way.

Even with all this great flexibility, try to keep your titles relatively plain and simple so that they are easy to read. Use fewer and larger words, with simple bolder fonts, colored and shadowed to stand out well from the background. ●

How to Create Title Objects

The Premiere Title window includes a drawing area and a toolbox with text and graphic drawing tools and attributes. You can also import a sample frame from a clip in your production to use as a positioning aid.

Begin

1 Open a Title Window

Open the **File** menu and choose **New, Title**.

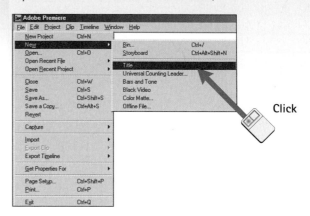

Click

2 Select the Type Tool

Premiere opens an empty **Title** window. Click on the **Type Tool** (with a "T" icon) in the toolbox at the top left, or press the **T** key.

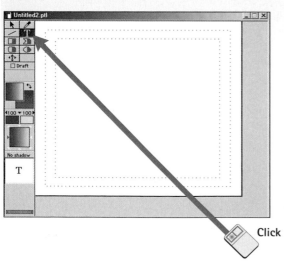

Click

3 Type a Title

Click inside the window and type a few lines of text. Click in the window when done. Premiere displays the text with the currently selected text attributes for font, size and style. The text is also filled with a gradient fill.

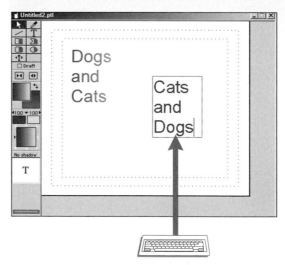

4 Display a Background Clip

Drag a clip from the **Project** window to the **Title** window to import a sample background frame. You can then use the frame to help in positioning the title text and in choosing appropriate colors. Premiere uses the first frame in the clip, or the current poster frame (marker 0), if specified. Use the pop-up context menu (or pull down the **Title** menu) and choose **Remove Background Clip** to remove the clip from the **Title** window.

5 Select Draft Display

Click the **Draft** check box under the tools to display the **Title** window in draft mode, which displays the text and graphics faster, but at lower quality than standard view mode does. The **Draft** option affects only the **Title** window display, and not how the title is rendered in a video program.

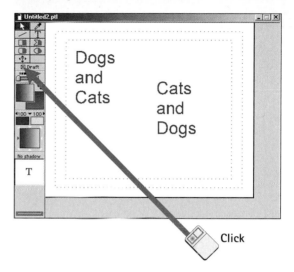

Click

6 Save the Title

Pull down the **File** menu and choose **Save As** to save the current Title window for use in your projects.

Click

How-To Hints

Selecting Tools

Click a tool in the toolbox to select it for a single use. The tool icon is highlighted in gray, and then reverts to the **Selection** tool after it is used.

Double-click a tool (except the **Type** tool) to select it for continual use. The tool is highlighted in black, and remains active until another tool is selected.

Formatting from the Menu

You can access most formatting options by right-clicking (Windows) or Control-clicking (Macintosh) an object and choosing a command from the pop-up context menu.

End

How to Set Title Window Options

Use the Title Window Options dialog to specify general options for the Title window, including its size, a safe zone overlay, and background color. Premiere also provides an option to automatically check and correct for NTSC-safe colors.

1 Open the Title Window Options

Pull down the **Window** menu and choose **Window Options, Title Window Options**, or choose **Title Window Options** from the pop-up context menu.

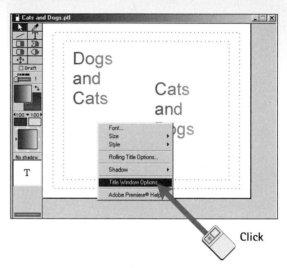

Click

2 Set the Title Window Size

Premiere displays the **Title Window Options** dialog. Enter a new **Size** (in pixels) and choose a new **Aspect** ratio, if desired, to better match your project and output video resolution.

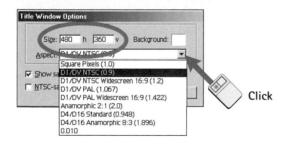

Click

3 Display the Safe Zone

If not already selected, click the **Show safe titles** check-box to display safe zone overlays on the **Title** window, such as in the **Monitor** window (see Part 11, "Editing in the Monitor Window"). The safe zone overlays provide guidelines for positioning your titles in the title-safe (inner) and action-safe (outer) regions of the frame. They are designed for NTSC video format.

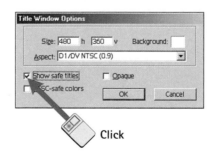

Click

4 Select NTSC-Safe Colors

Click the **NTSC-safe colors** check box to automatically adjust title colors that are outside the safe region for NTSC video displays. This can mute color intensity. If this option is not checked, colors outside this range might display badly and bleed on NTSC televisions.

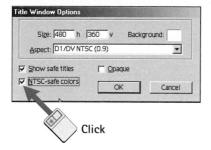

Click

5 Use the Color Picker

Click the **Background** color swatch to display the **Color Picker** dialog. Click and drag the cursor over the color area to choose a color, or type the **Red**, **Green**, and **Blue** color values. The bottom half of the color swatch in the top right of the dialog changes to show the current color, and the top half shows the original color.

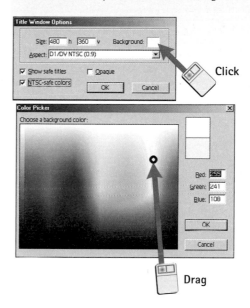

Click

Drag

6 Check the NTSC Gamut

If the selected color is out of the range that NTSC video can display accurately, the color swatch is displayed with a *gamut warning* symbol (yellow triangle with an exclamation mark). If you intend to show your production on NTSC video, click the swatch to automatically adjust the color into a safe range when the title is rendered. (The color is not changed until then.) Click **OK** to close the dialog.

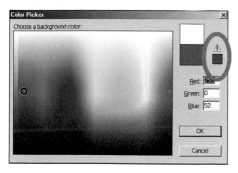

7 Set an Opaque Background

If desired, check **Opaque** to make the background color visible when placed on the Timeline. Click **OK** to close the dialog.

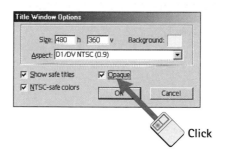

Click

End

How to Format Text

Premiere provides common text formatting and editing controls in the Title window, including text fonts and attributes, kerning, and paragraph layout. You can also add shadows to text and graphic objects to make them more readable and stand out better from the background.

1 Change the Text Attributes

Click the **Type** tool and click and drag to select a group of characters. Use the pop-up context menu (or pull down the **Title** menu) and choose **Font**, **Size**, or **Style** to change the text attributes as you would in a word processor.

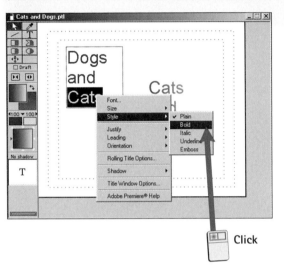

Click

2 Adjust the Kerning

Click between two characters, or select a group of characters and click the **Decrease Kerning** or **Increase Kerning** buttons to *kern* the characters, or change the spacing between adjacent characters.

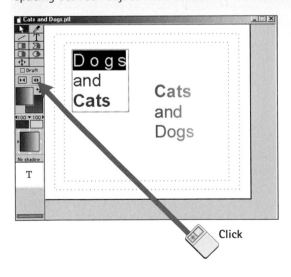

Click

3 Change the Paragraph Attributes

Click the **Selection** tool and then click a text block to select the entire text object. Use the pop-up context menu (or pull down the **Title** menu) and choose **Justify** to change the paragraph alignment to **Left**, **Right**, or **Center**. Choose **Leading** to adjust the line spacing to **More** or **Less**, or **Reset Leading** to restore the default. Choose **Orientation** to set the text direction to **Horizontal** or **Vertical**.

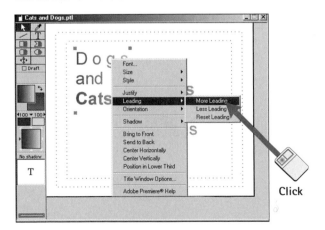

Click

4 Center the Text

Select a text object and then use the pop-up context menu (or pull down the **Title** menu) and choose **Center Horizontally**, **Center Vertically**, or **Position in Lower Third** to position the text in the window.

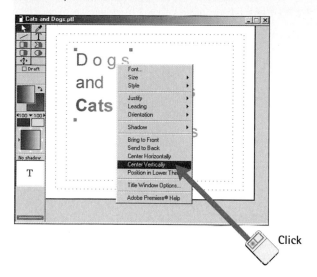

Click

5 Stretch the Text

Select a text object and then hold down the **Control** (Windows) or **Option** (Macintosh) key and drag an object handle to stretch the text.

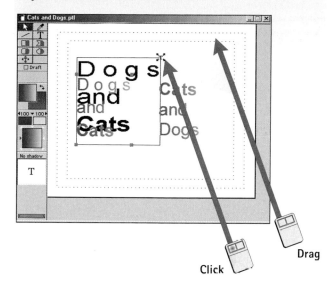

Click

Drag

6 Position a Shadow

Select a group of characters, or an entire text object, and then click and drag in the **Shadow Position** box to specify the offset of the shadow from the text. Hold down the **Shift** key as you drag to constrain the movement to 45-degree increments. Drag the offset off the edge of the area or back to the center to remove the shadow. The control will then display "No shadow."

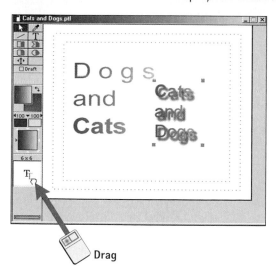

Drag

7 Choose the Shadow Type

Select a group of characters, or an entire text object, and then use the pop-up context menu (or pull down the **Title** menu) to choose **Shadow**, and **Single**, **Solid**, or **Soft** to choose the type of the shadow.

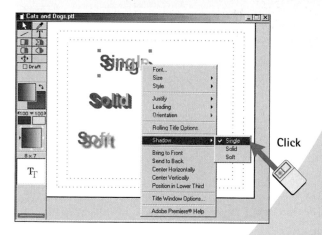

Click

End

How to Add Graphic Objects

Premiere also allows you to add graphics shapes to a Title window. You can create and edit shapes as in other graphics editors, including lines, rectangles, rounded rectangles, ovals, and polygons. Graphics objects can be framed (outlined) or filled, with adjustable line widths. The sharp corners of polygonal shapes and lines can also be smoothed to curves.

Begin

1 Draw Framed and Filled Objects

Click on the left side of the **Rectangle Tool** to draw framed (outlined) rectangles in the **Title** window, and then click and drag in the window to draw a rectangle. Click on the right side of the tool to draw filled rectangles.

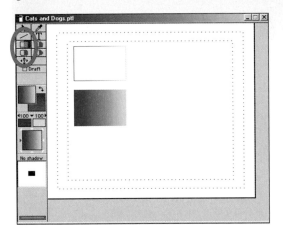

2 Draw Graphic Objects

Use the **Line**, **Polygon**, **Rounded Rectangle**, and **Oval** tools to draw other framed and filled graphical shapes. Use the Polygon tool to draw an open polygon as a series of lines. Hold down the **Shift** key as you draw to constrain the shapes to 45-degree increments.

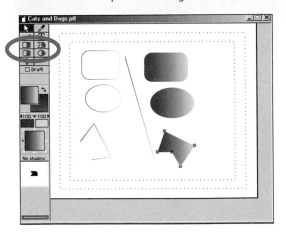

3 Change the Line Width

Select a line or a framed graphic object and then drag the **Line Width** slider to change the width of the line (in pixels).

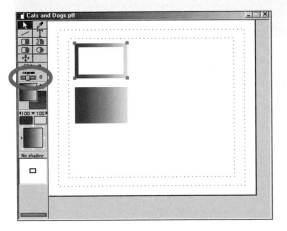

4 Smooth Polygons

Select a polygon object and then use the pop-up context menu (or pull down the **Title** menu) and choose **Smooth Polygon** to smooth the sharp corners of the polygon to curves.

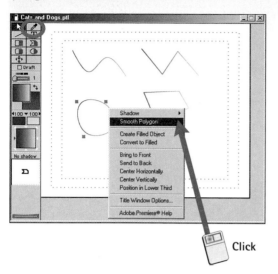

Click

5 Frame a Filled Object

Select a filled graphic object, and then use the pop-up context menu (or pull down the **Title** menu) and choose **Create Framed Object**. Premiere creates a duplicate object on top of the original. You can then change the color of the framed object to create the effect of a filled object with an outline.

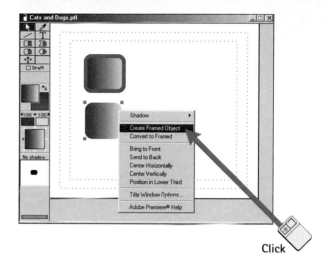

Click

6 Overlay Objects

Select an object, and then use the pop-up context menu (or pull down the **Title** menu) and choose **Send to Front** or **Send to Back** to overlay objects on top of each other. This is especially useful for positioning a framed object on top of a filled object.

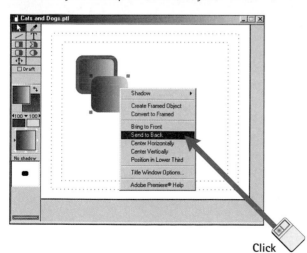

Click

How-To Hints

Convert between Framed and Filled

To convert a graphics object from framed to filled, or vice versa, select the object and then use the pop-up context menu (or pull down the Title menu) and choose **Convert to Framed** or **Convert to Filled**.

Select Multiple Objects

To apply an operation to multiple objects at the same time, click on one object to select it, and then hold down the Shift key and click on additional objects to add them to the current selection.

End

How to Use Color and Transparency

Premiere provides extensive control over the color and transparency of text and graphic objects, and even individual characters. Objects can have a solid color, or the color can be specified as a *gradient*, smoothly changing from one color to another in a specified direction. The gradient colors can also be opaque or transparent, varying in translucency from one side to the other.

Begin

1 Set the Object Color

Select a group of characters, or an entire text object, and then click the **Object Color** swatch to select a color for the text using the **Color Picker** dialog (see Task 2).

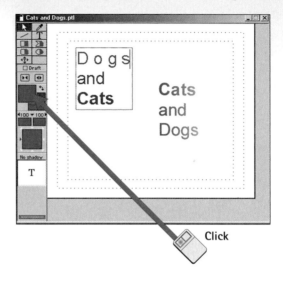

Click

2 Set the Shadow Color

Click the **Shadow Color** swatch to select a color for the shadow. Click the double-curved arrow to swap the object and shadow colors.

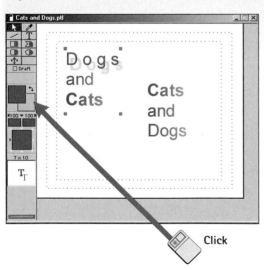

Click

3 Match a Color

To match another color in the **Title** window, click to select an object to be recolored. Click the **Eyedropper Tool** (or press I) to select it, and then click with the eyedropper cursor on the color you want to apply to the selected object (including a color from the background clip).

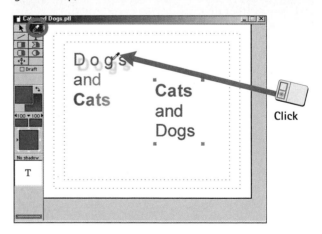

Click

4 Set a Color Gradient

Select a group of characters, or an entire text object, and then click the **Object Color** or **Shadow Color** swatch to select it. Then click the **Gradient Start Color** swatch (on left) and use the **Color Picker** dialog to select the start color for the gradient effect. Click the **Gradient End Color** swatch (on right) to set the ending color. The gradient effect is previewed in the swatch below.

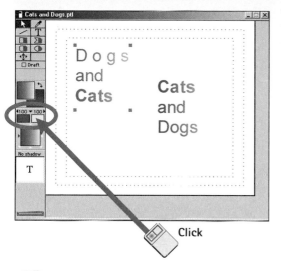

Click

5 Set the Gradient Direction

Click a **Gradient/Transparency Direction** triangle (located around the gradient preview swatch) to set the direction of the gradient.

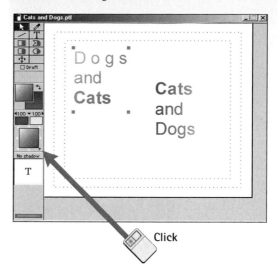

Click

6 Set the Transparency

Click the left **Start Transparency** triangle and click and drag in the menu to select the percentage opacity of the starting transparency value. Click the right **End Transparency** triangle to select the ending transparency, or click the center **Overall Transparency** triangle to set the transparency of the entire selection.

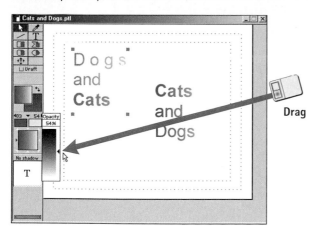

Drag

How-To Hints

Changing the Current Settings

If one or more objects are selected, the text and color settings are applied to those objects. If no objects are selected, then any changes become the current setting, and are applied to any new objects that are created.

You can also click any object to make its settings current, and then apply them to new objects.

Matching the Color for Individual Characters

Use the **Eyedropper** tool to change an entire object to match another color. To change individual characters to match another color, use the Color Picker dialog to display the color's values; and then enter those values for the new object.

End

How to Create Rolling and Crawling Titles

Premiere can create titles that move across the screen, either rolling (moving vertically up or down) or crawling (moving horizontally left or right). You enter the text in a Title window and specify the type of movement. When the Title clip is placed in a Timeline window, Premiere uses the duration of the clip to determine the speed that it moves.

Begin

1 Create a Rolling Text Title

Select the **Rolling Title Tool** (or press **Y**). Then click and drag to create a text window. Type multiple lines of text in the window to create a rolling title that will scroll up or down the screen. Add extra blank lines if needed to include enough text for the effect.

2 Create a Crawling Text Title

If you'd rather create a crawling text title, type a long line of text in the window to create a crawling title that will scroll left or right across the screen. Add extra blank spaces if needed to include enough text for the effect.

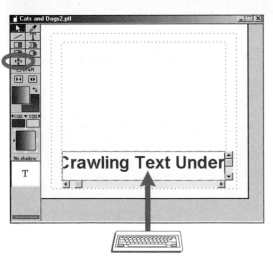

3 Open the Rolling Title Options

Use the pop-up context menu (or pull down the **Title** menu) and choose **Rolling Title Options**.

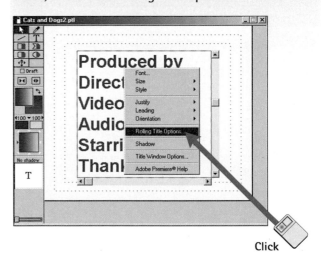

Click

4 Set the Direction of Movement

Premiere displays the **Rolling Title Options** dialog. In the **Direction** area, click to select the direction that the text is to move.

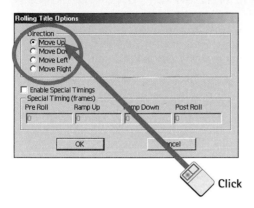

Click

5 Set Special Timings

Click the **Enable Special Timings** check box to control the text movement. Enter the number of frames of **Pre Roll** to wait before starting to move, the **Ramp Up** and **Ramp Down** frames to accelerate into and decelerate down from the movement, and the **Post Roll** frames to stay motionless until the **Out** point. Then click **OK** to close the dialog.

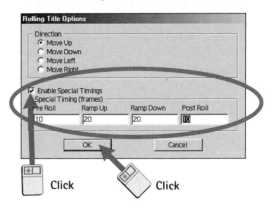

Click   Click

6 Preview the Movement

Drag the slider at the bottom-left corner of the **Title** window to preview the rolling or crawling type.

Drag

How-To Hints

Preview Special Timings

The preview slider does not allow you to preview special timings. They can be previewed only after adding the title to a Timeline.

Preview Duration

If a background preview frame has been imported into the Title window, the preview uses the duration of that clip.

End

7

How to Add Titles to a Project

Once you have edited and saved a Title window, Premiere treats the title like any other clip that you can import into a project and add to a Timeline. You can use the title clip either as a standalone title screen with a colored opaque background, or as a superimposed image, overlaid with transparency over video clips.

Begin

1 Add a Title to a Project

After you design a title, save it, and, Premiere will add it to the current Project window. To add a previously saved title to the project, import it like any other clip.

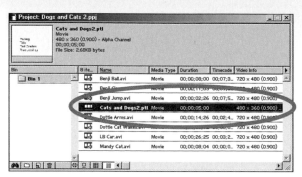

2 Add a Title Screen

To add a title screen to a production, drag it to the Video 1A or Video 1B track at the beginning of the Timeline.

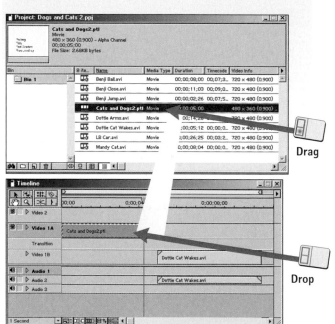

Drag

Drop

3 View the Title Screen

Press the **Alt** (Windows) or **Option** (Macintosh) key, and then click and drag the edit line in the time ruler to render-scrub though the Timeline and preview the title effect in the Monitor window. The title appears like any other clip, with its background opaque.

4 Add a Title Overlay

To add a title overlay to a video clip in a production, drag it to the Video 2 track or another superimposed track.

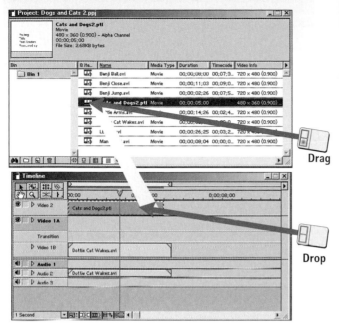

Drag

Drop

5 View the Title Overlay

Press the **Alt** (Windows) or **Option** (Macintosh) key, and then click and drag the edit line in the time ruler to render-scrub though the Timeline. The title appears in the Monitor window with its background transparent, and with transparent text and graphics objects blended over the underlying video clip.

6 Change the Title Timing

Change the duration of the title clip to change the timing of the title.

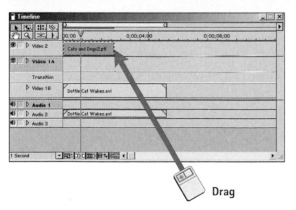

Drag

How-To Hints

Editing a Title on the Timeline

To change a title on the Timeline, double-click the title clip in the **Project** or **Timeline** window to open the Title window. Edit the title and then save it. The new, saved title will then be used wherever it appears in the Timeline.

End

Task

PART 13

Superimposing Video Clips

In Part 4, "Adding Transitions Between Clips," you saw how to use the Transition palette to create a variety of transition effects when playing from one clip to the next, including dissolves, wipes, and zooms. You can also use transitions to show two clips at the same time, for example, with a split-screen or inset.

But you can go further in combining two clips by using transparency, where one clip shows through another, or an image or shape in one clip is *superimposed* on top of another. This is particularly useful for overlaying a title, graphical logo, or translucent watermark on top of a clip.

Once you have laid out your main program in the Video 1 track in the Timeline window, Premiere provides up to 97 additional superimpose tracks, starting in Video 2. These tracks can be layered on one another, each with transparency settings to show though to the underlying tracks.

Premiere provides several different approaches for superimposing tracks. You can use the Opacity rubberband line to set the opacity or transparency of the entire clip to fade it in and out over time. You also can use the Transparency Settings dialog to define a *matte* shape as a transparent region in a clip, or to *key* the transparency on a color or range of colors to *composite* overlaid areas of one clip on another. In this way, you can shoot a person talking or moving against a color screen, and then use Premiere to key away the background and then composite them into a totally different video clip. ●

How to Fade Video Tracks

When you add a clip to the Video 2 or other higher superimpose track, Premiere displays it on top of the program in the Video 1 tracks. You must then change the transparency of the superimpose track to see through to the underlying program tracks. The simplest way of doing this is to use the Opacity rubberband line under the superimpose track to change the transparency of the track to provide simple fades, or to combine with mattes or keys (see Task 2).

Begin

1 Add a Superimposed Clip

Open a project and add a video clip to the Timeline in the **Video 1A** track. Then drag an image clip to the **Video 2** clip to superimpose over the **Video 1** track (for example you can use the **Veloman** clip from the **Sample Folder**, as in Part 1, "Getting Started with Premiere").

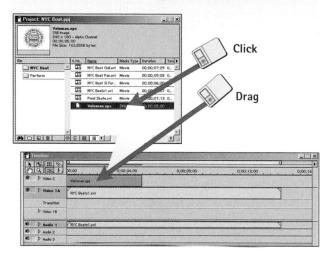

Click

Drag

2 Display the Opacity Rubberband

When you play through the Timeline, the image clip covers the video clip underneath it. Click the triangle to the left of the **Video 2** track name to expand the superimposed track. Then click the red **Display Opacity Rubberbands** icon under the track name to display the red **Opacity** rubberband line.

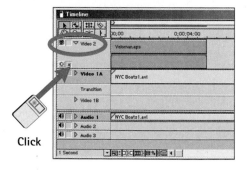

Click

3 Adjust the Opacity

The red **Opacity** rubberband line is at the top of the panel, indicating that the superimposed image is fully opaque. Click the **Selection Tool** (arrow icon) and move the cursor over the **Opacity** rubberband, and it changes to a pointing finger with red plus and minus signs. Click on the rubberband to create a handle (small red square) and drag it down to make the clip more translucent at that point, or fully transparent at the bottom of the panel.

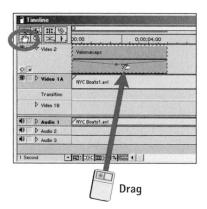

Drag

4 View the Info Palette

As you drag, Premiere updates the **Info** palette to show the percentage opacity.

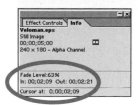

5 Create a Fade Effect

Add additional handles to the **Opacity** rubberband, for example, to fade the superimposed image in and out. Premiere adjusts the fade percentage over the duration of each line. Shorter and steeper lines cause faster fade effects.

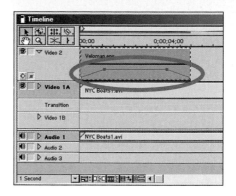

6 Preview the Result

Render-scrub through the Timeline to preview the effect: Press the **Alt** (Windows) or **Option** (Macintosh) key, and then click and drag the edit line in the time ruler.

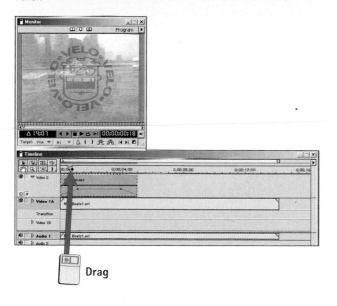

Drag

How-To Hints

Precise Percentages

To adjust the opacity percentage in exact 1% increments, hold down the **Shift** key as you drag the **Opacity** rubberband.

Delete Opacity Handles

To delete an **Opacity** handle, simply drag it outside of the track.

Opacity Adjustments

Premiere provides additional Timeline tools for adjusting the **Opacity** rubberband.

Use the **Fade Scissors Tool** (scissors icon, with the **Razor** tools) to click and add two adjacent handles to create a sharp transition.

Use the **Fade Adjustment Tool** (up and down arrow icon, next to the **Zoom** tool) to drag an entire segment of the line up or down.

End

How to Use Transparency Keys

Even better than changing the transparency of an entire clip in a superimposed track, you can also key on a range of colors in a clip to cut out an object, title, or logo and lay it on top of the clip. Premiere provides the Transparency Settings dialog to define the type of keying, adjust the effect, and preview the result.

Begin

1 Set the Transparency

Repeat the setup from Task 1, placing a simple image clip in the **Video 2** superimpose track. Select the image clip and click **Setup** next to **Transparency** in the **Effect Controls** palette, or pull down the **Clip** menu and choose **Video Options, Transparency**.

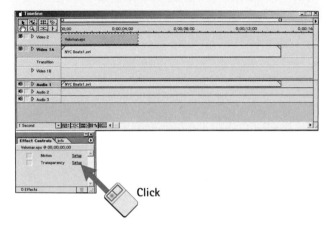

Click

2 Select the Key Type

Premiere displays the **Transparency Settings** dialog. Click the **Key type** drop-down menu and choose **Chroma** to key on a color value.

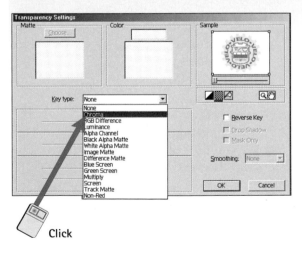

Click

3 Chose the Key Color

Click on the color swatch in the **Color** area to choose a key color, or click with the eyedropper cursor in the sample image.

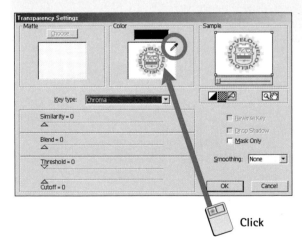

Click

4 Adjust the Keying Effect

Premiere previews the keying effect in the **Sample** area. Drag the key setting sliders to adjust the keying effect. The **Similarity** slider adjusts the range of matching colors, **Blend** controls the blending with the underlying clip, **Threshold** controls the amount of shadow in the color matching, and **Cutoff** darkens shadows up to the **Threshold** setting. Click the **Smoothing** drop-down menu to choose the sharpness or smoothing of edges.

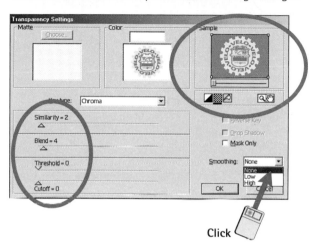

Click

5 Preview the Keying Effect

Click the background icons under the **Sample** area to better view the keying effect by placing the image against different backgrounds. Click the **Black/White** toggle for a simple black or white background, the **Checkerboard** pattern for a checked pattern, and the **Image** icon to display the underlying image (which can be slow to display).

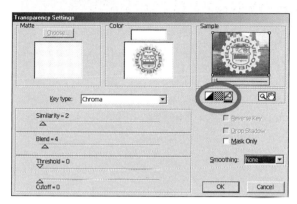

6 Examine the Sample Image

Click the **Zoom** icon and click in the sample image to zoom in for a more detailed view of the sample image, or hold down the **Alt** (Windows) or **Option** (Macintosh) key and click to zoom out. Click the **Hand** icon to click and drag in the sample image. Drag the slider under the image to view the transparency key effect across the duration of the clip. Click **OK** to close the dialog and preview the transparency effect in the Timeline.

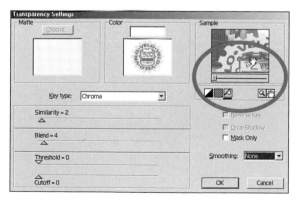

How-To Hints

Logos and Titles

You can use these Premiere tools to create interesting effects for logo and title overlays. Use the **Opacity** rubberband to fade a title in and out, and the Transparency effects to overlay a logo with transparent regions.

Key Options

Some key types support the additional key options under the **Sample** image area.

Use **Reverse Key** to reverse the opaque and transparent regions, and **Drop Shadow** to add a gray shadow to help a superimposed title or graphic stand out better from the underlying clip.

End

How to Use Transparency Mattes

Besides keying on a color in an image or a clip (as in Task 2), you can also explicitly define a keying region using a matte image to define which portions of the clip are transparent. You can create an overlay image such as a logo with a matte stored with the image, or you can use a separate image as the matte for keying.

Begin

1 Use an Alpha Channel Matte

Continuing from Task 2, display the **Transparency Settings** dialog. With the **Chroma** key set, all the white areas in the image are keyed out, including inside the logo. Click the **Key type** menu and choose **Alpha Channel**. Now only the area outside the logo is keyed out, because this image was prepared using a tool like Adobe Photoshop or Illustrator, and has an *alpha channel*, extra information stored with the image to define the transparent area.

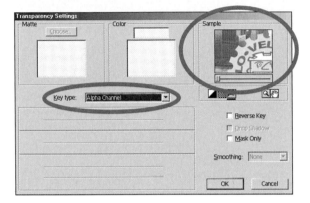

2 Use an Image Matte

Prepare a simple image in the **Title** window (see Part 12, "Adding Titles"), with plain, dark text against a white background. Reopen the **Transparency Settings** dialog, click the **Key type** drop-down menu, and choose **Image Matte**. In the **Matte** section, click the **Choose** button and open the title file.

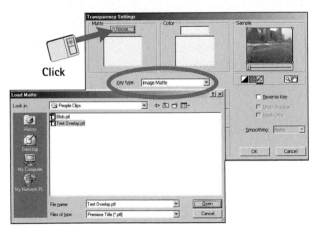

Click

3 Preview the Image Matte

Premiere displays a thumbnail of the title in the **Matte** section, and uses the non-white sections of the matte image to cut transparent areas in the superimposed track to see through to the underlying clip. Click **Reverse Key** to reverse the keying effect, and use the superimposed track as an image or video texture for the text and graphic overlays. Click **OK** to preview the matte effect in the Timeline.

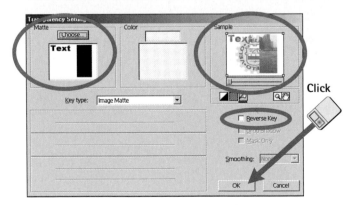

Click

4 Superimpose a Video Object

Delete the still image from the superimposed track, and drag a video clip to the **Video 2** track, with a foreground object (or person) shot against a relatively solid background. Even if the background was not shot carefully, you still can have fun with the clip. Reopen the **Transparency Settings** dialog, click the **Key type** drop-down menu, and choose **Luminance** to key against the brightness of the background. Preview the superimposed track in the **Sample** area.

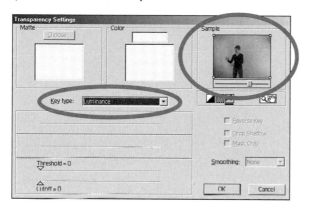

5 Key the Video Object

Adjust the **Threshold** and **Cutoff** sliders to mask out as much of the background as possible, without turning the entire foreground object transparent. Adjust the handles in the **Sample** area to include only the center region of the image with the foreground object. This creates a *garbage matte* to avoid keying in other areas of the frame.

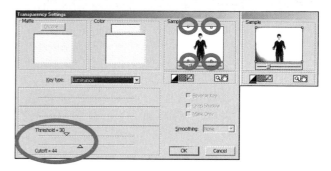

6 Preview the Video Composite

Premiere displays the Transparency setting name on top of the clip in the superimposed track. Render-scrub through the Timeline to preview the effect. Depending on how accurately you were able to key, you should have created a ghostly person moving in the scene.

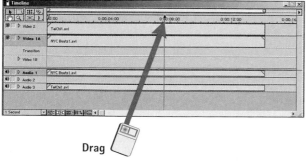

Drag

How-To Hints

Make a Split Screen

You can also use the corner handles in the **Sample** area of the **Transparency Settings** dialog to create a split-screen. Move the handles on one side of the thumbnail to the center of the screen, or use them to create a diagonal split instead.

Creating Mattes

You can create simple matte images with text and graphical shapes using the **Title** window. Or pull down the **File** menu and choose **New, Color Mattes** to create a solid color frame that can be used as a background image for titles.

End

Task

PART 14

Mixing Audio

*P*remiere can combine the visual effect of multiple video tracks with transitions (Part 4, "Adding Transitions Between Clips"), superimpositions (Part 13, "Superimposing Video Clips"), and effects (Part 15 , "Applying Audio and Video Effects"). You can also combine multiple audio tracks by *mixing* them together. For example, you can combine the audio recorded with a clip with voice-over narration and background music. Premiere also provides audio effects to *sweeten*, or enhance and manipulate, the audio (see Part 15).

When you play and edit an audio clip, Premiere helps you visualize it in a Clip window or a Timeline window track with a *waveform* display, showing the relative strength of the sound over time. You then use the Timeline controls to adjust the volume of individual clips over time, cross-fade between two clips, and pan or balance the sound of each clip between left and right stereo channels. You can also adjust the overall gain or volume of the entire production.

In addition, Premiere provides a separate Audio Mixer window that displays the volume and pan settings for each channel from the Timeline. The window shows them changing dynamically over time as you play the clip. You can also use the Audio Mixer to adjust the settings in real time as the program is playing and write them back to the Timeline.

When Premiere processes your program for preview, play, or export, it applies the audio settings in a specific order.

First, it converts the audio based on the Audio Settings dialog (see Task 1) and adjusts the stereo channels as set by the Audio Options menu (see Task 5).

Then it applies any audio effects (see Part 15).

Finally, it applies the pan/balance and volume settings for individual clips as set in the Timeline (see Tasks 4 and 2), and then performs a gain adjustment for the overall program (see Task 4). ●

How to Edit Audio Clips

You can view and edit audio clips in much the same way that you have been working with video clips. When you open an audio clip in a separate Clip window, Premiere provides an audio *waveform* display to help visualize the sound in the clip. Use the Audio Settings dialogs to convert audio clips between different formats, or to extract the audio channels from a video clip.

Begin

1 Open a Project with Audio

Open a project with a variety of clips, including clips captured from DV and audio-only clips. Click an audio-only clip (such as the **Music** clip from the **Sample Folder**) in the **Project** window to select it, and then pull down the **Clip** menu and choose **Open Clip**, or right-click (Windows) or **Control**-click (Macintosh) to display the pop-up context menu and choose **Open in Clip Window**.

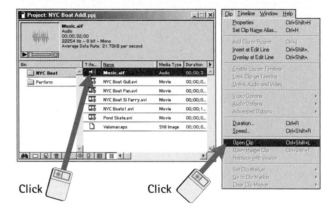

Click   Click

2 Play and Edit the Audio Clip

Premiere opens the audio clip in an individual **Clip** window that displays the audio waveform. Edit the clip as you would a video clip. Click the VCR controls at the bottom of the window to play through the clip, and the **In** and **Out** marker controls to trim the clip. Premiere displays the **In** and **Out** points with a green I and a red O mark. Pull down the **Clip** menu and choose **Properties**, or choose it from the pop-up context menu.

Click

3 View the Audio Properties

Premiere displays a **Properties** window for the clip. Click to select a stereo clip captured in DV format (see Part 8, "Capturing and Using DV") and also display its properties. The audio-only **Music** clip from the **Sample Folder** is recorded in mono with 8-bit samples at a 22254Hz sample rate. The DV clip is recorded in stereo with 16-bit samples at a 32000Hz sample rate.

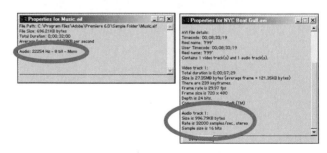

④ Export an Audio Clip

Close the **Properties** windows, click to select the DV clip from the **Project** window, and open it in a **Clip** window. Then pull down the **File** menu and choose **Export Clip, Audio** to export only the audio portion of the clip (see Part 6, "Exporting Video and Audio Projects").

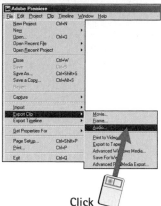

Click

⑤ Set the Audio Export Settings

Premiere displays the **Export Audio** dialog. Navigate to the project folder, and enter the output **File name**. Check the current audio export settings listed at the bottom left of the dialog. Click **Settings** to set the output audio file format.

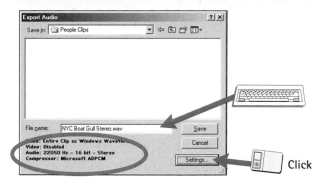

Click

⑥ Save as Stereo or Mono

Premiere displays the **Export Audio Settings** dialog. Click the **Next** button to change the **Audio** settings. Use the **Format** list to save the audio in a **Stereo** (or **Mono**) format. Click **OK** to close the dialog, and then click **Save** to save the audio-only file.

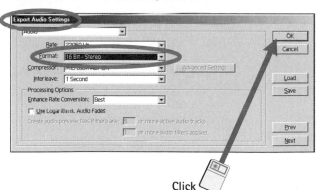

Click

How-To Hints

Rate Conversion

Converting between different audio formats often requires a *rate conversion* or *resampling* between the different sample rates.

Use the **Enhanced Rate Conversion** list in the **Audio Settings** dialog to choose the **Best** option, which offers higher quality results but longer processing time.

Logarithmic Audio Fades

Volume adjustments set using the **Volume** rubberband controls in the Timeline are linear, or ramped according to a straight line (see Task 2). Adjustments made using the **Audio Mixer** window can be linear or non-linear, depending on the speed at which you adjust the volume (see Task 5). However, linear volume changes might not sound natural to the human ear.

Use the **Logarithmic Audio Fades** option in the **Project** and **Export Audio Settings** dialogs to use more processing to convert linear volume changes to non-linear.

End

TASK 2

How to Adjust Audio Volume

Premiere provides rubberband lines for audio clips in the Timeline window to control their volume and pan/balance, similar to the Opacity rubberband line used for fading video clips (see Part 13). Use the red Volume rubberband line to adjust the volume within segments of an individual clip, and to cross-fade between two overlapping clips in different tracks.

1 Add an Audio Track

Open a project and add an audio clip to the **Timeline** window in the **Audio 1** track (for example you can use the **Music** clip from the **Sample Folder**, as in Task 1).

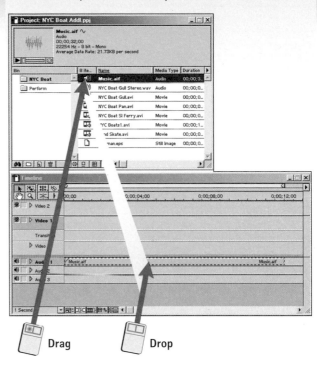

Drag   Drop

2 Display the Audio Waveform

Click the triangle to the left of the **Audio 1** track name to to display the expanded audio track, with additional buttons under the track name. Click the first **Show Audio Waveform** icon if needed to display the audio waveform in the Timeline. (This also might require changing the **Draw audio when view is n Seconds or closer** option in the **Timeline Window Options** dialog.)

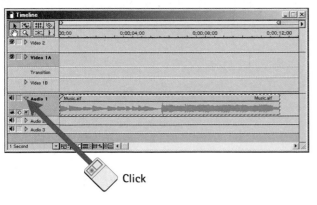

Click

3 Display the Volume Rubberband

Click the red **Display Volume Rubberbands** icon under the track name to display the red **Volume** rubberband line. The **Volume** rubberband runs through the center of the waveform, indicating that the volume is at 100% of the original setting for the clip.

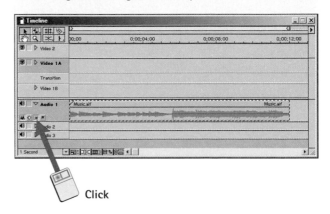

Click

4 Adjust the Volume

Click the **Selection Tool** (arrow icon) and move the cursor over the **Volume** rubberband; it changes to a pointing finger with red plus and minus signs. Click on the line to create a handle (small red square), and drag the handle down (to 0%) to lower the volume at that point, or up (to 200%) to raise the volume. As you drag, Premiere updates the **Info** palette to show the **Fade Level** as a percentage.

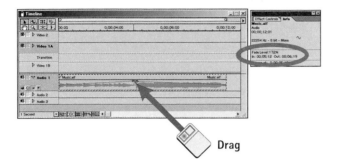

Drag

5 Fade In and Out

Add additional handles to the **Volume** rubberband, for example, to fade the volume up and then down over several segments. Premiere adjusts the fade percentage over the duration of each line. Shorter and steeper lines cause faster volume changes.

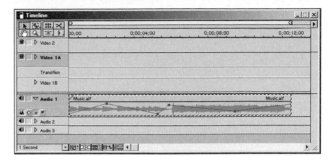

6 Adjust the Fade Effect

Premiere provides additional Timeline tools for adjusting the **Volume** rubberband. Use the **Fade Scissors Tool** (scissors icon, with the **Razor** tools) to click and add two adjacent handles to create a sharp transition. Use the **Fade Adjustment Tool** (up-and-down arrow icon) to drag an entire segment of the line up or down.

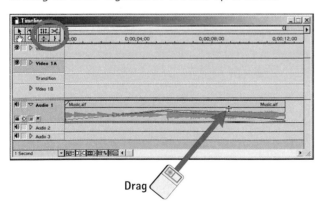

Drag

How-To Hints

Precise Percentages

To adjust the volume percentage in exact 1% increments, hold down the **Shift** key as you drag the **Volume** rubberband.

Delete Volume Handles

To delete a **Volume** handle, simply drag it outside of the track.

Audio Edits

Use the **Fade Scissors Tool** and **Fade Adjustment Tool** for simple audio edits, for example, to cut out a small section of a clip.

End

How to Cross-Fade Audio Clips

Premiere also provides a Cross-Fade Tool to automatically cross-fade between two overlapping audio clips, fading out the first while fading in the second. You also can cross-fade the audio between two adjacent video clips, even if they do not overlap, by performing a split edit. The idea with a split edit is to extend the audio track to overlap the adjacent video track, so the audio can lead in or fade out independently from the cut in the video. You do not want to simply shift the audio under the video because it would be out of sync.

Begin

1 Overlap Two Audio Clips

Clear the **Timeline** window and add two audio clips on different tracks so that they overlap in time, with one extending beyond the other. Click the triangle icon to expand the tracks to display the audio waveforms and click the red **Display Volume Rubberbands** icon, if needed (see Task 2).

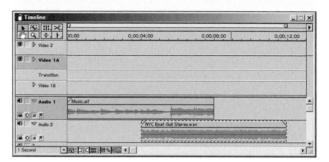

2 Select the Cross-Fade

Select the **Cross-Fade Tool** (next to the **Zoom** tool). Click one of the clips to select it. Move the cursor over the second clip, and it changes to the cross-fade icon. Then click to select the second clip to be cross-faded.

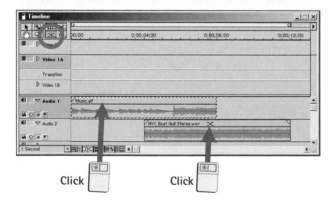

Click   Click

3 View the Cross-Fade

Premiere automatically adds volume handles to both clips, adjusted to fade out the volume of the first clip while fading in the second.

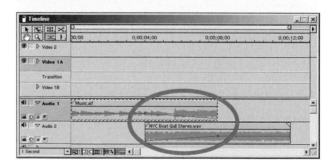

4 Overlap Video and Audio Clips

Clear the **Timeline** and add two adjacent video clips with audio. You can add a subtle transition between these clips, without needing to overlap them and add a video transition (see Part 4). Instead, you can perform a *split edit* on the independent audio and video tracks and cross-fade the audio while cutting the video. Click the **Toggle Sync Mode** button at the bottom of the **Timeline** window to unsync the video and audio tracks.

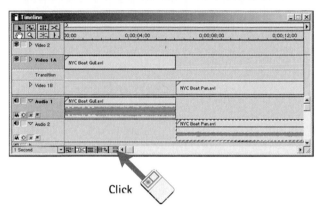

Click

5 Perform a Split Edit

Click the **Selection** tool and extend the end of the first audio track to the right so its Out point overlaps the second video clip. (First, trim the Out point of the entire clip, if needed, so that there is some extra material at the end.) This split edit is an *L-cut*, in which the audio Out point is extended beyond the video Out point so that the audio cuts after the video. You can now cross-fade the overlapping audio.

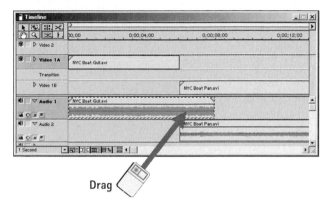

Drag

6 Perform the Cross-Fade

Click to select the **Cross-Fade Tool** and then click the two audio clips. Premiere adjusts the volume handles of both clips to create the cross-fade effect where they overlap.

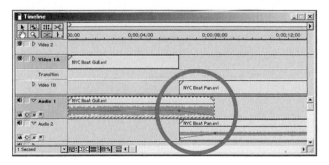

How-To Hints

J-Cuts

Another form of a split edit is the *J-cut*, or *audio lead*. In a J-cut, the In point of the second clip is adjusted to overlap the first clip, so that the audio portion of a cut starts playing before the video as a lead-in to the visual cut.

Trimming for Cross-Fades

Performing split edits for cross-fades requires that the clip has been trimmed by adjusting the **In** or **Out** points to provide some extra material at the beginning or end of the clip to overlap with the neighboring clip.

End

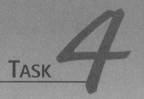

TASK

How to Pan/Balance and Set Gain

In addition to the Volume rubberband controls in the Timeline (in red), Premiere also provides similar Pan controls (in blue) for panning or balancing the audio between the left and right stereo channels. You pan the single channel of sound of a monophonic clip by setting its relative position from left to right, typically to match the position of the audio source in the video. You balance the two channels of a stereo clip between the left and right channels.

Begin

1 Add an Audio Clip

Clear the **Timeline** window and add an audio clip in the **Audio 1** track. Click the triangle icon to expand the tracks to display the audio waveforms (see Task 2). Click the blue **Display Pan Rubberbands** button under the track name.

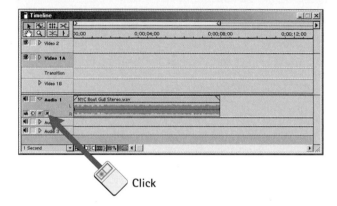

Click

2 Display the Pan Rubberband

Premiere displays a blue **Pan** rubberband line through the audio waveform. Click the **Selection Tool** (arrow icon) and move the cursor over the blue **Pan** rubberband line; it changes to a pointing finger with left/right arrows.

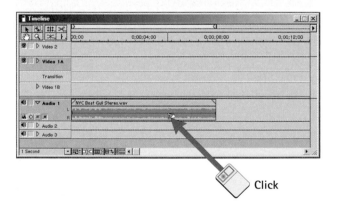

Click

3 Adjust the Pan Rubberband

As with the **Volume** rubberband, click to add a handle to adjust the **Pan** rubberband line, and drag the handle up or down to pan or balance to the left or the right. Set a straight ramp from left to right (top to bottom) and then back again, then listen while you play the clip to confirm that your audio hardware is set up properly. As you drag the **Pan** rubberband line, Premiere displays the pan/balance percentage in the **Info** palette.

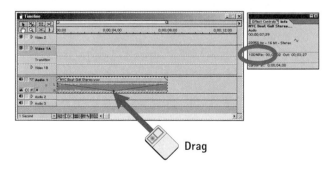

Drag

4 Adjust Overall Audio Gain

Pull down the **Clip** menu and choose **Audio Options**, **Audio Gain** (or choose it from the pop-up context menu).

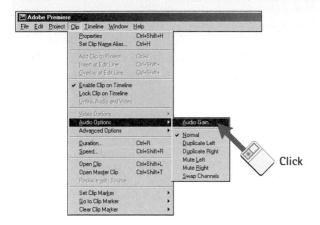

Click

5 Set the Audio Gain

Premiere displays the **Audio Gain** dialog. In the **Gain Value** field, type a percentage value for the overall gain. Enter a value greater than 100% to *amplify* the overall volume of the clip, or less than 100% to *attenuate* the clip, or make it quieter.

6 Automatically Adjust Audio Gain

Click **Smart Gain** to have Premiere automatically set the gain value, to boost the overall gain of the clip up to 200% so that the loudest part is at full volume. Click **OK** to close the dialog.

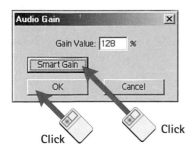

Click   Click

How-To Hints

Adjusting the Pan Rubberband Line

As with the **Volume** rubberband, specify precise percentages in 1% increments by pressing **Shift** as you drag the **Pan** rubberband line. To remove a handle, drag it outside of the track.

End

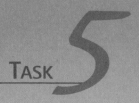

How to Use the Audio Mixer

Beyond setting handles on the Volume and Pan rubber-band lines in the Timeline window, Premiere also provides the Audio Mixer window to automate the viewing and setting of these controls in real time as the program is playing. The Audio Mixer has VU volume meters, Pan/Balance control knobs, and Volume fader sliders for each audio track, and a master control for the overall program.

Begin

1 Open the Audio Mixer

Open a new Project and add two clips with audio to the **Timeline** window. Adjust both the **Volume** and **Pan** rubberband lines for the two audio clips. Open the **Window** menu and choose **Workspace, Audio**.

Click

2 Use the Audio Workspace

Premiere rearranges the workspace with the **Audio Mixer** window. (You also can just pull down the **Window** menu and choose **Audio Mixer**.)

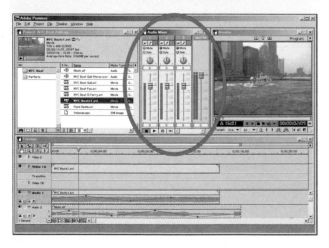

3 Play the Mixed Audio

Click the VCR controls at the bottom of the **Audio Mixer** window to play through the program on the Timeline. The **Audio Mixer** displays the audio level for each track with a VU meter, and the master audio level in the rightmost column. The small indicator above the VU meters turns red if the level is too high, and would result in *clipping*, or distortion.

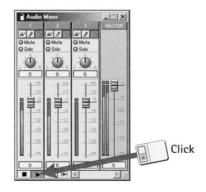

Click

4 Play Individual Tracks

Click the **Mute** button for a track to silence an individual track. Click the **Solo** button to listen to that track, and mute all others that do not have **Solo** selected. You can watch the video in the **Monitor** window to synchronize the audio with the video.

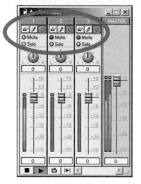

5 Adjust Stereo Channels

Pull down the **Clip** menu and choose **Audio Options** (or choose it from the pop-up context menu) to adjust the channels of a stereo clip. Choose **Mute Left** or **Mute Right** to mute an individual channel, or **Swap Channels** to exchange the two channels. Choose **Duplicate Left** or **Duplicate Right** to use one channel for the entire clip. Choose **Normal** to restore the original audio settings.

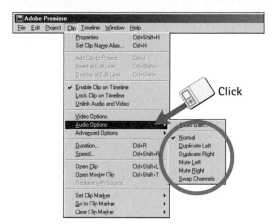

Click

6 Read the Volume and Pan

Click the **Automation Read** button (eyeglasses icon) in the top left of the individual tracks in the **Audio Mixer** window, and then click the **Play** button to play through the program on the Timeline. Premiere dynamically adjusts the **Pan/Balance** control knob and the **Volume** fader slider control to show the current settings at the Edit line in the Timeline. Click on the title bar of the **Audio Mixer** window and use the pop-up context menu to choose **Audio Mixer Options**.

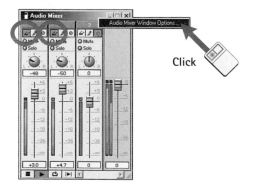

Click

7 Record Volume and Pan Changes

Premiere displays the **Audio Mixer Options** dialog. Use the **Display Options** section to customize the **Audio Fader** window to display only the individual **Audio Tracks** or **Master Fader** controls.

You can also use the **Automation Write Options** to have Premiere record your adjustments of the Audio Mixer controls to the **Volume** and/or **Pan** rubberband lines. Right-click (Windows) or **Control**-click (Macintosh) the **Volume** fader slider in the Audio Mixer to display the **Gang** pop-up context menu in order to group together multiple tracks to adjust them simultaneously.

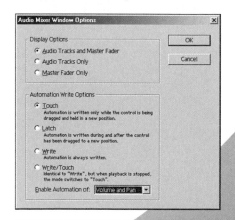

End

Task

15

Applying Audio and Video Effects

*P*remiere provides more than 70 predefined video effects and more than 20 audio effects for enhancing, improving, and distorting the clips in your productions with special effects. The available effects are listed in the Video Effects and Audio Effects palettes, organized into folders by category. Like the Transitions palette (see Part 4, "Adding Transitions Between Clips"), you can reorganize the folders to customize these palettes.

More than 25 of the effects included with Premiere are from Adobe After Effects, a professional animation, compositing, and effects program that integrates with Premiere and other Adobe products.

As you apply effects to the clips in the Timeline window, Premiere displays the list of effects for each clip in the Effect Controls palette. You can then adjust the effect settings and view the results in the Monitor window. As with other controls in Premiere, you can also add multiple keyframes to each clip to modify the effect settings and have Premiere interpolate the settings from keyframe to keyframe along the clip. ●

How to Use the Effects Palettes

Premiere organizes the available video and audio effects into different categories in the Video Effects and Audio Effects palettes. Much like the Transitions palette (see Part 4), you can customize these palettes by reorganizing the effects into folders. This makes it more convenient to find and apply your favorite effects to your productions.

Begin

1 Display the Effects Palette

Open a project with a variety of clips, and copy a video and an audio clip to the **Timeline** window. Pull down the **Window** menu and choose **Workspace**, **Effects** (or pull down the **Window** menu and choose **Show Audio Effects**).

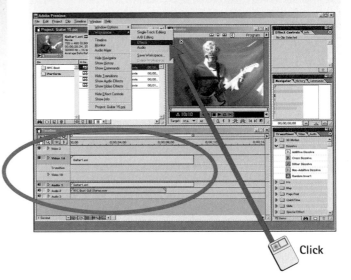

Click

2 Review the Effects Workspace

Premiere reorganizes the windows to make more room for the **Effect Controls** palette on the right side of the window.

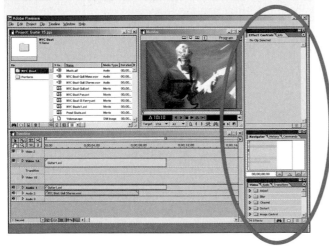

3 Expand the Audio Effects Palette

Click the **Audio** tab to display the **Audio Effects** palette window, with a collection of more than 20 predefined effects organized into categories as folders in the palette. Resize the window and click on the triangles to the left of the folders to expand them to show the included effects.

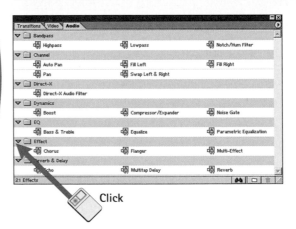

Click

4 Review the Video Effects Palette

Click the **Video** tab in the **Palette** window (or pull down the Window menu and choose **Show Video Effects**). Premiere displays the **Video Effects** palette, with a collection of more than 70 predefined effects organized into categories.

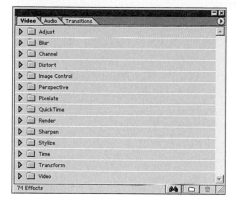

5 Expand the Video Effects Palette

Click on the triangles to the left of the folders to expand them to show the included effects. Premiere includes both built-in video effects (with a filmstrip icon and the letter "V") and many Adobe After Effects effects (with the After Effects icon).

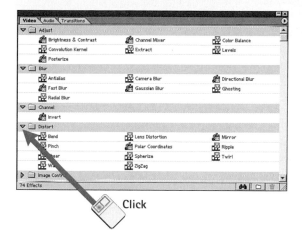

Click

6 Scroll Through the Effects

Click to open the **Effects** palette window menu to choose **Expand all Folders** or **Collapse all Folders**. These options will help you scroll though the effects in the palette.

Click

How-To Hints

Customizing the Effects Palettes

Like the Transitions palette, you can reorganize and customize the **Effects** palettes.

Use the pop-up palette menu (or palette buttons) to choose **Create Folder**, **Rename Folder**, and **Delete Folder**. Choose **Hide Selected** and **Show Hidden** to hide and reveal effects to simplify the list.

Then reorganize the effects as you like, and even drag your favorites into a new folder at the front of the list.

Finding Effects

You can also search for effects by name by choosing **Find** from the pop-up palette menu, or by clicking the **Find** button (binoculars icon) at the bottom of the window.

End

How to Apply Effects to Clips

You apply effects to clips in the Timeline window by simply dragging them from the Effects palettes. Since you can apply multiple effects to the same clip, and each effect might have several different controls you can set, Premiere provides the Effect Controls palette to view and tweak the effect settings. You can then preview the results of the effects in the Monitor window.

Begin

1 Add an Effect to a Clip

In the **Video Effects** palette, click on the triangle to expand the **Adjust** folder. Then click the **Posterize** effect, and drag it on top of the clip in the video track of the **Timeline** window.

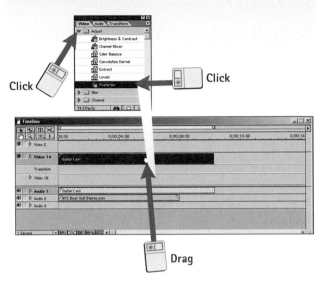

Click

Click

Drag

2 Adjust the Effect Controls

Premiere displays the **Effect Controls** palette, with the **Posterize** effect and its controls. Adjust the **Level** control to a low number to strengthen the effect. Premiere provides a preview of the result of the effect in the **Monitor** window each time you adjust the setting.

Drag

3 Add Another Effect

Click to select the **Color Balance** effect in the **Adjust** folder of the **Audio Effects** palette, and drag it into the open **Effects Control** palette (or drag it onto the same clip in the Timeline).

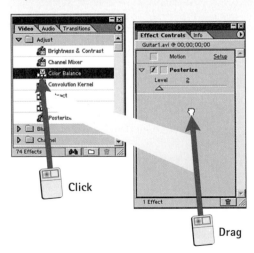

Click

Drag

4 Set Up the Effect

Premiere adds the **Color Balance** effect to the **Effect Controls** palette as a second effect to apply to the clip. You can click the **Effect Enabled** button (**"f"**) to the left of an effect name to temporarily disable that effect for the clip. This is a Premiere effect, and not an After Effects effect, so click **Setup** to the right of the effect name to set its controls.

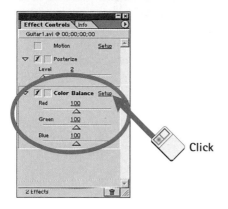

Click

5 Adjust the Effect Settings

Premiere displays the **Color Balance Settings** dialog, with the available controls for the effect and a preview image. Adjust the controls and then click **OK**.

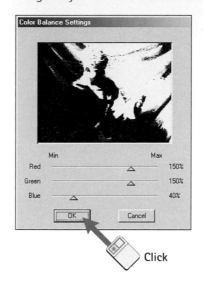

Click

6 Preview the Combined Effects

Premiere displays the result of applying both effects in the **Monitor** window. You can change the order of the effects in the list in the **Effect Controls** palette by clicking the triangle buttons to the left of each effect to collapse the list, and then dragging them to a new position.

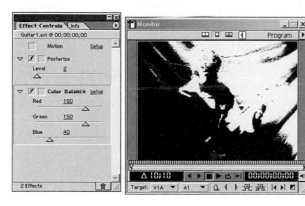

7 Edit the Effects List

Click to open the **Effect Controls** palette window menu. Use **Remove Selected Effect** and **Remove All Effects From Clip** to delete effects from the clip. Use **Preview During Adjust** to update the **Monitor** window continuously while adjusting the effects controls. Use **Best Quality** to improve the visual quality of the effect preview.

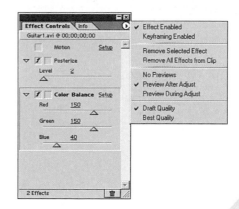

End

How to Use Keyframes

Premiere can also change the settings for each effect over time, by *interpolating* the values from one time point to another. You can add multiple *keyframes* to the Timeline window to define points where the settings for each effect change, and Premiere will adjust the settings from one point to the next.

Begin

1 Expand the Video Tracks

Continuing from Task 2, click the triangle to the left of the **Video 1A** track to expand it. Also expand the empty **Video 2** track. The **Video 1A** track is marked with the effect name and a blue line for setting keyframes. (For superimposed video clips in higher-numbered tracks, click the gray diamond **Display Keyframes** button to control keyframes for effects, or the red **Display Opacity Rubberbands** button to create handles for the fade controls.)

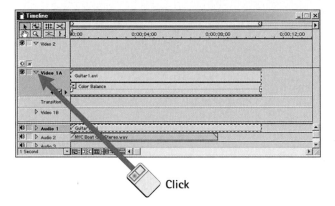

Click

2 Add a New Keyframe

The clip currently has two keyframes, one at each end, indicated by white boxes. When you added the effect to the clip, Premiere added both keyframes, with the same settings over the entire clip. Click and drag the **Edit Line** to a point in the clip where a new keyframe is to be added, and then click the **Add/Delete Keyframe** box to the left of the track.

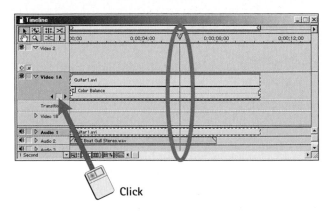

Click

3 View the New Keyframe

Premiere adds a new keyframe at the **Edit Line**, indicated by a white diamond, and the beginning and end keyframes change from boxes to diamonds because they can now be set independently. The **Keyframe Box** is also checked to indicate that the **Edit Line** is positioned on a keyframe. You can click the **Keyframe Navigator** arrows to jump to the **Previous Keyframe** and **Next Keyframe**. Or move the cursor over a keyframe so the cursor changes to a shaded finger, and then click to select it.

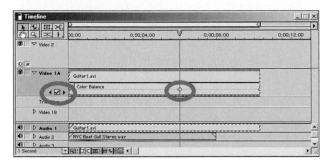

4 Change the Effect Settings

Premiere updates the **Effect Controls** dialog to display the timecode for the current keyframe on the first line of the palette. It also displays a stopwatch icon in the **Enable Keyframing** box to the left of the effect name. Use the effect controls to change the settings for the effect at the current keyframe, and view the result in the **Monitor** window.

5 Preview the Effect

Render-scrub through the Timeline to preview the effect. Watch as Premiere interpolates the effect values simultaneously for all the effects, in the **Effect Controls** palette and the **Monitor** window.

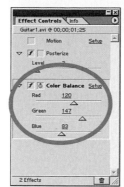

6 Select Other Effects for Keyframes

Click the effect pop-up menu to the left of the effect name on the **Keyframe** line to select from multiple effects applied to the selected clip. Then add keyframes for the other effects, as desired.

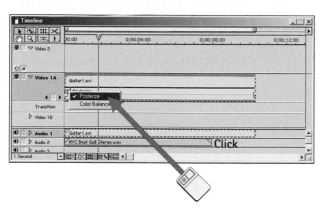

How-To Hints

Moving Keyframes

Click and drag the diamond icon to move a keyframe to a different point in the clip. Drag the beginning and end keyframes into the clip to change the starting and ending time for the effect.

Removing Keyframes

Uncheck the **Keyframe Box** to remove a single keyframe. Or drag the diamond icon off of the keyframe line.

To remove all keyframes from a clip, select the clip, and then click the stopwatch icon in the Effect Controls palette.

End

How to Choose Audio Effects

Premiere provides more than 20 audio effects, including filters to clean or enhance the audio signal (such as equalizing, boosting, or removing noise), and special effects to add more interest or detail to the sound (such as adding chorus or reverb). The available effects are organized into seven categories as folders in the Audio Effects palette. Here's a brief tour of the different audio effects.

Begin

1 Using Bandpass Effects

Use the effects in the **Bandpass** folder to remove specific frequencies from an audio clip. The **Highpass** effect removes low frequencies such as hiss and passes through high frequencies unchanged, and the **Lowpass** effect removes high frequencies such as high-pitched whines. The **Notch/Hum Filter** removes a specific frequency range, such as hum from a power line.

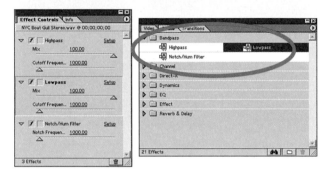

2 Using Stereo Channel Effects

Use the effects in the **Channel** folder to adjust the two channels of a stereo clip. The **Fill Left** and **Fill Right** effects place the entire audio clip in the corresponding channel, and **Swap Left & Right** exchanges the two channels. The **Pan** effect sets the pan/balance position between the two channels, and the **Auto Pan** effect pans back and forth between the two channels.

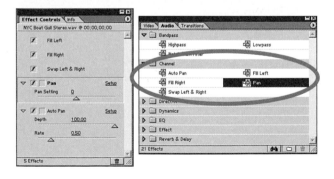

3 Using Dynamics Effects

Use the effects in the **Dynamics** folder to adjust the *dynamic range* (the difference between the loudest and softest sounds). The **Boost** effect raises the apparent volume of the clip by amplifying soft sounds without changing the loud sounds. The **Compressor/Expander** effect provides more precise control over the dynamic range. Compress to raise the level of soft sounds, or expand to increase the difference between volume levels. The **Noise Gate** effect silences quiet passages by removing background noise.

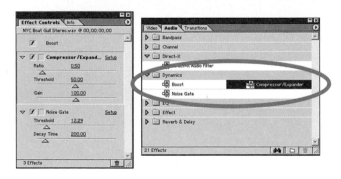

4 Using Equalization Effects

Use the effects in the **EQ** folder to adjust the tone and equalization of the audio, much as in home or auto audio equipment. The **Bass & Treble** effect boosts or weakens the low or high frequencies. The **Equalize** effect works like a graphic equalizer to adjust specific frequency bands. The **Parametric Equalization** effect provides more precise control of equalization over specific frequency ranges.

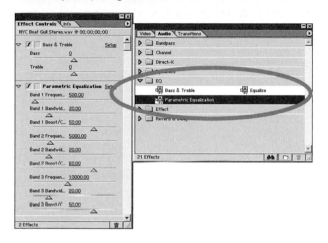

5 Using Audio Effect Effects

Use the effects in the **Effect** folder to add extra interest to the audio. The **Chorus** effect adds a second copy of the sound at a slight offset to add depth behind an individual sound. The **Flanger** effect provides a similar effect by inverting the phase of the audio signal at its center frequency. The **Multi-Effect** effect provides more precise control of echo and chorus effects by adjusting the delay and modulation of the audio.

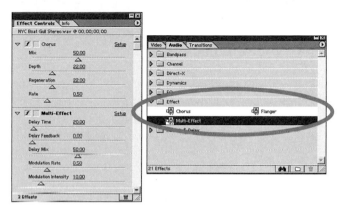

6 Using Reverb and Delay Effects

Use the effects in the **Reverb and Delay** folder to create a richer and more pleasant sound simulating a physical environment. The **Echo** effect provides an echo of the sound after a specified delay. The **Reverb** effect simulates the ambience of a room of a specific size and with different sound-absorbent properties. The **Multitap Delay** effect provides more precise control for delay effects, including a series of echoes.

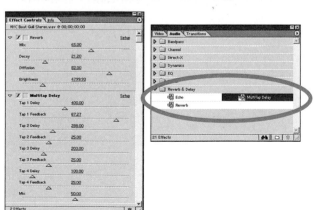

How-To Hints

Musical Time Calculator

The **Multitap Delay** effect dialog includes a **Musical Time Calculator** to calculate a delay time based on the **Time Signature**, **Tempo**, and **Note** value of the musical rhythm.

Direct-X Audio Filter

The **Direct-X** audio filter provides access to Windows Direct-X audio filters installed on your system.

End

How to Choose Video Effects

Premiere provides more than 70 video effects in 14 categories, including image and color adjustments, enhancements, and distortions and transformations. You can also use the Motions Settings dialog to animate clips and logos (see Part 16, "Animating Clips in Motion"). The available effects are organized into categories as folders in the Video Effects palette. The Premiere effects (with a filmstrip icon and the letter "V") provide a separate Setup dialog, whereas the Adobe After Effects effects (with the After Effects icon) are controlled directly from the Effect Controls palette. Here's a brief tour of the predefined video effects.

Begin

1 Using Adjust Effects

Use the effects in the **Adjust** folder to adjust the brightness and color of the image. Adjust **Brightness & Contrast**, change the **Color Balance** or use the color **Channel Mixer**, and **Extract** a range of colors. Perform more sophisticated brightness adjustments with a **Convolution Kernel**, and manipulations of brightness and contrast with **Levels**. Reduce the range of color tones for a **Posterize** effect.

2 Using Blur Effects

Use the effects in the **Blur** folder to smooth and blur the image. Simulate a **Camera Blur**, or a rotating **Radial Blur**. Smooth sharp edges with **Antialias**, or remove noise with **Gaussian Blur** or a simpler **Fast Blur**. Simulate motion with a **Directional Blur** or **Ghosting**.

3 Using Channel Effects

Use the **Invert** effect in the **Channel** folder to invert the colors in the image, and optionally blend the result with the original.

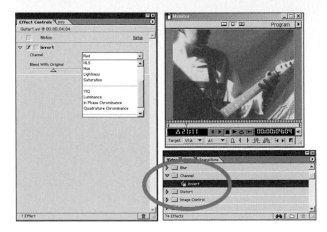

4 Using Distort Effects

Use the effects in the **Distort** folder to **Bend** and **Pinch**, **Mirror** and **Shear**, **Ripple** and **Twirl**, **Wave**, and **Zig-Zag** and otherwise mangle the original image. Distort the image in different directions with **Polar Coordinates**, simulate the effect of **Lens Distortion**, or **Spherize** to wrap the image around a 3-D globe.

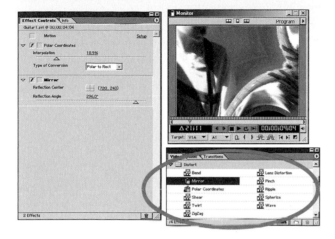

5 Using Image Control Effects

Use the effects in the **Image Control** folder to apply image color filters. Convert the image to **Black & White**, **Tint** it with color, or apply a **Color Pass** to retain only one range of color. Change the **Color Balance**, **Color Replace** a range of colors, or shift by a **Color Offset**. Apply a **Median** filter to remove noise or create a painterly effect, or use **Gamma Correction** to brighten or darken the image without washing it out.

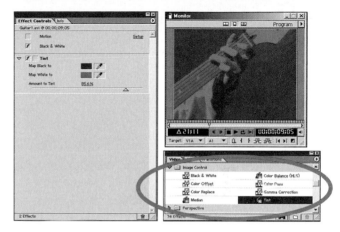

6 Using Perspective Effects

Use the effects in the **Perspective** folder to create 3-D effects. Add a **Drop Shadow** behind the image, or use **Bevel Alpha** and **Bevel Edges** to create chiseled, three-dimensional edges. Rotate the clip in two dimensions with **Transform**, or in 3-D space with **Basic 3D**.

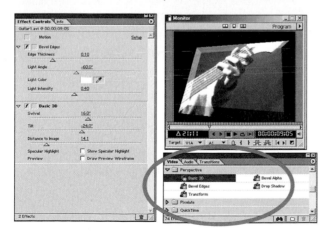

7 Using Perspective Transform

The **Transform** effect in the **Perspective** folder provides precise control over animating a clip with zooming, rotation, and other distortions along a motion path. The Motion Settings dialog (see Part 16) also provides a convenient interface for specifying similar effects.

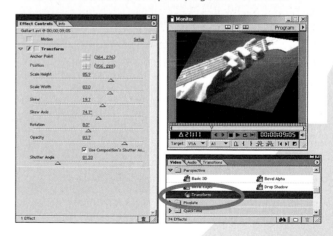

Continues

8 Using Pixelate Effects

Use the effects in the **Pixelate** folder to break up the image by merging adjacent pixels into larger clumps. **Crystallize** pixels into polygonal cells, or group similar colors into **Facets**, or **Pointillize** into dots.

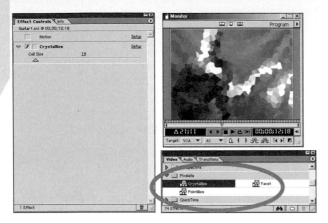

9 Using QuickTime Effects

Use the **QuickTime Effects** in the **QuickTime** folder to display the QuickTime **Select Effect** dialog box. From there, you can access the additional video effects built in to the QuickTime format.

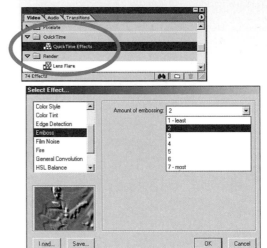

10 Using Render Effects

Use the Lens Flare effect in the **Render** folder to simulate the bright flare spot caused by a bright light shining into the camera lens.

11 Using Sharpen Effects

Use the effects in the **Sharpen** folder to **Sharpen** the image, or to **Gaussian Sharpen** it more, or to **Sharpen Edges** when there are large color changes in the image.

12 Using Stylize Effects

Use the effects in the **Stylize** folder to enhance the edges of the clip with **Find Edges**, **Emboss**, or **Color Emboss**. Distort the image with **Noise** or **Wind**, or brighten it with **Solarize**, or with periodic **Stobe Light** flashes. Break up the image with a **Mosaic** or into **Tiles**, or **Replicate** it in tiles. Use other images to **Texturize**, or apply an **Alpha Glow** around a masked alpha channel.

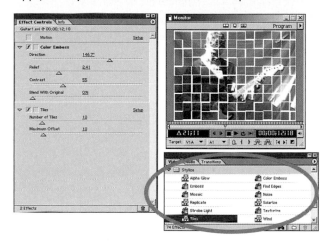

13 Using Time Effects

Use the effects in the **Time** folder to effect multiple frames over time. Combine and **Echo** multiple frames for a ghosting or streaking multi-image effect, or **Posterize Time** to strobe playback at a different frame rate.

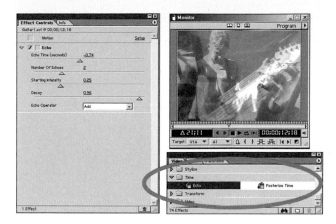

14 Using Transform Effects

Use the effects in the **Transform** folder to **Clip**, **Crop**, or **Resize** the image, or reverse it with **Horizontal Flip** or **Vertical Flip**. Adjust the image as if it were on a television screen with **Horizontal Hold** or **Vertical Hold**, or **Roll** the image on a cylinder. Simulate viewing the image by panning over it with **Image Pan**, or viewing it from different angles with **Camera View**.

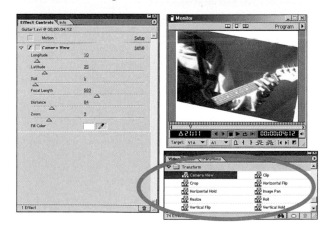

15 Using Video Effects

Use the effects in the **Video** folder to apply video corrections. Limit the clip to legal **Broadcast Colors**, or use **Field Interpolate** or **Reduce Interlace Flicker** to correct video footage with alternating odd and even interlaced lines.

End

Task

16

Animating Clips in Motion

*I*n this book, you have seen how to use Premiere to edit video and audio clips, organize them into a program in the Timeline, and then add interest with transitions, titles, superimpositions, and effects. But Premiere offers one more feature to combine these effects: the ability to animate clips, to put video and overlays in motion across the screen.

With the Motion Settings dialog, you can define a path for the clip to follow across the frame; coordinate the timing and speed of the motion; and cause the overlay to zoom in and out, rotate, and even distort its shape. This motion is controlled by keyframes, as other effects in Premiere are. Therefore, not only the motion, but also the zooming, rotation, and distortion can be smoothly interpolated from keyframe to keyframe across the screen.

You can also use the Transform effect in the Effects palette for even more precise control in animating clips (see Part 15, "Applying Audio and Video Effects"), but the Motion Settings dialog provides a convenient interface for performing a wide range of useful animations.

In this part, you will go back to the Sample Folder of clips installed with Premiere (see Part 1, "Getting Started with Adobe Premiere"). The Sample Folder includes video and audio clips and a still image logo, but also has a movie file (zfinal) that was edited together from the sample clips. The movie includes multiple video clips with a transition, an audio music track, and a superimposed logo that flies into the frame and then spins away off-screen. Even better, the folder also includes a Premiere project file (ztour.ppj) that you can open to see how the movie and the motion effect were created. ●

How to View the ztour Project

To understand how the zfinal movie in the Sample Folder was created, you can open the **ztour.ppj** Premiere project file. The Timeline window will show you the layout of the clips, transitions between clips, and where different kinds of effects have been applied to clips.

Begin

1 Open the Sample Project

Pull down the **File** menu and choose **Open** to display the Open dialog. Navigate to the **Sample Folder** and select the **ztour.ppj** project file. Then click **Open** to open the project.

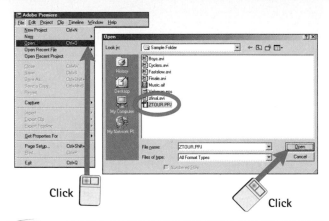

Click

Click

2 Display the A/B Editing Workspace

Premiere opens the **ztour** Project. Pull down the **Window** menu and choose **Workspace, Single-Track Editing** to use a single-track layout with the dual-view **Monitor** window. Then pull down the **Window** menu and choose **Workspace, A/B Editing** to reposition the windows in the layout you have been using with separate **Video 1A** and **Video 1B** tracks, and the Transition track in between them.

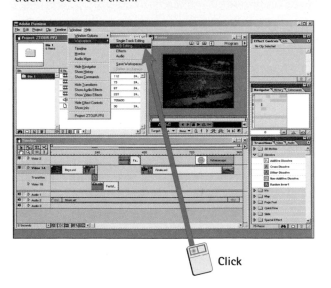

Click

3 Preview the Program

The program in the **Timeline** window has four video clips, one still image logo, and one audio soundtrack. The **Transition** track has a cross-dissolve between the first two video clips. Render-scrub through the Timeline to preview the program with all the effects. The program plays through the four video clips. Near the end, the logo image zooms into the frame and then spins away.

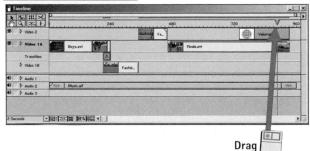

Drag

4 View the Video Effect

The **Finale** video clip has a blue line above it to indicate that it has an effect applied to it. Click on the triangle to the left of the **Video 1A** track name to expand the track. Premiere displays the name of the **Camera Blur** effect applied to the **Finale** clip.

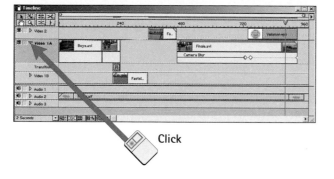

Click

5 View the Effect Keyframes

Click on the white diamond keyframes to see the settings applied to the effect in the **Effect Controls** palette (see Part 15). The effect starts at 0% in the middle of the clip, ramps quickly up to 80% blur as the **Veloman** still image logo starts to appear, and ramps back to 0% again at the end of the clip as the logo spins away.

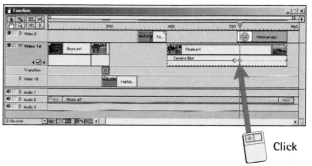

Click

6 View the Logo Transparency

Click the **Veloman** still image clip in the **Video 2** superimposed track to display its settings in the **Effect Controls** palette. You can click on **Setup** to the right of the **Transparency** item to display the **Transparency Settings** and see that the logo is superimposed using a **White Alpha Matte** (see Part 13, "Superimposing Video Clips").

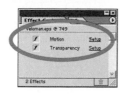

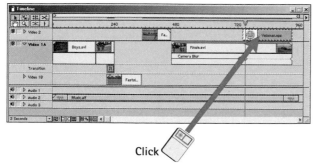

Click

How-To Hints

Time Display

The **Duration** field in the **Project** window lists the value for each clip as the number of video frames or audio samples, not the timecode that you have seen in earlier chapters. To change the time display for the project, pull down the **Project** menu and choose **Project Settings, General**. In the **Project Settings** dialog, change the **Time Display** item from **Frames/Samples** to **30 fps Drop-Frame Timecode**.

End

How to Define a Motion Path

The Motion Settings dialog provides a convenient visual summary of the animation applied to the clip, with its motion path across the screen, keyframes along the path, the timing between keyframes, and settings applied at each keyframe. Use the Motion Path window at the top right of the dialog to define the path and keyframe positions. The path can extend beyond the visible area of the frame so that the motions enters and exits at the edges of the screen.

Begin

1 Open the Motion Settings

Continuing with the results of Task 1, click the **Veloman** still image clip in the **Video 2** superimposed track to select it. Click on **Setup** to the right of the **Motion** item in the **Effect Controls** palette to display the **Motion Settings** dialog (or pull down the **Clip** menu and choose **Video Options, Motion**).

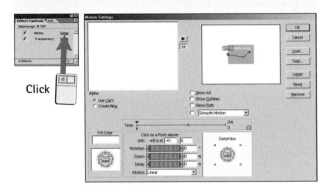

Click

2 Preview the Motion Effect

Premiere displays a visual summary of the motion effect in the **Motion Path** window at the top right, showing the path of the motion through the frame (the lines) and the keyframe points along the path (the squares). Click the **Play** button in the center of the dialog to preview the motion effect in the left **Sample** window; click the **Pause** button to pause it.

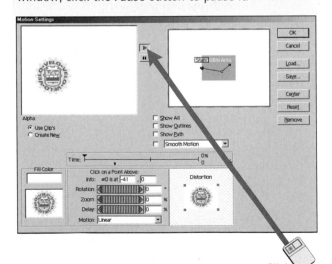

Click

3 Preview the Motion in the Program

Premiere also displays the keyframes as hash marks along the **Motion Path Timeline** in the **Time** area below. Click and drag the upward-facing arrow to play through the motion. Check **Show All** to display the motion as it would appear in the program, with transitions and transparency.

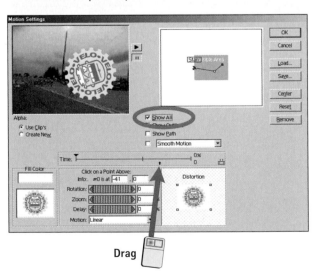

Drag

4 Change the Motion Path

Move the cursor over the first **Start** keyframe box in the **Motion Path** window, and it changes to a pointing finger icon. Click the **Start** box and drag it off the side of the visible area of the frame.

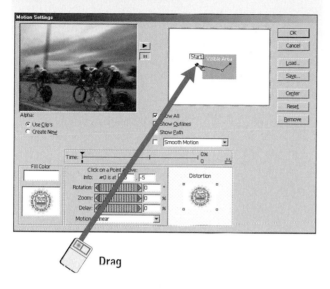

Drag

5 Preview the New Motion

Click **Play** or drag the upward-facing arrow in the **Motion Path Timeline** to preview the motion, as the logo now appears to fly in from off-screen.

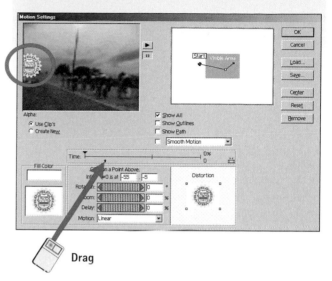

Drag

6 Add a New Keyframe

Move the cursor over the first line segment in the motion path and click to create a new keyframe point. Drag the keyframe box to near the bottom of the visible area to have the logo sweep down and then up into the frame.

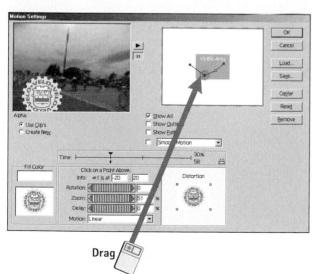

Drag

How-To Hints

Adjusting Positions

You can also adjust a keyframe position more precisely by clicking on it to select it, and then use the cursor control arrow keys to move it one pixel at a time. Or hold down the **Shift** key and press the arrow keys to move in 5-pixel increments. Click the **Center** button to move the keyframe to the center of the frame.

Entering Positions

When you view the keyframe information in the **Info** area below the **Motion Path Timeline**, the position for the current keyframe number is shown in pixel coordinates from the center of the image, relative to the pixel size of the image. You can also type coordinates directly into these fields, and use fractional decimal values for more precision.

Delete a Keyframe

To delete a keyframe, click to select it and then press the **Delete** key.

End

How to Change Speeds, Rotate, and Zoom

Once you define the overall motion path, and the keyframes along the path in the Motion Path window, you can adjust the timing of the motion between each keyframe in the Motion Path Timeline. You can also animate the motion by adjusting the Zoom and Rotation settings.

Begin

1 View Keyframe Timing

Continuing from Task 2, click the second keyframe (#1) to select it. Premiere updates the **Motion Path Timeline** to show the current position with a black downward triangle above the timeline mark for the keyframe. The number to the right of the **Timeline** shows that this keyframe is reached 30% of the way through the effect. Click the two red arrows to the right to switch between displaying the Time for the clip and the Time for the entire program.

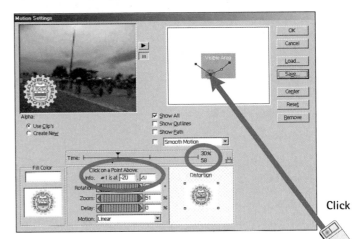

Click

2 Change Motion Speed

Click and drag the triangle to the left on the **Motion Path Timeline** so that this keyframe is reached 10% of the way through the effect. The motion of the first segment of the motion path is much faster than that of the second segment. Click **Show Path** to view a dotted motion path between each keyframe, with the dots spread farther apart to show a faster speed.

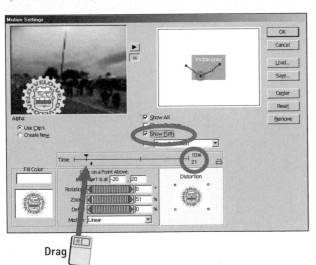

Drag

3 View Zoom Settings

Click the third keyframe (#2) to select it. Notice the **Zoom** value for the keyframes increases from 0% to 51% to 100%, causing the logo to grow in size as it moves onscreen.

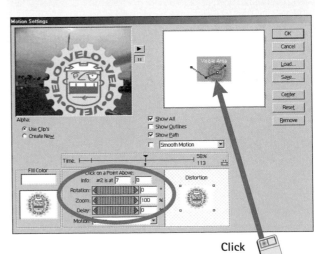

Click

4 Change the Zoom

Drag the **Zoom** slider, or type a value between 0% and 500%, to decrease or increase the size of the logo at that keyframe. Click **Show Outlines** to view an outline of the clip's size and rotation at each keyframe.

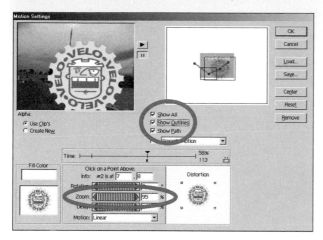

5 View Rotation Settings

Click on the **End** keyframe (#3) to select it. Notice the **Rotation** value for the keyframes changes from 0 to 720 degrees, causing the logo to spin though two full 360-degree rotations as it moves and shrinks offscreen.

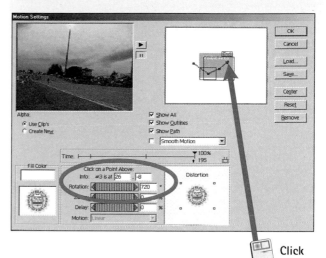

Click

6 Change the Rotation

Click to add another keyframe before the end, and drag the **Rotation** slider or type a value between -1440 degrees (counterclockwise movement) and 1440 degrees (clockwise), to spin the logo even faster, up to eight times between two keyframes.

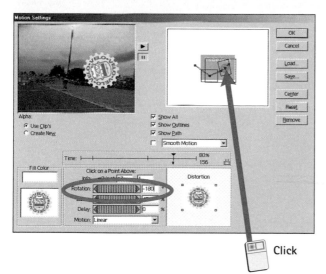

Click

How-To Hints

Undo Changes

When you complete a series of changes in the **Motion Settings** dialog, click **OK** to close the dialog and then re-open it again to experiment with the next set of changes. This way, you can always click **Cancel** to reject the new changes, or use **Undo** to step back though several sets of changes. You can also click **Reset** to remove all the settings for a specific keyframe.

Remove or Disable Motion Settings

Click **Remove** in the **Motion Settings** dialog to remove all the motion effect settings applied to a clip. Or click the **Enable Effect** button to the left of **Motion** in the **Effect Controls** palette.

Load and Save Motion Settings

Use the **Load** and **Save** buttons in the **Motion Settings** dialog to save settings before experimenting with them, and to share settings between different clips.

End

How to Delay and Distort Clips

Finally, Premiere provides several more controls to animate the motion more precisely. Use the Delay setting to pause the motion along the path, the Motion setting to add acceleration, and Distort to perform arbitrary distortions, resizing, and rotations.

Begin

1 Add a Delay

Click to select the middle keyframe (#2). Drag the **Delay** slider or type a value to have the motion settings pause at the keyframe for the specified time (up to the duration to the next keyframe). Premiere displays a blue bar on the **Motion Path Timeline** to show the delay period.

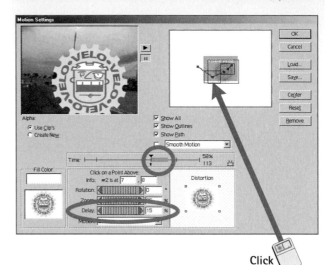

Click

2 Accelerate or Decelerate

Click the **Motion** drop-down list to choose the type of motion to use up to the next keyframe. The motion can be **Linear**, or constant, from one keyframe to the next, or can **Accelerate** or **Decelerate** to make the beginning and end of a motion seem more natural, or make a zoom seem smoother.

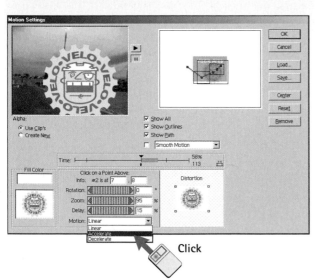

Click

3 Distort a Corner

Click and drag a corner of the sample image in the **Distortion** area to resize the image and stretch and distort its shape.

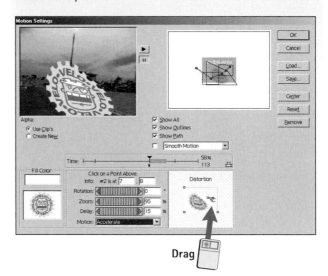

Drag

4 Distort and Rotate

Hold down the **Alt** (Windows) or **Option** (Macintosh) key and drag a corner to rotate the clip around its center to provide arbitrary rotation from keyframe to keyframe.

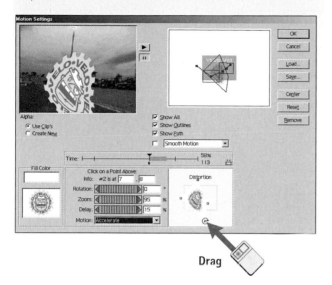

Drag

5 Distort and Move

Drag in the center to move all four corner points together to reposition the distortion.

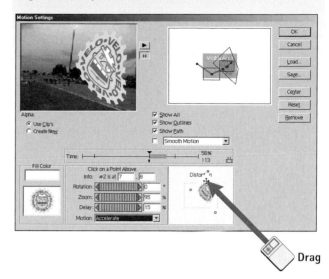

Drag

6 Smooth Motion

Click **Smooth Motion** and choose a smoothing option from the list to smooth out abrupt changes in direction, rotation, and distortion. Choose the amount of smoothing to be applied, from **Smooth Motion** (the least) to **Averaging-High** (the most).

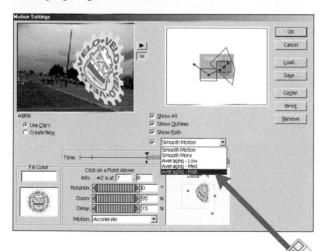

Click

How-To Hints

Moving Between Keyframes

After clicking on a keyframe in the **Motion Path** window, press **Tab** to move to the next keyframe, or hold down **Shift** and press **Tab** to move to the previous keyframe.

Selecting the Alpha Channel

Use the **Alpha** settings to control how the clip is superimposed, using the Clip's own alpha channel, or **Create New** for clips without an alpha channel (see Part 13).

Background Fill Color

Use the **Fill Color** area to specify a fill color to be used behind the clip for previews, or if the clip is in the **Video 1** track.

End

Glossary

Numbers

1394 A digital data interface, the IEEE 1394 standard, used for connecting DV camcorders to computers. Also known as Firewire.

A

A/B editing A style of editing in which you edit together clips in pairs—A and B—typically with a transition from one to the next. In Premiere, the A/B Editing workspace configures the Monitor window in Program view, and the Timeline with separate expanded tracks for Video 1A, Video 1B, and Transitions. This style is useful for assembling a program with simple drag-and-drop convenience. *See also* single-track editing.

alpha channel Extra information stored with an image to define transparent areas used for keying and superimpositions. Also called an alpha mask. Sometimes present in files prepared using a tool such as Adobe Photoshop or Illustrator. *See also* key.

amplify Increase the audio volume.

analog media Audio sources, such as audio cassettes and microphones, and video sources, such as VHS and 8mm VCRs and camcorders, that must be digitized and converted into digital format for processing by a computer. Newer digital formats such as DV and DVD have higher resolution and quality than older consumer formats like VHS, and also do not degrade in quality when they are copied from one generation to the next. *See also* digital media.

animate To move and manipulate an object over time, such as a title, a superimposed logo, or a transition between frames.

antialias To smooth out a jagged or stair-step appearance or motion between adjacent points so that it appears continuous.

aspect ratio The rectangular shape of an image or frame, expressed as the width-to-height ratio. *See also* Resolution.

attenuate To reduce audio strength or volume.

Audio Effects palette A small floating window along the right side of the Premiere work area that lists the available audio effects, grouped by type. Used to access effects to be applied to an audio clip. You can also reorganize and customize the list.

audio lead *See* J-cut.

Audio Mixer window The Premiere window used to dynamically monitor and control the volume level and pan/balance of multiple audio tracks on the Timeline in order to combine them into a final program.

audio waveform A graphical representation of an audio clip, helping to visualize the sound in the clip by showing the signal levels. Premiere can show a waveform in audio tracks in the Timeline, and in a separate Clip window when you open an audio clip.

AVI *See* Video for Windows.

B

balance To distribute two channels of a stereo clip between the left and right channels. *See also* pan.

bandpass effects Audio effects designed to remove specific frequencies from an audio clip (manifested as hisses, whines, and hums).

bandwidth The amount and rate of data that can be processed or transmitted by a given device. An analog modem has very little bandwidth compared to a high-speed cable modem, for instance, so the former cannot download video from the Internet nearly as quickly as the latter. *See also* data rate.

batch capture   The automated process of capturing an entire group of clips (such as from a DV camcorder) as defined by a batch list.

batch list   A list of clips with the timecode values for each In and Out point (also called a *timecode log*) to be used in a batch capture process. *See also* batch capture, log, timecode.

Bin window   The area of the Premiere Project window used to import and organize folders of source clips.

blue screen   A specially colored backdrop (typically blue or green) that can be matched with a color key and made transparent so that it can be replaced with another video layer. For example, you can cut out a subject from the blue screen background and composite it into another scene. *See also* matte, key.

BMP   The standard Windows Bitmap still image file format. Bitmap files are not compressed, and are therefore significantly larger than the same image stored in formats such as GIF and JPEG.

C

caption   Title text that labels a scene or identifies a location or person onscreen.

capture   To digitize, or import and convert, video and/or audio into digital format on your computer from external devices such as a camcorder or VCR. You typically use a special video capture card to input analog video into your computer, and then convert and save it into digital files on your disk. With DV camcorders, you transfer digital data directly into your computer over a 1394 interface. *See also* import.

channel   The sub-components of a clip. For images, an alpha channel can contain a matte or mask image to key certain regions of the image to be transparent. For audio, the separate left and right channels of a stereo clip.

clip   A short piece of video and/or audio, often containing an individual scene. When creating a video project, you import clip files into bins in your Premiere project, and often trim longer clips into individual scenes. You then edit the clips together on the Timeline to play in sequential order to tell the "story" of your production, with transitions between clips and other added effects.

Clip window   The Premiere window used to view and trim individual clips. *See also* Monitor window, Source view.

codec   A video or audio compression component that can both compress and decompress (encode and decode) files. Media formats and players such as Windows Media, RealMedia, and QuickTime have a selection of codecs built in, and can add additional codecs to support new file formats. *See also* compression.

Commands palette   A small floating window along the right side of the Premiere work area that contains a list of preset commands. You can customize the palette to define buttons and function keys for fast access to often-used commands.

composite   *See* superimpose.

compress   To reduce the size of audio or video data through the use of a compression scheme. *See also* lossy and lossless.

compressor   Program by which files are compressed. A compressor which also decompresses files (returns them to their original state) is called a *codec*. *See also* compress.

crawl   To scroll a line of title text sideways, left or right across the screen. *See also* roll.

credit   Title text that identifies the people who contributed to a production. Usually scrolled at the end of a show.

crop   To make an image physically smaller by trimming away one or more edges. This reduces the dimensions of the image, and reduces the size of the computer file.

cross-fade   *See* fade.

cut   To switch instantly from one clip to another. A video cut appears suddenly onscreen without any other kind of transition effect. The cut is the most basic kind of transition for changing scenes and dropping titles onto the screen. *See also* fade, transition.

D

data rate   The speed at which data is transferred, as in bytes per second. Also called bit rate. For example, the speed to download or stream a video file over the Internet, or the speed at which the file must play from a hard disk. When you create a video or audio file, you can specify the target bit rate at which the file will be played. *See also* bandwidth.

deinterlace   To process interlaced television video, in which each frame contains alternating pairs of lines from two separate fields captured at slightly different times. The motion between fields can cause visible tearing when displayed on a computer monitor. Deinterlacing uses every other line from one field and interpolates new in-between lines without tearing. *See also* interlaced video, NTSC.

delay   An audio effect that provides an echo of a sound after a specified time period.

digital media   Audio and video sources such as audio CD, DV, miniDV, Digital8 camcorders, and DVD that store the audio and video in digital format. As a result, the data can be imported and processed directly by a computer, and copied without any loss from one generation to the next. *See also* analog media, DV.

dissolve   A video transition in which one video clip fades into the next. *See also* fade, transition.

dub   To duplicate or make a copy of a production, traditionally from one tape (usually a master tape) to another tape.

duration   A length of time. For a clip, the length of time that it will play, determined by its overall length. Or if the clip has been trimmed, the difference in time between its In point and Out point. *See also* timecode.

DV   A Digital Video tape and compression format for consumer and professional video equipment. The DV compression format is used for DV and Digital-8 camcorders. DV format video and audio can be captured using an IEEE 1394 interface and then saved and edited in Premiere. The consumer tape format is more accurately called mini-DV.

dynamic range   The difference between the softest and loudest sounds. Decrease to compress the range and reduce noise, or expand to emphasize volume differences.

E

effect   The result of processing audio and video clips to enhance, improve, or distort them. *See also* filter.

Effect Controls palette   A small floating window along the right side of the Premiere work area that lists the current effects applied to an audio or video clip. Used to adjust the order of effects and change effect settings.

equalize   To adjust the tonal quality of an audio clip. As with graphic equalizers found in home or auto audio equipment, Premiere's equalize effect permits you to boost or cut the original signal at different frequency bands.

export   To save your production to a file or to an external video device. Premiere can export both individual clips and entire productions on the Timeline to a variety of disk and Web media file formats. *See also* import.

F

fade   A gradual transition from one clip to another. With video, the clip changes from transparent to fully opaque (or vice versa) to fade in or out. With audio, the gain changes between silence and full volume. A video dissolve transition or audio cross-fade fades one clip out while the next fades in.

field   For interlaced video sources, a full frame is constructed from alternating odd and even lines from two video fields captured at slightly different times. *See also* interlaced video.

filter   A transformation applied to a video or audio clip to enhance it or create a visual or auditory effect. *See also* effect.

FireWire   *See* 1394.

four-point edit   A method of setting In and Out points in order to precisely control where and how frames are inserted into a Timeline. In a four-point edit, you set all four In and Out markers, and Premiere will display a warning dialog if the durations do not match. *See also* three-point edit.

fps   Frames per second. *See also* frame rate.

frames   The individual video images that make up a moving sequence. Video formats and individual clips are typically described in terms of the resolution of the individual frames, and the frame rate at which they are played. *See also* frame rate, field.

frame rate   Video playback speed or capture rate as determined in frames per second. *See also* sample rate.

freeze frame   A technique in which a particular frame of video is held onscreen. Sometimes the audio portion of the scene continues playing.

G

gain   Overall audio output volume. Increase gain to amplify a clip, or decrease gain to attenuate a clip, making it quieter.

gamma   A display setting related to the brightness of the middle tones of an image. You can adjust the gamma of an image to lighten or darken the midtones (the middle-gray levels), without significantly changing the dark and light areas (the shadows and highlights).

gang   To adjust multiple tracks at the same time, as in the Premiere Audio Mixer window.

garbage matte   A mask used in a keying operation to remove a region of a frame that contains unwanted objects.

GIF   A still image file format commonly used on Web pages for simple images and animations. Use the JPEG format for photographic images.

gradient   Gradual change from one color (or intensity level) to another. Gradient colors can also become opaque or transparent, varying in translucency from one side to the other.

H

History palette   A small floating window along the right side of the Premiere work area that displays a list of your recent actions during the current working session. Used to undo recent operations and return to a previous state of the project.

Hz   Hertz. A measurement used for audio sampling rate, as in the number of audio samples per second. *See also* sample rate.

I

import   To bring media elements into your current working space. Premiere can import video and audio clips, still images, and animated sequences in a variety of formats. You can import both individual clips, and folders of clips, and add them to bins in an open Project. *See also* capture, export.

In point   A placeholder used to mark a specific time-code as the starting point of a segment in a longer sequence. You can use In and Out points to mark a clip to be captured from a source tape, to mark part of a clip to be trimmed, or to mark a portion of the Timeline to be played. *See also* marker, Out point.

Info palette   A small floating window along the right side of the Premiere work area that displays information about a selected clip or transition.

interlaced video   A technique used for television video formats such as NTSC and PAL, in which each full frame of video actually consists of alternating lines taken from two separate fields captured at slightly different times. The two fields are then interlaced or interleaved into the alternating odd and even lines of the full video frame. When displayed on television equipment, the alternating fields are displayed in sequence, depending on the field dominance of the source material. *See also* frame, field.

interpolate   To automatically create graduated steps between two or more keyframes to create smooth transitions for video, audio, and motion effects.

J

J-cut   A split edit in which the In point of a clip is adjusted to overlap the preceding clip, so that the audio portion of the later clip starts playing before its video as a lead-in to the visual cut. Also called an *audio lead*. *See also* L-cut.

jog   To move slowly through a program, as with frame advance or frame reverse VCR controls. Use the Premiere jog tread to step frame by frame through a clip or program to position to a specific frame. *See also* shuttle.

JPEG   A still image file format that can compress photographic images into much smaller file sizes while sacrificing only a little image quality. Great for Web pages and e-mail. *See also* GIF.

K

kerning   The spacing between adjacent characters in a text string, as in a title.

key   To specify a region of an image or video clip to be used as a mask for transparency. Used to make part of the scene transparent or semi-transparent, and then composite it with other superimposed images or video tracks. The region can be specified using features such as color (a color key) or intensity, or with a separate alpha mask or image matte. *See also* blue screen, matte.

keyframe   A point along a timeline or path that defines where and how the settings for an effect will change. Premiere can interpolate one or more settings from keyframe to keyframe to create the appearance of a smoothly changing effect over a series of frames or along a motion path. *See also* interpolate.

L

L-cut   A split edit in which the audio Out point of a clip is extended beyond the video Out point, so that the audio cuts after the video and continues playing over the beginning of the next clip. *See also* J-cut.

leader   The beginning of the physical tape on a video-cassette, or extra material before the beginning of a clip. A tape leader is a strip of nonrecording material that connects the actual recording tape to the spindle on the cassette. Most cassette tapes have about five seconds of leader before the actual recording media portion of the tape begins.

log   A list of clips in a longer sequence, identified by starting and ending timecodes. Use the Premiere batch log to build a list of clips to be batch captured from a tape.

lossless   Any compression scheme, especially for audio and video data, that uses a nondestructive method that retains all the original information, and therefore does not degrade sound or video quality.

lossy   Any compression scheme, especially for audio and video data, that removes some of the original information in order to significantly reduce the size of the compressed data. Lossy audio and video compression schemes such as MP3 and JPEG try to eliminate information in subtle ways so that the change is barely perceptible, and sound or video quality is not seriously degraded.

M

marker   A placeholder used to mark a specific time-code in a sequence. Use to keep track of changes, events, or synchronization points in a longer sequence. You can use the In and Out point markers to mark a clip to be captured from a source tape, to mark part of a clip to be trimmed, or to mark a portion of the Timeline to be played.

mask   An image which defines areas in a frame to be used as a transparency key or matte. Each pixel in the mask image indicates the degree of transparency to be used for the corresponding pixel position in each frame. *See also* key, matte.

master   The original video or audio source, or final video production with analog media, the first tape you create from your PC video file, also known as the first-generation tape. The master tape is a high-quality source to which you should return whenever you want to make more copies. Although you could use the file on your hard drive as a master, you won't want to keep that file forever because it takes up so much storage space. If you're using analog video, however, the PC file is your master source and first generation; the first physical tape you record is considered to be a second-generation tape. *See also* analog media, DV, digital media.

matte   An image mask used to define the transparent areas of each frame to be used in superimposing multiple clips. *See also* key.

Monitor window   The Premiere window used to preview and edit the Source view of individual video clips and the Program view of the material being assembled on the Timeline. *See also* Clip window.

motion blur   The effect of tracking a speeding object and thus blurring the background because of the motion.

MOV   QuickTime Movie format. *See also* QuickTime.

Movie Capture window   The Premiere window used to preview and record from DV and analog video and audio devices. Also used for batch capture of a group of clips.

MP3   An audio file format, especially popular for downloading songs over the Web. Named for Motion Picture Experts Group (MPEG) 1, Layer 3. Uses lossy compression to significantly reduce file size, but often with little perceptible loss in sound quality.

MPEG   A family of popular multimedia file formats and associated compression schemes defined by the Moving Pictures Expert Group. MPEG-1 video was designed for use on CD-ROMs and provides picture quality somewhat comparable to VHS. MPEG-2 video was designed for use on DVD, and can provide high-quality full-screen full-rate video with smaller file sizes. *See also* MP3.

N

narration   A voice that explains what is happening on a video. Voiceover narration can add tremendous value to a video by explaining the situation being shown to viewers.

Navigator palette   A small floating window along the right side of the Premiere work area that displays a miniature view of the current Timeline work area within the overall program. Used to scroll and zoom the program in the Timeline view.

NTSC   A television video format used in the United States and elsewhere. *See also* PAL, interlaced video.

NTSC safe colors   Colors that are displayable on NTSC television video. Title colors that are outside this range can display badly and bleed on NTSC televisions. *See also* safe area.

O

Out point   A placeholder used to mark a specific time-code as the end point of a segment in a longer sequence. You can use In and Out points to mark a clip to be captured from a source tape, to mark part of a clip to be trimmed, or to mark a portion of the Timeline to be played. *See also* marker, In point.

overscan   The outer edges of a video image that are typically cut off by consumer television sets in order to ensure that the image fills the entire display. *See also* safe area.

P

PAL   A television video format used in Europe and elsewhere. *See also* NTSC.

palette windows   Small floating Premiere windows that provide convenient access to information, options, and commands used in video editing. Palettes can be adjusted, hidden, and docked as desired to accommodate your editing style.

pan   To move the apparent location of a mono audio track to position it between the left and right stereo channels. With stereo clips, you adjust the balance between the two channels. *See also* balance.

PICT   The standard Apple Macintosh still image Picture file format.

pixel   The individual picture elements, or "dots" of color, that are arranged in a two-dimensional array to define a digital image or video frame. The dimensions or resolution of an image are described in terms of the horizontal and vertical pixel count.

preroll   To start a tape spinning up to speed before beginning playback or capture, in order to ensure that the operation is synchronized properly.

preview file   Temporary file created by Premiere to save the results of rendering a portion of the Timeline. With these files, Premiere can preview the results of your editing on the Timeline at full playback rate, including transitions and effects. *See also* scratch disk.

Program view   The Monitor window view that displays the production being assembled on the Timeline. Depending on the current settings, this can be a simple preview of the cuts between adjacent clips, or a fully-rendered preview with transitions and effects. *See also* Source view.

progressive download   A technique for downloading Internet video and/or audio clips so that they can be viewed at the same time that they are being transferred to your computer. This provides some of the benefits of streaming media without requiring a special streaming server. *See also* streaming media.

Project window   The main Premiere window, used to import and save clips used in the program you are editing and organize them into bins. You save each editing activity in a separate Project file, including the imported material and editing context.

Q

QuickTime   Multiplatform, multimedia Movie file format from Apple Computer (.MOV).

R

RealMedia   Multiplatform, multimedia Web streaming file format from Real Networks (.RM, .RAM).

render   To generate a video production in its final form, including transitions, effects, and superimposed tracks. You can render portions of a Timeline in order to preview your edits at that point, or render the entire production before exporting it in its final form, to a disk file or out to tape.

render-scrub   To preview a program in the Premiere Timeline and display the visual effects of transitions or other effects, but not at full playback speed. Used to preview a portion of the Timeline before rendering it. *See also* scrub.

resolution   The dimensions of an image, in pixels, typically expressed as the number of horizontal pixels across and the number of vertical pixels down. *See also* aspect ratio.

reverb   An audio effect that simulates the ambience of a room of a specific size and with different sound-absorbent properties.

RGB   The Red, Green, and Blue components used to define a specific color.

ripple edit   A method of editing in the Timeline so that when new material is inserted, or existing material is deleted, and other material is adjusted to fit. In a ripple edit, the change ripples through the rest of the material, as the existing clips slide apart to make room for the new material, or slide together to fill a gap. *See also* rolling edit, slide edit, slip edit.

roll   To scroll lines of title text vertically up or down the screen. *See also* crawl.

rolling edit   A method of editing in the Timeline by adjusting and trimming two adjacent clips. When you roll the cut point between the adjacent clips, the durations of the two clips are adjusted to keep the overall program duration unchanged. The Out point of the first clip is changed in tandem with the In point of the second clip so that, as one increases in duration, the other decreases to match it. *See also* ripple edit, slide edit, slip edit.

S

safe area   Also known as the safe zone. Margins left around the edge of the image. Used when working with material intended for display on television. Safe margins keep titles from bleeding off the screen. *See also* overscan.

sample rate   The rate at which samples of a continuous signal, such as music or a sound, are captured into a digital representation of the original signal. A higher audio sampling rate, with more samples per second, creates a more accurate representation of the original sound. *See also* frame rate, Hz.

scale   To reduce or enlarge an image or video sequence by squeezing or stretching the entire image to a smaller or larger image resolution.

scene   A single video sequence, typically shot in one continuous take. For editing purposes, it is useful to capture or trim your video material so that each scene is stored as an individual clip which can then be edited on the Timeline. *See also also* clip.

scratch disk   A dedicated work area on hard disk. Used by Premiere for temporary storage and for saving preview files.

scrub   To preview a program in the Premiere Timeline by dragging the edit line. You can also render-scrub to show the visual effects of transitions or other effects, but not at full playback speed.

shuttle   To move rapidly through a program, as with scan forward or scan reverse VCR controls. Use the Premiere shuttle slider control to scan rapidly through a clip or program to move to a general area in the material. *See also* jog.

single-track editing   A style of editing in which the Timeline is condensed to a single row per track. In Premiere, the Single-Track Editing workspace configures a dual-view Monitor window and a collapsed Timeline window showing a single row per track, without a separate transition track. This is the Premiere workspace used most often by video professionals. *See also* A/B editing.

slide edit   A method of editing in the Timeline by moving a clip, and trimming neighboring clips to adjust to the change. When you slide a clip earlier or later in the program, the neighboring clips are trimmed accordingly by changing their In and Out points so that the duration of the overall program remains unchanged. *See also* ripple edit, rolling edit, slip edit.

slip edit   A method of editing in the Timeline by changing the trim points in a clip. When you slip the trim points earlier or later in a clip, the In and Out points are adjusted correspondingly so that the duration of the clip is unchanged. A slip edit also does not affect the rest of the program on the Timeline. *See also* ripple edit, rolling edit, slip edit.

Source view   The Monitor window view that displays a source clip for viewing and editing on the Timeline. The source clip can be from a bin in the Project window, or from a track on the Timeline. *See also* Program view.

split edit   To adjust the video and audio portions of a clip separately so they start or end at different times. Used for audio cross-fading, so that the audio can lead in or fade out independently from the cut in the video. *See also* L-cut and J-cut.

split-screen   A divided display that shows two clips, or portions of clips, side by side.

still frame   A single image, or single frame of a video clip. *See also* freeze frame.

Storyboard window   The Premiere window used to organize a group of clips into a sequence. You can use this window to quickly lay out the scenes to include in your production into a rough cut, and then move them into the Timeline for further editing.

streaming media   Internet video and/or audio clips that can play directly over the Internet, without needing to be downloaded first onto a computer. Used to view and hear broadcasts, and to interactively play and seek in stored clips. *See also* progressive download.

stripe   To prepare a new videotape for a recording by prerecording a consistent timecode over the full length of the tape.

subtitle   Onscreen text that translates foreign-language dialog or transcribes hard-to-understand speech.

superimpose   To layer multiple tracks onto the Timeline. To composite portions of multiple clips into the final production by overlaying clips with transparent regions to allow the underlying tracks to show through. *See also* key.

superimpose track   In Premiere, the Video 2 track and above, which can include titles, logos, and other material to be overlaid on the bottom Video 1 track.

sweeten   To use audio effects to enhance and manipulate the audio sound.

synchronize   To keep two sequences playing at the same rate (in sync). A slide show or a series of video clips can be synced to the beat on an audio track. A talking-head video needs to maintain lip-sync, so that the audio matches the mouth movements of the speaker. Video and motion effects also are synced to the underlying video.

T

talking head   A clip that shows just the head and shoulders of a person who is talking. This tight focus is often used in interview situations where the background is not as important as the talking subject. It is also convenient in a movie destined for the Web because the small amount of movement in a talking-head shot compresses well for the Internet.

three-point edit   A method of setting In and Out points in order to precisely control where and how frames are inserted into a Timeline. In a three-point edit, you set any three such markers, and Premiere will determine the fourth to match the specified duration. *See also* four-point edit.

TIFF   A lossless image file format designed for photographic images that compresses the image size while preserving all the image quality. The resulting files are therefore larger than those with JPEG compression, which sacrifices some detail in order to significantly reduce the image size.

timecode   An exact time used to identify a specific point in a clip or production. Measured in hours, minutes, seconds, and frames. *See also* duration.

timecode log   *See* batch list.

Timeline window   The Premiere window used to assemble, trim, and arrange, superimpose video, audio, and image clips into a program. The Timeline provides a view of multiple sources being combined over time, with separate tracks for video, audio, and superimposed video, as well as transitions and effects.

title   Onscreen text (and associated graphics) that can be used to add information to your production. Used as a title screen at the beginning of your production, for subtitles superimposed under the video, and for rolling credits at the end.

Title window   The Premiere window used to lay out and design title text and graphics.

track   A sequence of video or audio clips in the Premiere Timeline that are to be combined and superimposed into a final production.

transition   A visual effect to segue from the end of one clip or scene and the start of the next. The most basic transition is a cut, in which the last frame of one clip is immediately followed by the first frame of the next clip. More interesting transition effects include fades, dissolves, and wipes between adjacent clips.

Transitions palette   A small floating window along the right side of the Premiere work area that lists the available video transitions, grouped by type. Used to access transitions to be applied to the Timeline. You can also reorganize and customize the list.

trim   To cut out a segment of a clip by removing frames from the beginning and/or end. To adjust the In or Out points of a clip to identify the portion to be used in the final production.

V

Video Effects palette   A small floating window along the right side of the Premiere work area that lists the available video effects, grouped by type. Used to access effects to be applied to a video clip. You can also reorganize and customize the list.

Video for Windows   The media file format used with Microsoft Windows (.AVI). Supports many different video and audio compression formats (codecs).

VTR   Video Tape Recorder. Also called VCR (Video Cassette Recorder).

VU meter   An audio mixer's display of audio levels for each track.

W–Z

watermark   A small, semitransparent graphic that identifies a scene or speaker. Many TV broadcasts use a watermark to let you know what channel you're watching.

WAV   The uncompressed Wave audio file format used with Microsoft Windows.

wipe   A video transition in which the new video physically moves into the frame while displacing the old video.

Index

How to Use *provides easy, visual information in a proven, step-by-step format. This amazing guide uses colorful illustrations and clear explanations to get you the results you need.*

Other How to Use Titles

Microsoft FrontPage 2002
Paul Heltzel
ISBN: 0-672-32140-8
$29.99 US/$44.95 CAN

Adobe Photoshop 6
Daniel Giordan
ISBN: 0-672-31954-3
$29.99 US/$44.95 CAN

Dreamweaver 4 and Fireworks 4
Lon Coley
ISBN: 0-672-32041-X
$29.99 US/$44.95 CAN

HTML and XHTML
Gary Rebholz
ISBN: 0-672-32031-2
$29.99 US/$44.95 CAN

Macromedia Flash 5
Denise Tyler
Gary Rebholz
ISBN: 0-672-32004-5
$29.99 US/$44.95 CAN

The Internet, 2001 Edition
Rogers Cadenhead
ISBN: 0-672-32000-2
$24.99 US/$37.95 CAN

Windows Me
Douglas Hergert
ISBN: 0-672-31937-3
$24.99 US/$37.95 CAN

Your Mac
Gene Steinberg
ISBN: 0-672-31827-X
$24.99 US/$37.95 CAN

Digital Video
Dave Johnson
ISBN: 0-672-31923-3
$29.99 US/$44.95 CAN

SAMS

www.samspublishing.com

Mount Laurel Library
100 Walt Whitman Avenue
Mt. Laurel, NJ 08054-9539
(856) 234-7319

All prices are subject to change.